Rallying the Whole Village

THE COMER PROCESS FOR REFORMING EDUCATION

Rallying the Whole Village

THE COMER PROCESS FOR
REFORMING EDUCATION

Edited by

JAMES P. COMER

NORRIS M. HAYNES

EDWARD T. JOYNER

MICHAEL BEN-AVIE

Foreword by Donald J. Cohen and Albert J. Solnit

TEACHERS COLLEGE PRESS

Teachers College, Columbia University
New York and London

Published by Teachers College Press, 1234 Amsterdam Avenue, New York, N.Y. 10027

Library of Congress Cataloging-in-Publication Data

Rallying the whole village : the Comer process for reforming education
   / James P. Comer ... [et al.] ; foreword by Donald J. Cohen and
   Albert J. Solnit.
         p.   cm.
    Includes bibliographical references and index.
      ISBN 0-8077-3540-X(cloth : alk. paper). — ISBN 0-8077-3539-6
   (pbk. : alk. paper)
      1. Educational change—United States. 2. School improvement
   programs —United States. 3. Child development —United States.
   4. Community and school—United States. 5. Educational evaluation—
   United States. 6. Teachers—Training of—United States. 7. School
   environment—United States. 8. Education, Urban—United States.
   9. Comer, James P.   I. Comer, James P.
   LB2822.82.S38   1996
   370'.973—dc20   96-2130

ISBN 0-8077-3539-6 (paper)
ISBN 0-8077-3540-X (cloth)

Printed on acid-free paper
Manufactured in the United States of America
03 02 01 00   8 7 6 5 4 3

WE DEDICATE THIS BOOK to the loving memory of Mrs. Shirley Comer, our spiritual mother and friend. Through her dedicated and faithful support of the Yale School Development Program, her love and caring have touched the lives of thousands of children across the United States. Her legacy of compassion and devotion to improving the lives of all children lives on in the spirit of collaboration and child-centered teaching and learning that now embues hundreds of schools throughout this nation. All of us are much richer and better for having known her and shared her wisdom. We are today—and will be always—grateful for Mrs. Comer's lifelong commitment to serving our children, community, and nation in her characteristically quiet and remarkably effective way. She gave us much and asked for nothing in return. We love her dearly.

Contents

CHAPTER ONE   1

THE SCHOOL DEVELOPMENT PROGRAM

James P. Comer, Norris M. Haynes, and Edward T. Joyner

With 28 years' experience and nationwide success as their vantage point, the authors recall the issues that triggered and shaped the School Development Program. They describe unflinchingly how some schools in the United States have become places that actively prevent success, and summarize the SDP's school reform initiative, in which redesigning engages all the influences of society to promote—rather than to erode—a community of healthy students, parents, and staff.

CHAPTER TWO   27

TRANSLATING THEORY INTO PRACTICE: COMER'S THEORY OF SCHOOL REFORM

Christine L. Emmons, James P. Comer, and Norris M. Haynes

The School Development Program model is a unique outgrowth from previous social theories. Comer's training gave him a deep understanding of individual and social psychology, community health, and psychiatry. Synthesizing and expanding these disciplines, he created a strong and novel theoretical framework for educational reform.

Foreword

The National Commission on Children, chaired by Senator John D. Rockefeller in 1991, called for a series of fundamental reforms in the curriculum, organization, and financing of schools as well as the training and treatment of teachers, the role of principals, and the quality of school environment. The Commission's recommendations were based on an extensive review of research assessing the state of American education, site visits to School Development Program (SDP) schools, and discussions with Dr. James P. Comer. The Commission report summarizes these contacts with the SDP: "The program builds strong and supportive relationships among students, parents, teachers and administrators by recognizing that they all share the same goal: to help children learn" (*Beyond Rhetoric*. Final Report of the National Commission on Children, 1991; p. 203). Nothing seems more simple than this shared commitment. After all, what are schools about?

James Comer asked this question almost 30 years ago. As a young child psychiatrist, he was recruited to the Yale Child Study Center to lead a new initiative bridging child psychiatry and education. James Comer entered anew the domain of assisting schools to promote the development of inner city children in this period of our history. Over the decades, he and colleagues he has brought into the field have mapped a powerful, effective methodology for reforming educational systems in order to facilitate learning and developmental progress.

In *School Power*, a description of the SDP, Comer (1980) provides the historical context:

> In 1966, after more than fifteen years of providing periodic consultation and in-service training in public schools, as clinical and educational scholars we planned to establish a systematic long-term collaborative exchange between a clinical cen-

ter and two primary schools. We planned to learn together and from each other by allowing clinicians to work together with teachers and educational administrators in the school setting, with the agreement and involvement of the parents. The clinicians knew that being able to observe children in the public schools would expose them to learning about a large sector of child life that otherwise they usually heard about only in an indirect fashion. The educators knew that clinicians used certain dynamic constructs and observational methods to understand the ailing child, which, when translated into an understanding of healthy or normal children, could be useful to teachers in their work with children and parents. Both groups spoke of adding a clinical dimension to the educational setting and process.... As we were planning our long-term collaboration, encouraged and supported by the Ford Foundation, we were aware that in the United States in the 1960s there was the impulse for a quantum jump in education and in democratizing our society (p. xiv).

The SDP grew out of James Comer's clinical talent for quiet observation, attentive listening, and respectful collaboration. With the patience of a dynamically oriented therapist, he has developed relationships with educators and joined with them in their work and aspirations. In *School Power*, he described, discussed, and evaluated:

> how a private university child study center, a public school system, and a community of teachers and parents could establish a long-term collaboration which would primarily benefit the children in the schools. (p. xvi)

He also noted:

> As additional yields from this collaboration, we have been concerned with a more satisfying and progressive professional development for the teachers involved; and for an appropriate and prideful participation and sense of ownership for the parents of our students. Also, we were committed to an evolving program, one that would go beyond the novelty effect, with self-critical and self-change capacities that were not artificially distorted or "psyched up" by funding crises. It could not succeed if it were totally dependent upon "outside" funds, or if it were so expensive it could not be useful to other school systems or to other schools in our system. (p. xvi)

Dr. Comer recognized the powerful conscious and unconscious forces that influence the perceptions of administrators and teachers concerning both the roles of schools and the needs and abilities of children and parents. He also appreciated the complexity of the relationship between mental health professionals relating to schools, and recognized that individuals such as himself could be seen both as useful and as threatening to staff and faculty. As an action-oriented researcher, Dr. Comer developed a general framework for changing schools based on interventions, outcomes, developmental theory, and a belief that teachers, parents, and administrators could define and pursue shared objectives. Over the years, his research, his reflections on his own life, and his understanding of history and

American society became the foundation of a vision about minority children, families, schools, and community.

The basic premises of the SDP are widely accepted today, in large part because of the success of James Comer and his many co-workers in the Yale Child Study Center and throughout the United States. Yet, these ideas remain quietly revolutionary, in some ways controversial, and not easy to actualize.

The SDP emphasizes the central role of schools in enhancing children's development; it recognizes that children's lives are shaped not only by their families and communities, but also by their relationship with teachers and administrators. The relationship between schools and children reflects their mutual perceptions and expectations. Importantly, for school reform, the texture of relationships within the school is deeply influenced by the principal's and teachers' portrait of the children and the vision of their future. This set of expectations, assumptions, and fantasies creates the background for moment-to-moment and daily engagements between teachers and children, and influences the ways in which children are heard, responded to, cared for, and instructed. Do the teachers see their students (and their parents) as neighbors, as the next generation of professionals and leaders of their community? Are the teachers supported in idealizing the future of their students, or do they see the students as heading toward dead ends?

Gifted teachers and administrators understand the many opportunities available to them to enhance children's social and emotional development. They can describe the role of schools in boosting self-esteem and fostering autonomy, and how such factors influence children's ability to attend and to be interested in learning and academics. They also know that at times teachers need to idealize their students and their potential—to enjoy and encourage their imagination and vitality and to recognize their special gifts of which neither the children nor their families may be aware. This hopefulness can become internalized by students when there is mutual trust and ongoing opportunity for real teaching.

There are overwhelming challenges to learning and teaching in today's inner city schools. In these schools, the most concerned teachers may be blocked in their attempts to relate to children with an authentic regard for their inner experiences, abilities, and needs. The schools are overcrowded and physically run down; children come to class tired, hungry, and anxious; many do not have the basic language, attentional, and cognitive skills that are the preconditions of mastering school material; too many children have attentional and behavioral problems and carry the emotional scars from years of physical and emotional strain. Dealing with discipline, finding good enough books and other materials, placating the demands of central and school administration, and adapting to high absenteeism and a constant flow of new students can exhaust the most dedicated, idealistic teacher. In many usual school environments, teachers and principals are swimming against the current. Is there, then, any sense in maintaining an expectation for authentic education in urban schools? Is this an illusion that will only continue to frustrate?

Dr. James Comer joined with administrators, teachers, and parents and showed that it was possible for a school to become a community in which they could join together to navigate through bureaucratic inertia, blaming, and pessimism. The SDP is not simply a "program" but a process of change that depends upon and is enriched by the perspectives and work of all the concerned sectors (central office administration, city leadership, principals, teachers, parents, the community, including those responsible for school maintenance and security, as well as the children themselves). The SDP training methods help administrators, teachers, and parents through a process that enables a school with low morale and low academic achievement to become a school in which there is a sense of purpose and demonstrated academic gains. The process, just like most clinical processes that lead to fundamental change, takes a long time, hard work, some pain, and a willingness to try new approaches and learn from errors. The transition from marginal to successful functioning can be observed by monitoring the "environment" or "climate" of the school—a phenomenon that can be operationally measured and reliably assessed by methods developed by the SDP.

There are fashions in education—new philosophies and approaches that are thought to guarantee success. Potentially good, useful ideas are promoted as the salvation for schools and rapid implementation is followed by disappointment and anger. Vouchers, for profit management of public school systems, and ideological (rather than developmentally sensitive) site-based management are among the currently fashionable solutions, as are methods that emphasize academic skills— "education without frills." Education is also a lightning rod: mayors become annoyed with superintendents for lack of success, administrators blame politicians for lack of resources; and parents vent anger. As panaceas fail and tempers flare, children suffer.

In this ever-changing environment, the SDP stands as a well-marked channel for slow, thoughtful planning and implementation of programs based upon well-defined principles of administration and child development. The SDP makes no extravagant claims; instead, it rests its case on empirical data, on a demonstrated record of gradual improvement in environment and student achievement.

Even with a well-implemented SDP, schools cannot provide everything that children need to move ahead in their personal, social, and academic development. In the past, schools could count on families and communities to do a great deal for children, both before they arrived for formal education and throughout their developmental years. It is now all too clear that for many children these resources are not available or that their neighborhoods and experiences at home are sources of unhappiness, danger, or worse. A premise of the SDP is not to blame, but to recognize problems and develop clearly defined, shared courses of action.

Thus, James Comer's increasing recognition of the limitations of what schools can do or, more precisely, of the need for broader social supports working in synergy with schools, does not shift "blame" for schools' problems, nor "blames" families or neighborhoods. The data, however, demonstrate that schools will not be able to do their share without fundamental changes in the social and economic context of family and child life in America, particularly in the inner city. In his forthcoming book, James Comer will address this broader "environment"—the condition of American society at the end of the millennium.

The future of American economic and national stability rests, to a large extent, on how we deal with the issues that James Comer and the co-authors confront in this book. As a nation, we cannot afford the widening gap between high achieving and economically affluent children and families and the expanding group of economically and educationally disadvantaged. As a nation, we cannot continue to focus on the end results of poor school achievement, truancy, and the risks for delinquency and social maladaptation. Unless we find ways of ensuring that most, if not all, children succeed in school and can enter into lives of independence, security, and satisfaction, there will be a looming threat and an increasing burden on everyone and all social institutions.

The scholarship, clinical care, and advocacy that have characterized James Comer's career have also proven to be magnets for others. There are now several generations of educators, researchers, and clinicians mentored by James Comer and nurtured by the SDP. Through the SDP network and the energetic dissemination of SDP ideas, James Comer's work now suffuses many school districts and the ideas of others. As with other successful approaches, one of the best compliments for SDP is that the concepts are often borrowed without recognition of their origin.

This newest publication by the Comer School Development Program forces into view in a scholarly manner the scope and limits of what the school experience can enable each child to gain if the adults, parents, and teachers form a positive collaborative relationship in establishing a socializing, learning environment appropriate for each child. Parent-teacher collaboration helps children extract from their school experiences what they need. Their positive school experiences influence their progressive development and systematic learning. As they socialize in their school communities, they develop their increasing capacity to use thought as trial actions.

The assumptions and expectations on which the Comer School Development Program is based have been productive. They are:

1. School experiences can evoke the strengths of children, their parents, and their teachers if the collaboration of administrators, teachers, and parents is fostered and enhanced;
2. Schooling cannot replace family and cultural conditions and expectations but can promote the positive health and social ingredients that are present in potential and active forms in each family, cultural, and social setting;
3. Teacher preparation, especially in colleges of education, can benefit from and contribute to the promotion of these assumptions and expectations;
4. The continuity of school reform is ensured if guided by a systematic evaluation process designed to sustain the energy of change in the service of children's progressive learning and socializing.

The SDP has been taken up by other cities and states. The manifold imple-mentations of the SDP process have added to the lessons learned yesterday and are broadening today's understanding of how to bring about improvement in our public schools, very much in the spirit of Maggie's American Dream (Comer, 1988). At a time when it seems that our society is bent on critically weighing its priorities and values in reducing services and support for our children and their parents, it's refreshing to read about the progress of the SDP in this new volume.

References

Comer, J. P. (1980). *School power: Implications of an intervention project.* New York: The Free Press.
Comer, J. P. (1988). *Maggie's American dream.* New York: New American Library.

November, 1995

DONALD J. COHEN, M.D.
Irving B. Harris Professor of Child Psychiatry,
    Psychology and Pediatrics
Director, Yale Child Study Center

ALBERT J. SOLNIT, M.D.
Sterling Professor Emeritus
Pediatrics and Psychiatry
Senior Research Scientist
Yale Child Study Center

Commissioner
Department of Mental Health and Addiction
    Services
State of Connecticut

Preface

Next to the family, the school has the most significant impact on children's growth and development. In school, children acquire many of the psychosocial and cognitive skills that they need to realize and actualize their full potential to become productive and successful adults. A nurturing, challenging, and supportive school environment provides the nourishment that children need to be healthy, whole, and successful. Therefore, effective schooling cannot be a unidimensional enterprise. It must be grounded in a holistic educational philosophy and must incorporate sensitive practices of authentic teaching and learning that are implemented according to sound principles of collaboration and empowerment and that are undergirded by a respect for the dignity of all children.

Traditionally, schools have not been organized and managed to allow for the empowerment and full participation of parents and staff as true partners in addressing children's psychoeducational and developmental needs. This fact was very evident when Dr. James P. Comer began to work with the two pilot schools in New Haven in 1968. As he tells it:

> Reports from teachers, principals, and social workers indicated that a high percentage of inner-city children were not motivated, were disruptive or apathetic in class, were unable to profit from time to time in school and appeared to be disinterested in school materials. Parents and community workers complained that schools did not create the kind of self-esteem needed for adequate academic achievement and that parents felt cut off from the school. The school staff felt abandoned, left to do the best they could and then criticized for not overcoming their personal limitations, those of the schools, the problems of families, and society as a whole. (1993, p. 60)

These observations reflected then, and to some degree, continue to reflect the realities in many of the public schools throughout the United States.

The School Development Program (SDP), a school reform initiative, was designed by Dr. Comer in response to the problems and needs that he discerned and that parents, staff, and students themselves identified. It is a process that unites, empowers, and inspires significant adult caretakers and caregivers, parents, and teachers to make an individual and collective difference in children's lives. The program emphasizes the importance of mutual respect and collaboration among and between parents and school staff in creating a positive school climate and developing effective school- and classroom-level activities that support and nurture all children along multiple pathways.

Many public schools, a large number within the School Development Program network, have experienced significant improvement in climate and in teaching and learning, resulting in impressive student psychosocial and academic growth. The program has been credited with turning these schools around. Our research and evaluation findings support the testimonies by staff, parents, and students that our work has made a significant positive difference in children's lives.

This book shares the story of the School Development Program, chronicling its history and explicating its philosophy, principles, operations, and mechanisms.

In Chapter 1, Comer, Haynes, and Joyner outline the chronological development of the program and describe its major components. The authors analyze and discuss the sociological and psychoeducational issues that helped to inform and shape the development of the program.

In Chapter 2, Emmons, Comer, and Haynes explain the theroretical framework that undergirds the program. The authors show how Comer's child development and educational perspective has been synthesized from several social-psychological theories and how it is applied through the program.

In Chapter 3, Haynes, Ben-Avie, Squires, Howley, Negron, and Corbin describe the SDP school. They highlight the role of parents, school staff, and community members in helping children develop well. They discuss the need and importance of collaboration, consensus, and no-fault in building a caring school community and emphasize the value of a proactive, responsive, and sensitive school climate.

In Chapter 4, Smith and Kaltenbaugh give an informative and insightful explication of the partnership between Southern University at New Orleans and the New Orleans Public School system in implementing the School Development Program. They describe the teacher preparation program, including courses that discuss Comer's child development perspective and the nine components of the program. They also discuss the practicum experiences that preservice teachers receive in program schools.

In Chapter 5, Squires and Joyner clearly articulate a methodology for improving student achievement at the classroom level. They discuss the importance of curriculum alignment and the efficient use of instructional time within the context of the program.

In Chapter 6, Haynes, Emmons, Gebreyesus, and Ben-Avie discuss the research and evaluation framework, process, and findings. They share data on the relationship between the level and quality of program implementation and program results. They also share cross-sectional data, longitudinal profile school-level aggregated data, and findings from qualitative studies.

In Chapter 7, Gillette and Kranyik discuss insights gained from the implementation of the program over its 28-year history. They share some lessons learned from the explosive growth of the program during the past decade.

It is our hope that this book will inform and inspire everyone who reads it. We sincerely believe that all children can and will learn if we provide appropriate levels of challenge and support for each and every child in our schools.

Reference

Comer, J. P. (1993). *School power: Implications of an intervention project* (2nd ed.). New York: The Free Press.

Norris M. Haynes

Acknowledgments

We extend our sincere thanks to the SDP facilitators, superintendents, principals, school staff, parents, and students within the SDP network.

Every national SDP staff member, regardless of position or unit, contributed to this book. Our deepest appreciation.

We would like to acknowledge the kind and generous support of the various philanthropic organizations that have supported our work over the years, including the Ford Foundation, Carnegie Foundation, MacArthur Foundation, Exxon Foundation, and the Melville Corporation. We are particularly thankful to the Rockefeller Foundation for its extensive support of our work. Without their support we could not have achieved as much as we have in recent years both in terms of implementation and research. Specifically, we appreciate the confidence in our work expressed by Hugh Price and Marla Ucelli, and for their unwavering support.

We are also grateful for the inspiration and support that we have received from our colleagues at the Yale Child Study Center. In particular, we would like to thank Drs. Albert Solnit and Donald Cohen for their leadership and vision in helping to realize the mission of the SDP.

Trudy Raschkind Steinfeld significantly contributed to this book and to the SDP. In the process of guiding us in the preparation of the book, she became special to us and a cherished member of the SDP's "village."

We extend special thanks to Faye Zucker and Susan Liddicoat, Teachers College Press, for their encouragement and support.

We would like to acknowledge the technical assistance of Scott LaMontangne, M.P.H., in the design and production of many of the diagrams found in the book.

Chapter 1

The School Development Program

JAMES P. COMER, NORRIS M. HAYNES,
AND EDWARD T. JOYNER

With 28 years' experience and nationwide success as their vantage point, the authors recall the issues that triggered and shaped the School Development Program. They describe unflinchingly how some schools in the United States have become places that actively prevent success, and summarize the SDP's school reform initiative, in which redesigning engages all the influences of society to promote—rather than to erode—a community of healthy students, parents, and staff.

When children are developing well, they learn well. When the adults in their lives show trust, support, positive regard, high expectations, affiliation, and bonding, learning comes naturally. But what happens when children aren't developing well, aren't learning well? What should we do when students don't do well in their schools? Some educators blame these children and their families, concluding that there is something inherently wrong with them. But we have demonstrated again and again that the same children who fail to thrive in a specific setting can become eminently successful *in the same school* when the adults in their lives take the time to create a healthful climate. This climate supports a no-fault approach to identifying and solving problems, it fosters processes that generate consensus decision making, and it employs structures that promote collaborative working relationships. This climate takes a while to teach and some dedication to practice. After a while, it becomes as natural as breathing and as natural as learning, for in this climate, children and the adults around them develop well.

When we became engaged in the New Haven, CT school system in 1968, and discovered how alienated and unchallenged children could be, we were gripped by sorrow and fury. James P. Comer, M.D. (1980), recalls that on his very first day at Baldwin School, a teacher grabbed his arm and cried, "Help me! Help me!"

> What I saw was almost unbelievable. Children were yelling and screaming, milling around, hitting each other, calling each other names, and calling the teacher names. When the teacher called for order, she was ignored. When I called for order, I was ignored. That had never happened to me before. We headed for the hall, confused and in despair. (p. 76)

The most appalling thing was that the school staff were trying, but because they were working in isolation, without support, and at odds with one another, they could make no progress.

In response to this horrendous situation, Comer formulated a school-level systemic approach to educational change that addressed all aspects of a school's operations. This model, referred to fondly as the Comer Process by the parents, school staff, and students whose lives have been touched by it, is the core of the School Development Program.

Now after 28 years of experience, we have clearly defined what needs to be done, we've done it, and we've proved that it works. We are constantly changing as an organization, building on our strengths, willing to undergo the same processes that we ask schools to undergo. Our experiences, both as an organization and as workers in the field, have shown us that people are really willing to modify the way they work with one another when the outcome is their students' development as healthy, whole children.

Opening the School Door and Walking In

In 1963 and 1964, we were beginning to be concerned about problems with children who were being locked out of the economic and social mainstreams. We saw youngsters who were not going to be able to contribute to society. Albert Solnit, then director of the Yale Child Study Center and today Connecticut's Commissioner of Mental Health, had a philosophy that research is done by service in the community. The approach that we decided on finally was to immerse ourselves in schools, and really learn about them, and learn through them about people in systems: how systems work and how they function. The school is the most natural place to help children, for there is no stigma attached: To be helped is the very reason the children are there. The school is also the venue in which we have the most potential to guide the life paths of the greatest number of children. "Schools are the final common pathway in our society and are more accessible to systematic change than the family" (Comer cited in Schorr, 1988, p. 232).

The SDP was established in 1968 in two elementary schools, Baldwin and Martin Luthor King, Jr., as a collaborative effort between the Yale Child Study

Center and the New Haven Public Schools. (Later Katherine Brennan replaced the Baldwin School which eventually closed.) The two schools involved were the lowest achieving in the city, had poor attendance, and had serious relationship problems among students, staff, and parents. Comer (1980) provided a description of the neighborhood of the schools:

> If you had walked up Dixwell the year our program began, 1968, you might well have felt a peculiar mixture of joy and hope, despair and hopelessness so often found in struggling black communities. Decay and promise were in competition everywhere... On Sunday, you might have seen a black bride and groom and their wedding party, resplendent and beautiful, leaving church after a traditional wedding ceremony, probably still including a pledge of obedience from the bride to the groom. On Monday you might have seen the numbers man (illegal gambling) and even the pusher doing business on the same block... The Dixwell Community House stood aging with the promise that it would be rebuilt as an attractive modern structure. Empty lots where houses were leveled to make way for redevelopment stood gathering weeds, whiskey bottles, and tin cans. (pp. 47–48)

The conditions at these initial schools mirrored the conditions in many if not most of the schools in the city. Staff morale was low. Parents were angry and distrustful of the schools. Hopelessness and despair were pervasive.

As we looked around at schools, we saw a teacher orienting the children on the first day of school and a child politely raising his hand to say, "My mama said I don't have to do anything you say." Behind that comment was the distrust that community had of schools, as schools represent mainstream institutions. We saw teachers who really believed that the children could not control themselves and therefore had to be controlled. We saw a 230-pound, 6'2" teacher squared off against a 3-foot-tall student. The teacher explained, "He called me a name." The understanding of children and the way they interact, and the ways we can respond to support their development and their desirable behavior within the school, simply were not there. Ed Joyner, director of the SDP's implementation wing, recalls that when he became a school principal:

> The attitude among the school staff was that some kids who come here will learn and some won't. That's the way it is: It's okay for some kids to learn fairly well and go on to work after school, and it's okay for some kids not to learn a great deal at all.

We also saw social workers, psychologists, and special education teachers working differently, separately, and never talking to each other. Nine different people were helping one child, Comer remembers, all of whom "jumped in and out of the classroom, each doing his or her little thing, with the kid pieced up all over the place, with nobody thinking about what the kid needs altogether, and who should address what" (Comer cited in Schorr, 1988, p. 235).

The school staff lacked training in child development and behavior, and understood school achievement solely as a function of genetically determined intellectual ability and individual motivation. Thus, the schools were ill prepared to modify behavior or to close developmental gaps. The staff usually responded with punishment and low expectations. Such responses were understandable given the circumstances, but they usually led to more difficult staff–student interactions and, in turn, to difficult staff–parent and staff–community interactions, staff frustration, and a lower level of performance by students, parents, and staff.

We were almost kicked out of the schools the first year. Instead of bringing in from the outside a school initiative packaged and guaranteed to improve the achievement of the students, we learned together with the school staff how to change the way we interact with each other in schools for the children's sake. Comer recalls:

> At the end of the first year we had an event, and we talked about how much better it was. Most of the parents agreed. I was cleaning up in the gymnasium with one of the parents who had been very tough on me at that event. We were working together, and I thought she was angry with me and did not like me. But as we finished she said, "Well, I look forward to seeing you next year. I sure enjoyed fighting with you." I was amused, but I also began to realize that people who live under difficult circumstances and who are powerless and who have not been able to make things work for themselves and for their children over the years often begin to establish a pattern of fight and struggle. The pleasure and excitement comes from the fights and the struggles rather than the successful outcome.

We began to realize that we had to create many, many successful outcomes and help people move in the direction of success so that they could see that long-range success is possible.

▰▰▰ Comer's Problem Analysis

Our Yale Child Study Center staff—social worker, psychologist, special education teacher, child psychiatrist—provided the traditional support services. But we focused more on trying to understand the *underlying* problems and how to correct them, or on preventing their manifestations wherever possible, than on treating individual children or finding deficiencies among staff and parents. We eventually identified underlying problems on both sides: family stress and student underdevelopment in areas necessary for school success, as well as staff needs for organizational, management, and child development knowledge and skills. Comer recounts:

I began to think of the larger systems and how they have an impact on individuals, communities, and in turn, on families. Yet the methods they used to study schools, it seemed to me, did not address all of those issues. It had to be addressed if we wanted to understand children in schools and why children weren't doing well in schools and weren't being prepared for life and participation in society. While I was in the public health service in 1967 and 1968, after I finished my residency in psychiatry at Yale, I was concerned about the issues of relationships. My own experience, my low-income background, and my work in public health all came together as I began to consider another way of thinking about how we observe and how we develop research approaches that would allow us to initiate ventures that could truly be helpful to the children we were concerned about. And I made a deliberate return to Yale and the Yale Child Study Center because one of the things I realized is that the kind of interventions that we wanted to do required trust. The interventions were asking for a new way of working and a new way of thinking and people don't change easily, especially when they are being helped to change by strangers. So I came back to New Haven because I had spent 3 years training in psychiatry here and knew lots of people in the community and the people were willing to try to change.

It was obvious to us that we needed to understand the interactions that took place in the schools. Comer analyzed the school as a system, and analyzed how the families and communities around that school building and the central office all influence life within both school life and learning. We developed a research design that would help us use the clinical eye that came from child psychiatry in that setting, and the epidemiological, ecological eye of public health.

Any understanding of the present plight of schools is helped by widening the frame for a moment to discuss the impact of U.S. economic and social trends over the last several decades. Children who underachieved in school and left school without adequate cognitive skills and knowledge were not in significant trouble in our society until about three decades ago. Only within the last decade has widespread attention been given to the detrimental impact these unsuccessful students will have on the nation's future. Schools and other institutions whose mandate is to foster children's growth and development have lagged in their response to the major changes in our economy and to other societal factors. Even now criticism and reform efforts often focus narrowly on the underachieving student and the underachieving school, ignoring the underlying structural changes that have precipitated the growth of a large body of educationally disadvantaged young people.

The rapid application of scientific and technological knowledge to industrial production after 1945 required the work force to have higher levels of cognitive development. High levels of education became the ticket of admission to the primary job market, even when the job did not require it. It became increasingly difficult for young people to leave school and meet their adult responsibilities without education credentials and a reasonably high level of cognitive skills and knowledge.

The acquisition of these skills and knowledge is most often made possible through adequate overall development. Parents in reasonably well-functioning families, enmeshed in reasonably well-functioning social networks of friends, kin, and social and spiritual institutions, have the best chance of supporting the growth and development of their children to an adequate level of cognitive skills and knowledge. And when the skills and knowledge have utility and reward in their social networks and the larger society, young people are more often motivated to acquire them.

Also, before television and high mobility, the major sources of knowledge, information, and expectations were powerful community figures who greatly influenced parents, and they, in turn, greatly influenced their children. Teachers, religious and civic leaders, and other authority figures were often a tangible part of most neighborhoods and social networks. The school was a natural part of the community, and there was an incidental and automatic transfer of the authority of parents to the school. This minimized behavior that could have greatly interfered with teaching and the acquisition of cognitive skills and knowledge. School staff, reinforced by parental and community sanctions, were able to support overall student development and learning.

In the 1970s and the postindustrial age after the 1980s, the level of development needed for children to succeed in school and in life rose rapidly. The families most adversely affected by conditions of the past have been least able to give their children the kinds of preschool experiences that would prepare them for the expectations of the school. As a result, a disproportionate number of such children enter school underdeveloped and, sometimes, simply differently developed. They have attitudes, values, and ways that work successfully for them on the playground, in the housing project, and in a variety of other areas in their neighborhood and social networks, but that work to their disadvantage in school. Their social and interpersonal underdevelopment is often viewed as bad or troublesome behavior in school. Their linguistic and cognitive underdevelopment is often viewed as evidence of limited intellectual ability.

On the other side of the equation, school reforms in the 1930s through the 1950s were driven by scientific and technological changes. Attention was given to cognitive development and academic achievement as if they were isolated from overall development. The fact that community and its support for overall development and learning was weakened or lost to changes created by high mobility and mass communication was largely overlooked. The size, organization and management, and location of schools largely ignored community and relationship issues and needs. Neither preservice nor inservice training of school teachers and administrators considered these issues in a meaningful way. Even today many school personnel receive no training in the application of child development and relationship knowledge to their work with their students and to the management of their schools; in fact, many educators (e.g., researchers, public policymakers, and practitioners) do not appreciate the relationship between home–school congruence, overall development, and the ability of students to function in the cognitive area.

Without adequate preparation, school people respond by punishing what they understand as bad behavior and they hold low expectations for underdeveloped or differently developed children. This leads to difficult interactions between students and staff and between staff and parents, and eventually, to a culture of failure in school. In such a climate, distrust, anger, and alienation often develop between home and school. The outcome is that most schools are unable to address the educational needs of underdeveloped or differently developed children from families marginal to the mainstream of the society.

Difficult initial social interactions between student and school compound cognitive skill and knowledge underdevelopment and lead to early school failure. Early school failure contributes strongly to increased interpersonal or behavior problems, which in turn lead to failure in later schooling and eventually to dropping out. With no realistic chance of succeeding in school, and with the universal need to establish identity and belonging, many young adolescents cannot embrace mainstream attitudes, values, and ways, including a commitment to academic learning. In fact, when they are asked to do so they are often being asked to be different from their own parents; and often the parents are opposed to mainstream goals. There is objective evidence that the limited mainstream opportunities in school and in the community begin to lower the school achievement trajectory even among many who were doing reasonably well in early school years. This, of course, limits employment opportunities and makes it difficult for such young people to carry out expected adult life tasks.

Our most successful students in school are those from better functioning families, students who attend schools where there is home–school social congruence, and students whose schools have not developed a culture of failure. The schools, therefore, are in the strategic position to remove educational and life disadvantage, but most have not done so, except by chance, because of particular staff or community attributes and conditions, or in model or demonstration programs.

The School Development Program

Our School Development Program, through basic and applied research, has addressed these issues since the 1970s. As we began to collaborate with parents, school staff, and community members, we kept in mind that every action we took had to be on behalf of the children. We had to facilitate interactions that would help the adults in the setting to be predictable and caring so that they would be able to provide guidance and support for children. The school staff members themselves had to grow so they would be responsible to themselves and the children in the system. We also knew, even then, that children learn best through activities and that they learn best through interacting with peers and with adults. At the time people frowned on the idea of activity learning. Moreover, we knew that all adults want to succeed in working with children. The interventions that we had to develop had to disrupt harmful interactions in schools and replace them with interactions that enabled all of the adults to help all of the children to grow and learn.

▨▨▨▨ *Program Description*

We found that, even when there was a desire to work differently, there was no mechanism at the school level to allow parents, teachers, and administrators first to understand one another's needs and then to collaborate with and help one another address those needs in an integrated, coordinated way. This situation led to blaming, fragmentation, duplication of effort, and frustration. There was no sense of ownership and pride in the school. The result was frequent and severe behavior problems and a sense of powerlessness on the part of all involved. The kind of synergism that develops when people work together to address problems and opportunities could not exist.

One thing was clear: the need for an organizational and management system based on knowledge of child development and relationship issues. It was also clear that a comprehensive approach would be best, rather than one that addressed particular areas of need.

During the early years of our program a number of realities about the educational system in the United States became apparent to us. Many of these realities are still true today. The organization and management of the vast majority of American schools are deeply entrenched in the attitudes, values, and ways of the larger society, and are maintained by traditional training and practice. Since most individuals and systems generally resist change, efforts toward improvement such as providing knowledge of research findings, inservice education, and mandates from administrators or outsiders rarely bring about significant or sustained change.

In order to promote such change, mechanisms must be created that allow parents and staff to engage in a process in which they gain knowledge of systems, of child development, and of individual behavior and apply it to every aspect of school programs in a way and at a rate that is understandable and nonthreatening. When faithfully adhered to from the start, these mechanisms help the people involved achieve the kinds of small, early successes critical to reinforcing confidence in the new program. Success encourages the staff to use these ways of working again, until the new ways eventually replace the old. Comer (1988) notes:

> All the money expended for educational reform will have only limited
> benefits—particularly for poor minority children—as long as the underlying

developmental and social issues remain unaddressed. [Yet,] most teachers and administrators are not trained to organize and manage schools in the ways that support the overall development of students. Nor does their training enable them to analyze, much less solve, the social misalignment problems of children from outside the mainstream. The first step toward improving the education of these children then, is to induce teachers' colleges and schools of education to focus on student development. Teachers who invest time in training will have an incentive to use what they have learned. The efforts of individuals will not be enough; the entire staff of a school must embrace new ways of thinking. (p. 48)

The SDP's approach, with parents and families at the center of change, is a critical missing link in education reform. It permits schools to transform and improve their programs and, with adequate staffing and appropriate teaching and curricula, to achieve high levels of student performance.

The SDP is not a quick fix, nor is it an add-on. It is not just another new activity to be carried out along with the other experiments and activities already underway in a school. Implementation of the SDP takes significant time, commitment, and energy. It represents a different way of conceptualizing and working in schools and completely replaces traditional organization and management. All of the activities in a school are managed through the SDP process. And, most important, the SDP produces desirable outcomes only after a cooperative and collaborative spirit exists throughout a school.

The SDP model is a school-level participatory approach that addresses all aspects of a school's operation, not a particular group of individuals or any particular pre-targeted aspect of a school (see Figure 1-1). The school staff and the stakeholders organize themselves into the three teams that are the hallmark of the SDP: the School Planning and Management Team (SPMT), the Parent Team (PT), and the Student and Staff Support Team (SSST), formerly known as the Mental Health Team (MHT). These teams are referred to in the model as the *three mechanisms.*

In order to sustain a learning and caring community in which all adults feel respected and all children feel valued and motivated to learn and achieve, the work of the teams is driven by *three guiding principles*—consensus, collaboration, and no-fault—that nurture a positive climate. These principles allow the school to review its aims and methods and to identify problems in a no-fault atmosphere. Consensus allows for brainstorming, in-depth discussion, cross-fertilization of ideas, and a plan for trying different solutions in some sequence. Decision by consensus discourages voting on issues because voting results in losers who may feel that they have no stake in the decision that is made. Collaboration without paralyzing the principal or any other individual requires respect for other points of view and a willingness to work cooperatively as part of a team (Haynes and Comer, 1993). In the no-fault approach to problem solving, "fingers of blame" are not

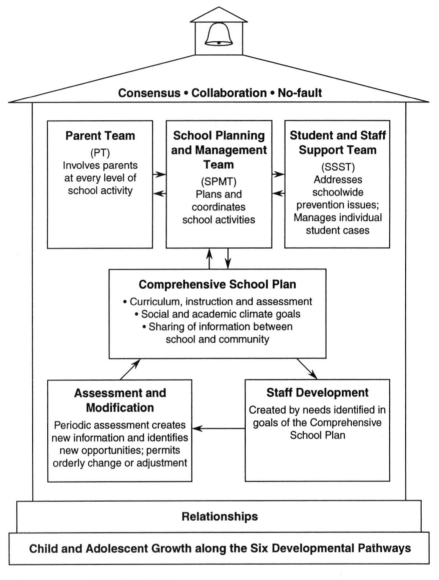

Figure 1-1. Model of the SDP Process

pointed at others, but everyone accepts equal responsibility for change. These guiding principles permit the development and implementation of creative ways of dealing with problems, using the collective good judgment (based on social and behavioral science knowledge) of school staff and parents.

The Parent Team and the Student and Staff Support Team provide meaningful input and uphold the members of the School Planning and Management Team as they engage in three primary activities: developing a Comprehensive School Plan, ensuring staff development, and monitoring and assessing program implementation and outcomes. These primary activities are referred to in the model as the *three operations*. Joyner employs the metaphor of a ship to describe the teams:

> The School Planning and Management Team is a lot like the big sail on a three-sail ship. You might be able to sail the ship with two of the smaller sails or maybe one by itself. But you can go forward faster if you have all the sails up catching the wind.

It takes plenty of work to change a school, but everyone in that school is working very hard, anyway. The difference is that in dysfunctional schools, people work alone and hopelessly, always sliding backward. The SDP allows them to be members of teams working with enthusiasm toward goals that everyone envisions at the same time. They measure their progress and the outcome data feeds back into the process so that the next achievement is way ahead of the last one. Instead of reacting to crisis after crisis, team members begin to engage in preventive planning to address global issues. And they have a cadre of professionals actively working in the field and at the Yale Child Study Center on whom they can call for help.

The key professional in the field is the SDP facilitator in each school district. The SDP facilitator's duty is to disseminate information about the SDP process in the district, to help schools organize the major program components, and to monitor program implementation. The SDP facilitator receives intensive training in the SDP process and its theoretical perspectives at the Yale Child Study Center before assuming his or her responsibilities. The SDP staff at the Yale Child Study Center provide district-level support by training school district staff, monitoring SDP implementation, and providing technical assistance.

▰▰▰ *The Three Mechanisms*

▰▰▰ The School Planning and Management Team (SPMT)

This team is the central organizing body in the school. It is usually led by the building principal and includes teacher, parent, and support staff representatives. Its major function is to develop and monitor a Comprehensive School Plan for the academic, social climate, and staff development goals of students and adults in the school. Specific programs are developed and/or selected by the SPMT to accomplish these goals. All school activities are coordinated by the SPMT. The presence of parents and teachers on this decision-making body balances representation and input. The decision-making process that characterizes an effective SPMT is one of collaboration and consensus.

▊▊▊▊▊▊▊ The Parent Team (PT)

This team is intended to involve parents at all levels of school life, especially parents who have typically not been involved in their children's education due to feeling uncomfortable in the school environment. The majority of parents serve at the first level, which involves general support activities, including attendance at Parent Teacher Association (PTA), Parent Teacher Organization (PTO), or Parent Teacher Student Association (PTSA) meetings, social events, and other school activities. At the second level, some parents serve in school buildings as volunteers or paid assistants in the library, cafeteria, or classrooms. At the third level, parents are selected by their fellow parents to represent them on the SPMT. As members of the SPMT, parents transmit the views and opinions of the general parent body on issues related to academic, social, and staff development needs of the school. The PT bridges the gap between home and school. It reduces the dissonance that disadvantaged students experience as they attempt to adjust from one environment to the other. By empowering parents, schools provide continuity in the socioeducational lives of children. Empowerment can also serve to strengthen families and help them become resilient supporters of their children's development. The SDP views parental involvement as the cornerstone for success in developing a school environment that stimulates the total development of its students. Parents are expected to:

- Select their representatives to serve on the SPMT
- Review the school plan developed by the SPMT
- Work with staff in developing and carrying out activities of the parent–teacher general membership group (PTA, PTO, PTSA) in line with the overall school plan
- Support the efforts of the school to assist students in their overall development
- Encourage new parents to become involved in school activities (Joyner, Haynes, and Comer, 1994; Corbin, private communication)

▊▊▊▊▊▊▊ The Student and Staff Support Team (SSST)

This team includes staff with child development and mental health knowledge and experience: the school psychologist, guidance counselor, school nurse, special education teacher, attendance officer, pupil personnel workers, and any other appropriate staff persons. The SSST addresses schoolwide climate and psychosocial issues that are likely to have an impact on the students' adjustment and life path choices; it also deals with individual student concerns. Rather than being reactive, the SSST works preventively and prescriptively, and consults with teachers and the governance and management body on child development and behavior. It meets weekly to:

- Apply, through its representative on the SPMT, child development and relationship knowledge and skills to the social climate, academic, and staff development programs developed by the governance and management body

- Facilitate the many interactions between parents and school staff
- Consult with classroom teachers to assist them in responding to students in a way that promotes growth and development
- Assist classroom teachers in developing strategies that prevent minor problems from becoming major ones
- Set up individualized programs for children with special needs, which involve outside services when necessary and possible
- Assist all staff in bridging the gap between special education and regular classroom activities
- Provide consultation to and training workshops for staff and parents on child development, human relations, and other mental health issues
- Make recommendations for building-level policy changes designed to prevent problems (Joyner, Haynes, and Comer, 1994)

In addition, the SSST provides a forum for psychologists, social workers, and community health people, teachers, and parents to talk collectively about a child and figure out ways in which they can provide unified support for that child's development.

The Three Operations

The Comprehensive School Plan

Writing the Comprehensive School Plan gives direction and specific focus to the school improvement process. This document provides a structured set of activities in academics, social climate, staff development, and public relations which enables the SPMT to establish priorities and to approach school improvement in a well-coordinated and systematic fashion. Using data on student achievement, behavior, and attendance, and the felt needs of the school's educators and parents, the Comprehensive School Plan generates goals and objectives (Joyner, Haynes, and Comer, 1994).

Staff Development

Staff development requires the continuous examination of skills and their effectiveness. Joyner notes:

> Clearly the skills that I brought to education in 1970 when there was no such thing as crack, when homelessness was something unheard of, and when the majority of the people in the community supported education—and that was only 24 years ago—are different from the skills that are required now.

Staff development activities are based on training needs that stem from the Comprehensive School Plan. Decisions about staff development are made by the SPMT with support from central office personnel. This program for staff development:

- Organizes periodic workshops for teachers and parents based on identified needs and program objectives at the building level
- Creates workshops to provide teachers with skills proven to be most effective in working with underdeveloped student populations
- Allows the staff to integrate academic, arts, social, and extracurricular activities into a unified curriculum
- Encourages teachers to develop special curriculum units in the skill areas most needed in an underdeveloped student population (e.g., government, business, health and nutrition, and leisure time/spiritual activities) (Joyner, Haynes, and Comer, 1994)

Monitoring and Assessment

Monitoring and assessment generates useful data on program processes and outcomes, feeds back information to inform program modification where necessary, and establishes new goals and objectives. Joyner recalls that when he became a principal in 1982 he found that the previous administrators of his school had never looked at the data on achievement, suspensions, and attendance, and so had no sense of how well their school was fulfilling the mission charged to it by society.

An illustration of the monitoring and assessment process is provided by Vivian Williamson-Johnson, project director of the SDP for the Dallas Public Schools. (In Dallas, the SDP is referred to as School-Centered Education.) During the 1991–1992 school year, 10 "campuses" (schools) began implementing the SDP. As of March 1995, every Dallas campus in the district had begun implementation. Monitoring and assessment activities are conducted by the school-level Evaluation and Modification Committee (EMC). The committee is headed by the principal and includes one representative from each stakeholder group: teachers, parents, support staff, community, campus administrators, and where appropriate, students. The committee's function is oversight to determine progress and achievement of the goals, objectives, and strategies of the SPMT and the comprehensive school plan. The EMC: (1) organizes the process for collection of all relevant data; (2) collects and interprets data for the SPMT in order to facilitate continuous improvement; (3) develops an internal evaluation procedure for each committee's or team's plan of work; (4) reviews work plans of all committees and teams; and (5) submits a plan of periodic assessment to the SPMT. The Dallas Public School's Department of Program, Evaluation, and Accountability provides technical assistance and resources to each EMC.

Society, Schools, and Child Development

When we think back to those first classrooms in which a culture of failure was so manifest, we can see clearly that the misalignment between the students and the

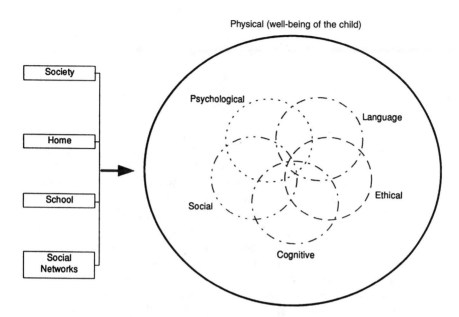

The Six Developmental Pathways

Physical (well-being of the child)

Society

Home

School

Social Networks

Psychological

Language

Social

Ethical

Cognitive

Figure 1-2. *Early childhood: Potential development.* All children can learn and develop well. Children are social beings who need the support and involvement of caring adults for their five internal developmental pathways to become fully realized and to grow physically. If children's physical needs are met, they have the potential to develop psychosocially. For some children, the home, school, social networks, and society nurture and facilitate development. For other children, however, negative influences in their environment inhibit their total development.

school was a direct result of child development being ignored. Looking around and seeing what was so terribly wrong clarified for us how much more there is to the student than a brain on a stick, to borrow a phrase from Jonathon Gillette, coordinator of professional development at SDP's national office. Our experience working with parents and school staff prompted us to explain child development in terms of six developmental pathways. Although the child is a seamless whole, a high level of development along the physical, cognitive, psychological, language, social, and ethical pathways is critical for academic learning (Figure 1-2).

A child develops a strong emotional bond to competent caretakers—usually parents—that enables the child to develop. The attitudes, values, and behavior of the family and its social networks strongly affect such development. A child whose development meshes with the mainstream values encountered at school will be prepared to achieve at the level of his or her ability. In addition, the meshing of home and school fosters further development: When a child's social skills are considered appropriate by the teacher, they elicit positive reactions. The bond that develops between the child and the teacher supports the development of the whole child. Comer (1989) explains the idea of whole child development:

> Development takes place in very indirect ways and through many little incidents as children grow and live with their parents. For example, if 2-year-old Johnny wants to play with a ball that 2-year-old Michael has, he will get up and try to take the ball away from Michael. If Michael objects, he might pop Johnny in the mouth. The adult caretaker who is present has to say, "Johnny, you cannot take Michael's ball. You must go do something else until he is through," or "Maybe you and Michael can work it out so that you can play together," or "Just go away, Johnny." If one thinks about it, what is involved in a situation like this is that the caretaker is spelling out the options for Johnny, thus helping him to grow along all of the critical developmental pathways. Michael learns not to hit, to control the impulse to hit, and to work out something that meets his needs without compromising the needs and rights of others. This is the beginning of ego development. As the adult attends to Johnny's upset feelings, psychoemotional development also takes place within the child. He learns a moral lesson on what is right and wrong. Thinking, speech and language lessons are also involved in that single incident. If we multiply one incident times the many, many other such incidents that occur in the lives of children, we can begin to understand how these combined experiences contribute to children's growth and development prior to their entering school. (p. 127)

A child from a poor, marginal family is likely to enter school without adequate preparation. The child may arrive without ever having learned such social skills as negotiation and compromise. A child who is expected to read at school may come from a home where no one reads and where no parent ever read a bedtime story. It is because such circumstances are at variance with mainstream expectations that these children are often considered aggressive or "bad" and often judged to be of low academic potential.

Parents, for their part, interpret these judgments as personal failure or as animosity from the mainstream. They lose hope and become less supportive of the school. Some parents, ashamed of their speech, dress, or failure to hold jobs, may become defensive and hostile, and avoid contact with the school staff. The result is a high degree of distrust between home and school. This alienation between home and school makes it difficult to nurture a bond between child and teacher that can support development and learning.

As with all systems, any underdevelopment or constrained development in one part has an impact on the whole system (see Figure 1-3). For example, in healthy

The Six Developmental Pathways

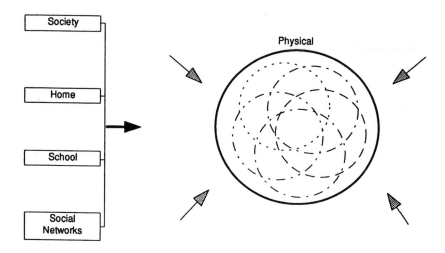

Figure 1-3. *Unmet physical needs: Constrained development.* If the physical pathway is not adequately addressed, physical development would be impaired. Unmet physical needs, including lack of immunizations, result in the diversion of energy toward the fulfillment of these needs and away from the realization of potential along other pathways.

development, the child develops an awareness of what it takes to be healthy with respect to nutrition, fitness, and responsible decision making about his or her body. Growth results in the proper functioning of the body, which means that the child is able to master critical developmental tasks at appropriate biological milestones. This development assumes that the child receives adequate support during the early stages when he or she is dependent on adults for nurturing. With increasing independence, the child can and should become more responsible for his or her physical well-being. If, however, the child's physical well-being has been impaired due to prenatal exposure to alcohol, drugs, and smoking, lack of immunizations after birth, lack of nutrition, or physical harm inflicted by self or others, then the internal aspects of development will be constrained.

Overemphasis on one pathway to the detriment of the others promotes uneven development (see Figure 1-4). Because of preschool experiences in families under stress, a disproportionate number of low-income children behave in ways that reflect overemphasis on a type of social development that is appropriate on the playground, at home, or at other places outside of school, but is inappropriate to the culture of the school. In a school environment that overemphasizes the cognitive pathway to the detriment of the others, a child may acquire basic academic skills and engage in higher-level thinking and problem-solving skills when faced

The Six Developmental Pathways

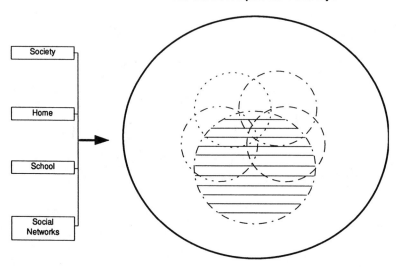

Figure 1-4. *Detrimental overemphasis on one pathway: Unbalanced development.* Development is a holistic process. Sometimes development in children is uneven—there is significant growth along one pathway but not along others, resulting in an imbalance in children's overall development. Adults can help children by structuring environments to support and facilitate children's simultaneous development along all the pathways.

with increasingly complex cognitive tasks. Yet without support and guidance along the psychological and ethical pathways, the same child will not learn to respect the rights and integrity of others. Nor will the child learn to manage his or her emotions and to uphold and defend his or her own rights and integrity.

Balanced development, or maturity, is characterized by strong linkages among all of the developmental pathways (see Figure 1-5). This metaphor of linkages among pathways enables us to explain simultaneously the complexity of development and the urgency of paying attention to all aspects of development. In our ordering of the pathways, for example, the language pathway precedes the social. These two pathways precede the ethical in order to express that carrying our civilization into the future depends on our having a shared language, so that we can talk together and make ethical decisions for the common good.

Talking with parents and educators about balanced development enables us to highlight, for example, that since language mediates all learning, it is a powerful factor in facilitating cognitive development. A strong linkage between the physical and ethical pathways precludes the child from engaging in high-risk, self-destructive behaviors. A strong linkage between the cognitive and psychological pathways allows

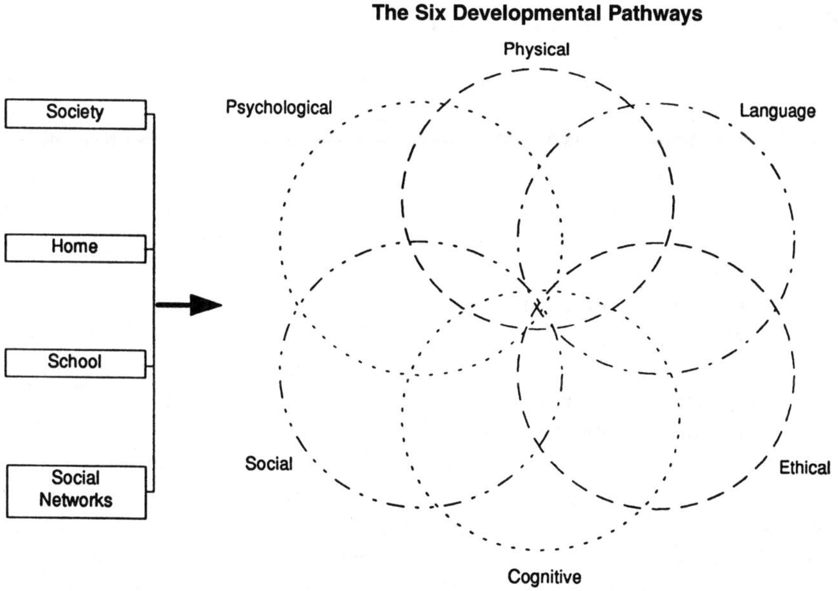

The Six Developmental Pathways

Figure 1-5. *Maturity: Balanced development.* The circles that represent the developmental pathways are intertwined and of equal size. Development is occurring in a balanced manner along all the pathways. The circles are not encased in an outer circle. Because development along each pathway is unconstrained, children can realize their fullest potential.

the child to explore and engage in discovery. We challenge school principals during the national SDP's Principals' Academy to categorize the manifold educational initiatives currently in their schools according to the developmental pathways. For many it is the first time that they are able to articulate what they hope to accomplish with the math initiative, the language program, school uniforms, the drug-free school campaign, the student council, cooperative learning, the health program, the social studies curriculum, and so on. When school staff have a framework based on child development, they are able to determine the effectiveness of each initiative, which allows them see if they are focusing on some pathways to the detriment of others.

Because of its emphasis on child development and positive relationships, the SDP is an effective socioeducational intervention for empowering schools to influence positively the life paths of students. The well-functioning SDP school is a social system in which the developmental needs of students can be addressed in the school's curriculum, pedagogy, and social activities. The empowered school reinforces the positive factors of the students' homes and social networks and helps everyone connected to students. Children in SDP schools have been given back their futures. And through the children we can see a brighter, alternative future for our whole society realized in a single generation.

▮▮▮▮▮ *SDP Program Expansion*

We recognize three broad stages in the evolution of the SDP from its inception in 1968 to the present time. The first stage was the pilot from 1968 to 1978 during which the program was designed, developed, and tested in the two pilot schools in New Haven. The second stage was the field testing of the program from 1978 to 1987 in more schools in New Haven and in three other school districts: Prince George's County, Maryland; Benton Harbor, Michigan; and Norfolk, Virginia. Between 1968 and 1988, the pilot and field testing stages, we used a direct service approach to inform, train, and support districts and schools that were part of our relatively small SDP network. During this time period, the staff at the SDP national office were few in number. SDP staff meetings were held around kitchen tables. We focused on refining and testing the replicability of our early work in New Haven and in a few other school districts.

In the mid-1980s, a major thrust of the SDP was training school personnel from various school districts to implement the program in their own schools. Change agents known as SDP facilitators were selected and trained to implement the SDP, under the direction of their local school superintendent, with minimal direct support from the Yale Child Study Center. In addition, small representative groups of parents, teachers, administrators, and district office staff participated in orientation workshops at Yale. The training and orientation enabled the change agent and the groups to work together to implement the process in their home districts.

In 1985, Norris M. Haynes, director of the SDP Research and Evaluation Unit, joined the staff. One of the first priorities, he recalls, was the undertaking of short-term, cross-sectional comparison studies in New Haven, Benton Harbor, and Norfolk. In these studies, students in SDP schools were compared with students in matched non-SDP schools on achievement, attendance, behavior, self-concept, perceptions of school and classroom climate, and social competence. These studies showed significant student gains in achievement, attendance, behavior, and overall adjustment in SDP schools when compared to students in the matched schools (Becker and Hedges, 1992; Haynes and Comer, 1990, 1993; Haynes, Comer, and Hamilton-Lee, 1989a, 1989b). Analyses of aggregated data in Prince George's County also showed impressive gains for students in schools with the SDP.

Our ethnographic studies and process documentation studies also showed that parents felt more connected to their children's schools and that some of them were motivated to go back to school to obtain their high school equivalency diplomas or pursue meaningful work, including volunteering. Some went to college and obtained graduate degrees including doctorates. Teachers also reported increased feelings of efficacy and satisfaction with work. Evidence suggested that the early positive effects of the program endure beyond elementary school grades into the middle and high school years and may carry over into young adulthood. Our findings, based on correlational and path analytic studies, also showed that when the SDP model is implemented well, schools experience significant positive changes in global and classroom-level climate. These positive changes in climate, in turn, mediate appropriate student behaviors and attitudes, and result in successful student outcomes (Haynes and Bility, 1994; Emmons et al., 1992).

The third stage from 1988 to the present time is regarded as the dissemination stage, during which new strategies for disseminating the program have been explored and supported by the Rockefeller Foundation. The Rockefeller Foundation felt that a gap existed in the school reform movement. It was attracted to our conceptual views and the demonstrated effectiveness of our work. The foundation decided to support an expanded training program that we named the Comer Project for Change in Education (CPCE). The idea was to begin to build greater capacity in the school districts to sustain the implementation of the program by using a trainer-of-trainers model. This coincided with another Rockefeller-supported initiative, the formation of partnerships between universities and schools, and between schools and state departments of education. The goal of these partnerships was to strengthen the school districts' capacity to implement the program and to inform and help change the preservice preparation of teachers and other school-based professionals.

In 1990, we began developing partnerships with schools of education, state departments of education, and other institutions. The partnerships have taken on two distinct forms: university partnerships and Regional Professional Development Centers (RPDCs). Today, the SDP's university partners are New Orleans School District and Southern University of New Orleans, Cleveland Public School District and Cleveland State University, and San Francisco School District and San Francisco State University. The schools of education involved in these partnerships have modified their preservice teacher preparation programs based on the principles and practices of the SDP (see Chapter 4).

The Regional Professional Development Centers hold SDP trainings and support developmental activities in their regions. The current RPDC sites are Prince George's County, Cleveland, and San Francisco. These partners are now able to support the efforts of local and neighboring school districts. It is our plan that three or four of these partnerships in different parts of the country will evolve into semi-autonomous Regional Professional Development Centers.

In 1990, there were 70 schools in the SDP network. In 1991, the SDP had grown to 165 schools. In 1992, the number was 200 schools, and in 1993, 267 schools. In June 1994, the program expanded to 382 schools, reaching a total of 500 schools by the year's end. As of fall 1995, the count of schools implementing the SDP had grown to 433 elementary schools, 85 middle schools, and 45 high schools—563 schools in more than 80 districts in 21 states and the District of Columbia. In addition, numerous other schools are implementing the SDP as an integral part of the CoZi and ATLAS initiatives that we describe later in this chapter and in Chapter 3.

Within the past year, we have embarked on two new, major initiatives: Systemic Implementation (SI), and the launching of the SDP longitudinal cohort study (from the year 1994 to the year 2000). Systemic Implementation infuses SDP principles at the district level and trains key central office staff, school board members, and members of professional and support staff. Our experience shows that schools that have improved using our process must be supported systemically or they may decline or persist with difficulty when administrative or other change events occur. In order for the SDP to be implemented effectively at the school level, there has to be total commitment to the process on the part of the district's superintendent of schools and the motivation of district-level administrators charged with overseeing its implementation. The change in the organization, management, and process of schooling requires the approval and full support of the superintendent of schools and the school board. Efforts to develop facilitative relationships with community agencies, unions, and leadership groups in the school system and the larger community also need to take place. The SDP's district-level Systemic Implementation initiative is discussed in Chapter 7. Accompanying the Systemic Implementation initiative is the SDP's longitudinal cohort study in the SI districts. The study is described in detail in Chapter 6.

We had long recognized the need to address family support, child rearing, and education issues for preschool-age children. In 1993, we joined forces with Dr. Edward Zigler, former director of the federal Office of Child Development and currently Sterling Professor of Psychology at Yale, the director of the Yale Bush Center, and founder of School of the 21st Century (21C). Together, we established the Comer–Zigler (CoZi) project. In this project, family and community services are mobilized to prepare children for school. Child development principles and practices are involved in the organization and management of the before-school and in-school programs.

Through our involvement in a project entitled Authentic Teaching, Learning, and Assessment for all Students (ATLAS), funded by the New American Schools Development Corporation, we are extending our work through high schools and are addressing how curriculum, instruction, assessment, and technology may enhance student learning and understanding. ATLAS is a cooperative effort that will fuse the principles and practices involved in Theodore Sizer's Coalition of Essential Schools at Brown University, Howard Gardner's Project Zero at Harvard University, and Janet Whitla's teacher preparation and educational technology utilization work at the Education Development Center in Newton, Massachusetts. The design of the ATLAS model began in 1992; implementation is underway in K-12 feeder pathways in three school districts.

Since 1990, the SDP has used a number of traditional dissemination tools such as a quarterly newsletter, the *SDP Newsline,* as well as several telecommunications strategies such as the Internet and satellite broadcasting. The SDP has a web site on the World Wide Web at http://info.med.yale.edu/comer which includes an overview of the program, a staff and national SDP network directory, a bibliography of publications produced by the SDP staff since 1990, and more.

In collaboration with EVT Productions, Inc., we have developed a series of how-to videotapes, entitled *For Children's Sake: The Comer School Development Program,* and an accompanying manual that complements our work in school districts where we are directly involved. The tapes and manual will enable some school districts to implement the model without our presence.

The SDP has also worked with the Association for Supervision and Curriculum Development and N.A.K. Production Associates to produce two national satellite broadcasts about the SDP in 1993 and 1994. The 1994 program, *The Comer Process: Education, Health and Family Services Collaborating for Children's Sake,* won best direct satellite application as a one-time special event at the 13th annual TeleCon Awards sponsored by *TeleConference,* the business communications magazine.

Through a collaboration with Cleveland State University and the SDP schools in Cleveland, the national SDP office is working to develop a professional development model that uses a variety of telecommunications strategies including distance learning, e-mail, desktop videoconferencing, and web pages for individual schools and classrooms. The lessons we learn from this pilot project will help us to build a national SDP telecommunications network city by city.

Policy Implications

Our work in the SDP has significant implications for the reformation of national education and social policy and the refocusing of educational practice across the United States. Since the mid-1980s, and most recently, with former President Bush's New American Schools initiative, we have informed and, in some cases, led the debate about what true educational reform means and what it must entail. We have asserted time and time again that genuine reform in education must address a number of key issues:

1. We need a greater focus on and support for preschool readiness programs, such as Headstart and Zigler's School of the 21st Century. The CoZi project is a good example of future directions.
2. The school must become an important, integral service component of the community. The mission of the school changes from being only the purveyor of knowledge to being a central, coalescing agent where vital services for children and families are provided in an integrated way. The relationship between learning and socioeconomic development is clearly recognized, and the school's action plan reflects this awareness. The Comprehensive School Plan in all of our schools includes goals that address the relationship between the school and the community. Also, activities are designed that promote an interface between services and school programs. Thus, the school becomes a true part of the community.
3. Schools' hierarchical management systems must be transformed into systems of collaboration and involvement of all the key stakeholders in the

education of the children. This reorganization requires that the power to make decisions and establish policy should not be the domain of any one individual or a few individuals, but should be shared equally among school administrators, staff, and parents who work in mutually respectful, supporting ways, with decision-making guided by considerations of what is best for children.

4. School curricula and the social developmental experiences of children must teach children respect for themselves and for others, together with the responsible behavior and values that are an integral part of good citizenship and exemplary lives.

5. We must recognize the centrality of the family in the child's self-definition and development, and we must seek to involve parents and guardians in meaningful ways in children's school experiences. Families and schools must be seen as partners, not as antagonists; parents must not remain on the periphery of the educational enterprise. This approach requires well-defined mechanisms and strategies for ensuring meaningful parent involvement, including workplace policy adjustments that are flexible enough to allow parents to participate more in their children's education.

6. We must increase student achievement through examining time use and curriculum/test alignment in classrooms. Chapter 5 explores this topic in depth.

7. We must develop curricula and pedagogical approaches that are sensitive and responsive to the diverse needs of children from various cultures, racial groups, and ethnic groups, and to those children with special physical, cognitive, or psychological needs.

8. We must pay attention to child development issues, and we must incorporate child development knowledge into teacher preparation programs and the inservice training of practicing teachers. Schools of education have failed in large part to prepare teachers who are sufficiently knowledgeable about child development issues and sensitive to the influence of experience on learning. In our partnerships with universities and school districts, we seek to have an impact on the curriculum and educational experiences the universities provide to their prospective teachers, professional support staff, and other school personnel in training.

Many school improvement approaches have emerged in recent years. Most differ from our approach in at least three significant ways. First, most give specific attention to one major group within a school setting—either the students, or the teachers, or the parents—or to one program area, such as curriculum, social skills, or artistic expression. We use a *comprehensive* approach in which *all* groups work in a collaborative fashion, coordinating resources and programs to establish and achieve school objectives and goals.

Second, most programs are not driven by child development and relationship concepts at all—or else they utilize such concepts only in regard to the students. By contrast, all aspects of our work are driven by relationship and child development imperatives, focusing most on institutional arrangements that hinder adequate functioning of all members of the school community.

Third, many programs focus exclusively on academic achievement. The SDP's approach to school reform acknowledges that creating a climate conducive to successful teaching and learning requires an organizational structure that decreases the friction, resistance, and interference to authentic learning and healthy development. We begin by creating a school climate that permits parents and staff to support the overall development of all students in a way that makes academic achievement and desirable social behavior both possible and expected. We believe that such an approach has a much greater potential for improving students' chances of achieving school success, decreasing their likelihood of being involved in problem behaviors, and increasing their chances for life success.

We believe that insights gleaned from the School Development Program have implications for education in the United States and other countries. This book underscores the need for us to operate in a way that will make the knowledge from our work, and that of others throughout the country, available to other researchers, practitioners, policymakers, and all others with a stake in positive educational outcomes.

Historically, educational reform efforts have not adequately addressed many of the underlying causes for school failure among U.S. students. Reform initiatives have tended to be knee-jerk reactions to perceived threats to the international competitiveness of U.S. students and the U.S. work force, rather than sustained, proactive attempts to change the culture, contexts, and focus of schools. By focusing attention on the interactions that occur in schools, we pave the way for the emergence of self-perpetuating school structures designed to sustain educational change and promote the development of the whole child.

References

Becker, B. J., & Hedges, L. V. (1992). A review of the literature on the effectiveness of Comer's School Development Program. Report prepared for the Rockefeller Foundation, University of Michigan and University of Chicago.

Comer, J. P. (1980). *School power: Implications of an intervention project.* New York: The Free Press.

Comer, J. P. (1988). Educating poor minority children. *Scientific American, 259* (5), 42–48.

Comer, J. P. (1989). Child development and education. *Journal of Negro Education, 58* (2), 125–139.

Emmons, C., Owen, S. V., Haynes, N. M., & Comer, J. P. (1992). *A causal model of the effects of school climate, classroom climate, academic self-concept, suspension and absenteeism on academic achievement.* Paper presented at the 1992 Conference of the Eastern Educational Research Association, Hilton Head, South Carolina, March 3–8.

Haynes, N. M., & Bility, K. (1994) Evaluating school development. *School Development Program Research Monograph.* New Haven, CT: Yale Child Study Center.

Haynes, N. M., & Comer, J. P. (1990). The effects of a school development program on self-concept. *The Yale Journal of Biology and Medicine, 63,* 275–283.

Haynes, N. M., & Comer, J. P. (1993). The Yale School Development Program: Process outcomes and policy implications. *Urban Education, 28* (2), 166–169.

Haynes, N. M., Comer, J. P., & Hamilton-Lee, M. (1989a). The effects of parental involvement on student performance. *Educational and Psychological Research, 8* (4), 291–299.

Haynes, N. M., Comer, J. P., & Hamilton-Lee, M. (1989b). School climate enhancement through parental involvement. *Journal of School Psychology, 27,* 87–90.

Haynes, N. M., & Joyner, E. (1992). *Proposal for Developing a Framework for the Comer Developmental Pathways Curriculum.* New Haven, CT: Yale Child Study Center.

Joyner, E., Haynes, N. M., & Comer, J. P. (1994). Implementation of the Yale School Development Program in two middle schools: An ethnographic study. In Norris M. Haynes (ed.), *School Development Program Research Monograph.* New Haven, CT: Yale Child Study Center.

Schorr, L. B. (1988). *Within our reach: Breaking the cycle of disadvantage.* New York: Anchor Books, Doubleday.

Chapter 2

Translating Theory into Practice: Comer's Theory of School Reform

CHRISTINE L. EMMONS, JAMES P. COMER, AND NORRIS M. HAYNES

The School Development Program model is a unique outgrowth from previous social theories. Comer's training gave him a deep understanding of individual and social psychology, community health, and psychiatry. Synthesizing and expanding these disciplines, he created a strong and novel theoretical framework for educational reform.

Why a Theory of School Reform?

To be coherent, action that will bring about long-lasting change needs a theory that organizes and directs it. This theory acts as litmus to check the appropriateness of what is included in the solution. If such a theory does not exist, the goals and procedures of a plan of action will have no organizing principle and, as a result, will become subject to passing whims. Therefore, in his conceptualization of a school reform plan of action, Comer researched the literature of psychiatry, psychotherapy, and psychology for ideas that would form an organizing base or theory. Failing to find any one theory adequate for this purpose, Comer created "a theoretical formulation that combined elements from several models" (see Figure 2-1; Comer, Haynes, and Hamilton-Lee, 1987, p. 192). These models included elements of:

- Lewin's (1936) social psychology theory (field theory)
- Human ecological systems theory, particularly as explained by Kelly (1966)
- The population adjustment model by Becker, Wylan, and McCourt (1971), and Hartman (1979)
- The social action model by Reiff (1966)

Population Adjustment Model
Becker, Wylan, and McCourt (1971)
Hartman (1979)

- Identify populations at risk for developing mental illness.

- Intervene through modifying the environment to promote mental health.

Social Action Model
Reiff (1966)

- Program planning should be a collaborative effort between professionals and community members.

- Professionals should have an integral knowledge of the community in which they are working.

Comer's Theoretical Framework of Child Development

- A child's behavior is determined by his or her interaction with the physical, social, and psychological environments.

- Children need positive interactions with adults in order to develop adequately.

- Child-centered planning and collaboration among adults facilitate positive interactions.

- All planning for child development should be a collaborative effort between professionals and community members.

Comer's Framework Applied
The School Development Program

- Three Guiding Principles
- Three Mechanisms (Teams)
- Three Operations

Field Theory
Lewin (1936)

- Everything an individual knows, feels, and perceives is done in a subjective reality.

- This subjective reality is known as a person's psychological field or life space; only those things present in the life space influence behavior.

Human Ecological Systems Theory
Kelly (1966)

- Behavior is an interaction of human beings with the physical, social, and psychological environments, making behavior adaptive.

- The theory's four principles are:
  — The community is the client.
  — Reduce those community services that maintain the status quo.
  — Strengthen community resources.
  — Plan for change.

Figure 2-1. The foundations of Comer's theoretical framework of school reform.

These ideas were refined through application in the New Haven Public School system and emerged as the School Development Program (SDP).

Comer's Synthesis

Comer's synthesis begins with several postulates. Humans are social beings who need community support and involvement to develop adequately. Their behavior is an adaptation or reaction to their environment as they build that necessary community, and is based on their perceptions of their environment, rather than on any "objective" reality. Human behavior is consistent in given situations within a range of similar perceptions. To change an individual's behavior, therefore, one must be able to understand that individual's perceptions, including feelings, attitudes, and abilities, at the given time. Desirable behavior change is that which results in the optimal development of the individual and the common good.

To change any individual's behavior one must be able to understand that individual's perceptions. To change a child's behavior one must be able to understand that child. School is designed for the development of the child: to elicit behavior change that results in development, school personnel must understand each child in their care. Understanding a child requires prolonged focus. Hence, in Comer school reform theory, the child is the focus of all school activities. The school is child-centered. The first measure of whether or not a school is an SDP school is the extent to which it addresses the total development of all children.

According to Comer, each school is an ecological system in which behavior, attitude, and achievement levels of students reflect the school's climate (defined as the frequency and quality of interactions among parents, teachers, students, the principal, administrators, and adjunct staff). It follows that to change the students' attitudes, behavior, and achievement, one must change the interactions within the system, or the parts of the system that have an impact on the individual. Change in the interactions within the system results in change in the environment (social, academic, instructional, physical). With each change in the environment, students adjust their behavior. To change the interactions, Comer uses a notion from systems management theory (Comer, 1988); changes in the inputs and processes will result in changes in the products (e.g., student attitudes, student behavior, and student achievement).

The social action model provides a mechanism for changing systems. If the school is a social system that needs to be changed, then the behavior of individuals within this system must change. If behavior is to be changed, then the environment must be changed. If the environment is to be changed, then professionals and clients must work collaboratively to solve problems. The School Planning and Management Team (SPMT), the Student and Staff Support Team (SSST), and the Parent Team (PT) of the School Development Program provide the necessary structure. Through participation in these teams, a wider variety of people are involved in the life of the school. This tends to lead to a greater number and a wider variety of resources being available to the school. A second measure of whether a school is an SDP school, therefore, is the existence of these three teams in the school.

In the SDP, the implementation of the population adjustment model is manifested in the functioning of the SSST. The role of this team is to focus on primary prevention through the development of a warm and supportive climate that fosters optimal development of the students along the six developmental pathways. For the supportive climate, and, in turn, for development to occur, children must see positive images of the significant adults in their lives, adults who feel empowered and who are empowered by having some say in the events that affect their lives.

Participation in the three teams gives school and community people the opportunity to share in the decision-making power. However, if they are to participate, they must feel comfortable and valued. The consensus, collaboration, and no-fault approach to teamwork and problem solving creates such a climate. This approach results in improved relationships among the adults and a greater sense of security among the students who see their parents, teachers, principals, and counselors all working with each other (and with the students) sharing a common mission: the development of each child. A third measure, therefore, of whether a school is an SDP school is the extent to which consensus, collaboration, and no-fault are practiced in the functioning of the teams and in other school-based relationships, and between the school and the community at large. A fourth measure is the extent to which the school is organized around preventing problems as well as dealing with them when they occur.

Because the school is a system, change in any part will affect the entire school. Therefore, all aspects of school life must be coordinated. The Comprehensive School Plan, the plan for change, is the document through which this coordination takes place. This plan is developed and administered by the SPMT, with input from the other teams or any interested stakeholder. If there is a plan, it must be assessed and modified as needed. Areas of training and development for students, staff, and parents must be identified and implemented as needed to ensure the proper implementation of all school activities. To accomplish this, the three processes of Comprehensive School Plan, staff development, and assessment and modification are monitored and administered through the three teams: the School Planning and Management Team, the Student and Staff Support Team, and the Parent Team. Teams use the three principles of consensus, collaboration, and no-fault with the aim of the optimal development of each child along the six developmental pathways.

The remainder of this chapter is a specific discussion of the four theoretical models from which Comer's model grew, with particular attention to the application of each one to the SDP.

▓▓▓▓ Social Psychology Theory (Field Theory)

▓▓▓▓▓▓ Exposition

Lewin's (1936) social psychology theory, also called field theory, states that the individual functions in a psychological environment that is composed of feelings about
objects, situations, self, and others. According to field theory, behavior is determined
by this immediate psychological environment and the state (physical, social, intellectual) of the person at the time. In social psychology, behavior is driven not by the
individual as an isolated entity, but by the interaction of the individual with the environment. Lewin's work on field theory was influenced by Gestalt theory with respect
to the relationship of individuals to the psychological environment (Watson, 1979).

In field theory, the environment is defined psychobiologically, not physically
(Lewin, 1935). That is, the environment includes not only what can be seen and
touched but also what is felt. According to Lewin (1935), "a person lives in a psychological field" and only facts that have a position in this psychological field can
influence behavior. This psychological field, the immediate social and psychological contexts in which an individual functions, is referred to as that person's life space
(for a child in the classroom, his or her life space could consist not only of the other
people and objects in the room but of this child's feelings of anxiety about learning,
parental pressures, and feelings of helplessness). The life space of a person at any
particular time includes all that affects behavior at that time but nothing else (Lewin,
1951). The life space contains situations or regions, subregions, positive and negative valences, barriers, and paths (Lewin, 1938). A situation or region is the psychological meaning of an object or activity and includes self-perceptions, feelings,
and activities (Bigge and Hunt, 1980). Regions and subregions are also described as
goal areas (Lewin, 1936), because inherent in the psychological meaning of an object
or activity is its purpose or aim. Valences are positive or negative pulls that draw
people toward or away from various objects and activities to which the individual
has ascribed psychological meaning. Valences may be of varying strengths (Lewin,
1936). Barriers, according to the theory, are boundaries or hindrances to achieving
any goals. For example, a region may be computer competence: An individual may
want to be an expert in word processing and database management because of
increased opportunities for promotion and increased marketability. This constitutes
a positive valence toward computer competence. On the other hand, the same individual may have reservations about being computer competent because of the probability of being assigned additional work and more difficult work. This is a negative
valence. A barrier to that person's achieving computer competence may be fear of
destroying files on the computers, or lack of funds to pay for computer courses to
upgrade and enhance one's knowledge of computers.

A person's psychological field or life space also includes paths between regions,
movement along these paths, and force. A path is defined as the actions an indi-

vidual takes to achieve a particular goal. This path may not always be a direct one (for example, a child who wants the teacher's attention and concern to deal with a problem may not feel comfortable enough to approach the teacher and might act up in class instead to get the teacher's attention). Direction in field theory is, therefore, not physical direction but psychological direction. When a problem can be viewed as a whole so that actions needed for its solution are clear, regardless of how indirect the path, this person's field or life space has been restructured. In field theory, Lewin was concerned with the individual's environment that includes other people. "Hence, his was a social psychological approach to the motivational forces working on the individual" (Watson, 1979, p. 316).

An individual's life space becomes increasingly complex with age and development. This complexity results from "differentiation, integration, and restructuring" (Lewin, 1936, p. 155). Differentiation is the cognitive ability to make increasingly fine distinctions among what seem to be similar things. Integration is the cognitive ability to see commonality among apparently different things. Restructuring is the cognitive ability to make connections that lead to new and different meanings of desires and activities in life. Children learn what actions will bring what results; individuals identify with groups (Bigge and Hunt, 1980). Identification with a group influences individual behavior, and groups are more powerful and more effective levers for change than individuals (Frank, 1978). The ideologies of these groups then become a motivating factor (Bigge and Hunt, 1980). Bodily changes throughout childhood, adolescence, and adulthood also bring about restructuring that includes the expansion of the time dimension, as children move from existing only in the present to the ability to imagine the past and the future. Things are seen in a new light as redefinitions take place (Bigge and Hunt, 1980). The life space is organized in a hierarchy that increases with age (Lewin, 1951).

If behavior is to a large extent determined by changes in an individual's life space, then for explaining or predicting behavior it is essential to be aware of the linkages in that person's current life space (Lewin, 1951). Lewin (1938) notes that perception is extremely important to the life space, because, he says, the behavior of individuals is influenced not by the way the world "objectively" is but by how they perceive it to be. Nonetheless, their perceptions are real in their consequences.

According to Lewin (1936), the first prerequisite for understanding a child is to determine the psychological place in which this child is currently situated and his or her freedom of movement region or "space of free movement" (p. 42). A space of free movement is an area of behavior that is either available to the child or that exists psychologically for the child (i.e., the child knows that it is an option) but is at that time unavailable because of the constraints of others (such as adult forbiddance) or because of his or her limited physical, social, or intellectual skills. The size of a child's space of free movement "is of decisive significance for the whole behavior of the child" (Lewin, 1935, p. 80). *In other words, if it does not occur to a child that a particular behavior can be performed, that behavior will not be performed.*

Summary

In field theory, everything an individual knows, feels, perceives, and experiences, occurs in subjective reality, at a particular time, in a particular situation. That constitutes that person's psychological field or life space, and only those things present in the life space can influence the individual's behavior. To understand and influence someone's behavior, one has to understand that person's life space, including the range of behavior available to that individual. To influence someone's behavior, one has to (1) know that person's goal region, and (2) introduce into that person's psychological field those experiences that either change the valences of selected goal areas or that remove barriers to goal areas. Thus, the individual can view the problem in a holistic manner and see ways to achieve his or her goals. Because the size of the freedom of movement region is a decisive factor in an individual's behavior, it is important to introduce into the person's life space those experiences that will broaden the range of possible behaviors available to that person.

Application in the School Development Program

Comer applied Lewin's theory to the world of schools. He formulated the following basic assumptions that undergird the SDP:

- School reformers must stress the importance of understanding child and adolescent development along all critical pathways, so that they can arrange the school environment to enhance the life space of all students.
- School reformers should learn about the child's family and community, and anything that influences the child's life space. They must try to understand the child's behavior before proposing any intervention.
- School reform programs should provide experiences that expand options for behavior—the freedom of movement—both for children and for the significant adults in their lives. Enhancing their physical, social, and psychological development is a prerequisite to increasing behavior options.

The Comer theory of school reform places the child at the center of the process. Such a child-centered focus demands an understanding of the child through a study of what is known about child development in general, about children in a given situation, and about each individual child situated in the family, school, community, and society at large. In the SDP, Lewin's (1936) model of action, training, and research for implementing and maintaining institutional change is translated into:

- Implementation—the operationalization of the three teams (the School Planning and Management Team, the Student and Staff Support Team, and the Parent Team)
- Staff development
- Assessment and modification

▧▧ Human Ecological Systems Theory

▧▧▧ Exposition

Human ecological systems theory merged human ecological theory with organizational systems theory. This synthesis resulted in a theory of optimal service delivery to people in communities. The theory of human ecology came out of the study of general ecology. Wilkinson and O'Connor (1982) credited Park and Burgess with the first direct transfer of general ecological concepts to human behavior. Wilkinson and O'Connor noted that the notion that environment influences behavior also has its roots in Lewin's field theory. Hawley (1944) described the study of ecology as the examination of the ways in which

> growing, multiplying beings maintain themselves in a constantly changing but ever restricted environment. [Ecology] is based on the fundamental assumption that life is a continuous struggle for adjustment of organism to environment. (p. 403)

Hawley noted that human ecology describes the "adjustment of human populations" to their physical, moral, and psychological environment. According to Hawley, the distinguishing characteristic of human ecology is the idea that human adjustment to habitat is a community development process.

Kelly (1966) and Wilkinson and O'Connor (1982) applied human ecological systems theory to the design and delivery of mental health services. They were disaffected with the approach of treating individual patients as entities in isolation, while the contexts in which the mental illness developed were ignored. In his application of this theory to the delivery of mental health services, Kelly listed three questions that must be answered before optimal service delivery can occur:

1. How can an organizational systems model be used to link mental health services and other community services?
2. What is the relationship between individual behavior and the physical environment?
3. What is the relationship between individuals and their immediate social environment?

The assumption underlying the first question is that because the operation of one unit will affect the functioning of all other units, the coordination of all services to a community improves delivery. The assumption underlying the second and third questions is that individual behavior occurs through interaction with defined physical and social environments, and that to understand and treat pathology, one must understand and change the context in which it occurs (Kelly, 1966).

The assumptions underlying the three questions set the stage for the four principles (consistent with the ecological thesis) for programming community mental health services (Kelly, 1966):

1. *The community is the client.* Therefore, the focus of assessment is the total population, rather than individuals.
2. *Reduce the use of those community services that maintain the status quo* because a prevention focus requires change in the social structure of the population being served. Those at risk can be identified in their natural setting.
3. *Strengthen the community resources.* Mental health programming should function as a resource, thus helping to create a basis for problem solving (Kelly, 1966, p. 537) and for "professional and research services to the local community resources" (Ibid., p. 537). Mental health programming should help to coordinate existing services and so help to create new services as needed, examples of which are "collaboration of activities, the creation of staff development institutes, and provision of multiple research services" (Ibid., p. 537).
4. *Plan for change.* Anticipate problems for both clients and professionals. Planning can cause short-term disruption and discomfort, but it leads to long-term increased effectiveness and efficiency. Kelly (1966) stated:

   The elements of the planning cycle include data sources which provide continuous input of the interdependent and reciprocal effects of three elements: the plan, community services, and the population at risk. (p. 537)

Kelly stressed the importance of socially effective indigenous leaders. According to Kelly, behavior is not viewed as sick or well but as adaptive: Behavior is the result of interaction between individual and social situation.

Wilkinson and O'Connor (1982) developed a model based on the APA Task Force concept name *ecopsychiatry* that "is based on a systemic model derived originally from biological ecology" (p. 985). Ecopsychiatry is the study of the person–environment interactions that affect an individual's mental health. Its model takes into account the familial and social factors that affect mental health, merging clinical and community treatment with prevention interventions. The unit of analysis and intervention from an ecological perspective is "a population and its environment" (Wilkinson and O'Connor, 1982). For an individual, the ecological focus is the individual in complete physical, organizational, social, cultural, and psychological contexts (ibid). According to Wilkinson and O'Connor, the main advantage of an ecological model is the conceptualization of the individual, community, or organization functioning in a consistent manner. Use of such a model should result in interactions between individuals and the environment that are mutually beneficial.

All systems—from physiological to sociocultural—influence individual behavior. Therefore, before acting one must decide on the significant contexts for assessment and interventions, and determine whether the intervention should take place on the individual or systemic level.

According to Wilkinson and O'Connor, "Assessment and intervention in an ecosystemic framework extend beyond the individual, to the interactions within the individual's ecosystem" (p. 987). The intervention focus is placed on processes of the ecosystem that are dysfunctional, rather than on the individual's adaptation (Stokols, 1977). Wilkinson and O'Connor defined adaptation as the individual's ability to cope with the environment. They state that optimization includes adaptation but extends to the maintenance and modification of the environment to meet needs more adequately.

Existing techniques are not discarded but assessed for their suitability. When the intervention is aimed at the broader context, the psychiatrist often becomes the advocate for the patient with the community agencies. The advocacy may be as a case coordinator to monitor and facilitate contacts with agencies or as a community consultant who identifies the organization–patient dysfunction and facilitates organizational change (Wilkinson and O'Connor, 1982, p. 988; citing F. V. Mannino and M. F. Shore, paper presented at the 1980 annual meeting of the American Psychological Association, Montreal).

Summary

Human ecological systems theory is the study of the individual in the context of the environment. It describes behavior as the interaction of human beings with the physical, social, and psychological environment and views behavior as adaptive, rather than sick or well. It states that the context in which individuals function influences their behavior. Because the context influences behavior, treating individuals and returning them to the same environment will almost guarantee a return to the previous pathological behavior. Optimization of an individual's ability to cope goes beyond adaptation; it requires the modification and maintenance of the changed environment. Therefore, the community, not just the individual, should be the client.

Because communities and organizations are systems in which change in one part affects the other parts, services to the community should be coordinated so that a coherent and consistent approach can be presented. To maintain change in the community or institution, there must be deep-rooted changes in the structure of the community and its level of functioning. Such changes can be maintained only if self-sustaining community resources are developed. This necessitates training effective local leaders.

There should be symmetry between the functioning of the individual and the community. This requires not only the coordination of services and resources, but a plan of action for change that identifies problem areas and develops and applies solutions.

Application in the School Development Program

Comer's theory of educational reform is based on the assumption that the process of change in schools is the process of relationship and community building. This is reflected in the "whole village" concept (see Chapter 3) and in the emphasis on building good relationships among the relevant adults—the school staff, the principal, and community members—for the benefit of the children.

From the four principles of human ecology (the community is client; reduce the use of those community services that maintain the status quo; strengthen community resources; plan for change) emerge part of the theoretical basis for the SDP. Although the focus of school reform is the individual child, the SDP views the child as a part of the family unit and neighborhood as well as a part of the school community. The intervention is, therefore, made at the school level rather than at the individual child level. Because the emphasis is on changing the social structures and building local capacity and expertise, the governance of the school is placed under the auspices of a School Planning and Management Team (SPMT) that is composed of all the stakeholders, including parents. The SPMT organizes and integrates the various school and community resources available to the school. SDP staff serve as consultants to the process, functioning as part of the professional and research services to the school community. The Student and Staff Support Team (SSST) allows for the identification of maladaptive behavior in the natural school setting, where both curative and preventive measures are taken. Staff development and assessment and modification are two of the processes through which SDP effects school reform. The plan for change in the SDP is the Comprehensive School Plan, the third SDP operation.

The SDP facilitators and members of the three teams can be considered effective indigenous leaders. It follows that if the social situation is changed, the type of interaction that the individual has with the social environment must necessarily change. Therefore, the SDP emphasizes improving school climate as a means of changing behavior.

The Population Adjustment Model

Exposition

The population adjustment model proposed by Becker, Wylan, and McCourt (1971) and by Hartman (1979) is a primary prevention model of mental health services. Becker et al. (1971) affirmed that the role of mental health centers stretched beyond treatment to primary prevention—identifying populations and individuals at risk for developing behavior pathology and designing preventive interventions. The premise on which the interventions are based is that pathology is the result of stressful life events coupled with lack of the necessary behavioral or coping skills to deal with these events (Hartman, 1979). People less skilled in stressful situations need a greater amount of social and environmental support "in order to continue to function effectively" (Hartman, 1979, p. 123). Hartman stated that primary prevention "calls for the identification of a symptom-free population at psychological risk for developing behavior pathology" (p. 122). One such population is the poor, who, according to Becker et al. (1971), are particularly vulnerable to feelings of inadequacy and powerlessness—feelings that adversely affect their mental well-being. Becker et al. stated that in every field, program planners were recognizing the need to consult the clients of prospective services before developing their programs. They noted that "consumer involvement in program planning and decision-making [was] absolutely crucial" (p. 45).

According to Hartman (1979), "the central tenet of this [population adjustment] approach is that disorder is the consequence of ineffective coping techniques employed by persons in a variety of life situations" (p. 123). Therefore, the solution is to prevent vulnerable individuals from developing behavior pathology by providing them with coping strategies, for example, social skills training to deal with the stressful situations and events of life. A study conducted by Hartman supported this hypothesis.

Summary

In the population adjustment model, primary prevention is key. The aim is to identify populations at risk for developing mental illness or behavior pathology. After the populations are identified, two interventions are implemented to prevent the manifestation of pathology:

1. The environment is modified to promote mental health.
2. Members of the population are provided with coping skills to improve the chances of adjustment.

Because feelings of inadequacy and low self-worth contribute to pathology, clients should be involved in the planning of their mental health services.

Application in the School Development Program

Parent participation at every level of school building activity is illustrative of the assumption that the clients for whom a service is being provided should be involved in the design and implementation of that service. This involvement becomes a vehicle for empowering parents and school staff, improving their sense of accomplishment and motivating them to take ownership of the service. Opportunities for empowerment come especially through the three teams of the SDP; other avenues are also available simply through the way each person is treated with respect and the way the opinion of the person is valued.

The modification of the environment takes the form of improved relationships among the adults through the consensus, collaboration, and no-fault approach to teamwork and problem solving. The SSST is charged with identifying students at risk for behavior problems and helping them develop coping skills, as well as providing everyone with a healthy, safe, caring, and stimulating environment in which to learn and function.

The Social Action Model

Exposition

Reiff's (1966) social action model is a social systems change model that urges the collaboration of professionals with clients in the development of programs that bring about societal change for the benefit of the whole community. In applying this model to the delivery of mental health services, Reiff (1966) stated:

> A really innovative community mental health program requires greater clinical skill, knowledge about social process and social organization, and an ability to be versatile in shifting one's focus from individual, to group, to social systems. (p. 543)

Reiff raised two interrelated concerns: sensitivity to the needs and perceptions of low-income people, and delivery of services that change the environmental conditions that foster mental illness. Reiff noted that low-income people were suspicious of mental health services rendered by strangers to the community, and that they were wary of being treated by the same person who treats serious mental illness. Reiff stressed the need for primary prevention and the need to change social systems for the common good, but noted the difficulty of changing institutions.

According to Reiff, there was a need for an adequate theory, body of knowledge, or set of concepts on which to base training for a social action approach. He stated that there should be a new set of experts in "changing social systems for prevention of mental illness and for the improvement of the psychological effectiveness of all individuals in society to deal with problems of living" (p. 544). Reiff identified the need for social scientists and clinicians to come together and for an integrative theory to allow them to come together. He suggested that social and behavioral scientists and mental health professionals become "participant conceptualizers" with nonprofessionals from the poor in the community in order to influence policy. According to Reiff, people who decide to enter the domain of institutional change must confront issues of power, which he considers a strong determinant in the outcomes of institutional change efforts.

Summary

Reiff's social action model changes social systems for the common good. This model is based on the theory that environmental conditions influence human behavior, sometimes pathologically. Therefore, to change behavior, one has to modify the environment or social system. But one cannot successfully change the social system without having the professional service providers work collaboratively with the clients (including the poor, whose needs and concerns must be addressed) to solve problems and influence policy. In doing so, one must confront issues of power and control that are sure to surface.

Application in the School Development Program

In Comer's school reform theory, the school is a social system. This social system needs to be changed if it is not working well, as manifested by degree of student development along the physical, cognitive, psychological, language, social, and ethical pathways. (Comer believes that development along these six pathways is critical for a child to become an optimally functioning human being). To achieve the common good of children and all concerned, the change agent must plan with the local people, school staff, parents, community members, and where appropriate, students. That is why the SDP is not prescriptive. It provides a framework within which professionals and clients (that is, school personnel, parents, and community members) can collaborate. This structure includes the three teams and the guiding principles of consensus, collaboration, and no-fault, within which issues of power are addressed. Because the SPMT, composed of all stakeholders, is the governing body, all constituents are represented. Because decisions are made by consensus, there are no losers. The no-fault principle reduces individual feelings of vulnerability. In addition, the SPMT cannot be a rubber stamp for the principal, nor must it completely thwart the will of the principal. Using the guiding principles, even the implementation of the teams themselves creates change in the social environment through the development of improved interpersonal relationships. These improved relations set the stage for tackling serious and deep-rooted problems.

References

Becker, A., Wylan, L., & McCourt, W. (1971). Primary prevention: Whose responsibility? *American Journal of Psychiatry, 128,* 412–417.

Bigge, M. L., & Hunt, M. P. (1980). *Psychological foundations of education.* New York: Harper & Row.

Comer, J. P. (1988). Educating poor minority children. *Scientific American, 259* (5), 42–48.

Comer, J. P., Haynes, N. M., & Hamilton-Lee, M. (1987). School power: A model for improving black student achievement. *Urban League Review, 11,* 187–200.

Frank, J. D. (1978). Kurt Lewin in retrospect—a psychiatrist's view. *Journal of the History of the Behavioral Sciences, 14,* 223–227.

Hartman, G. W. (1935). *Gestalt psychology.* New York: Ronald Press.

Hartman, L. (1979). The preventive reduction of psychological risk in asymptomatic adolescents. *American Journal of Orthopsychiatry, 49,* 121–135.

Hawley, A. H. (1944). Ecology and human ecology. *Social Forces, 22,* 398–405.

Kelly, J. G. (1966). Ecological constraints on mental health services. *American Psychologist, 21,* 535–539.

Lewin, K. (1935). *A dynamic theory of personality: Selected papers.* New York: McGraw-Hill.

Lewin, K. (1936). *Principles of topological psychology.* New York: McGraw-Hill.

Lewin, K. (1938). The conceptual presentation of the measurement of psychological forces. *Contributions to Psychological Theory, 1* (4).

Lewin, K. (1951). *Field theory in social science.* New York: Harper & Brothers.

Reiff, J. (1966). Mental health manpower and institutional change. *American Psychologist, 21,* 540–548.

Stokols, D. (1977). Origins and directions of environment–behavioral research. In D. Stokols (ed.), *On environment and behavior: Theory, research and applications.* New York: Plenum Press.

Watson, R. I. (1979). *Basic writings in the history of psychology.* New York: Oxford University Press.

Wilkinson, C. B., & O'Connor, W. A. (1982). Human ecology and mental illness. *American Journal of Psychiatry, 139,* 985–990.

Chapter 3

It Takes a Whole Village:
The SDP School

NORRIS M. HAYNES, MICHAEL BEN-AVIE,
DAVID A. SQUIRES, J. PATRICK HOWLEY,
EDNA N. NEGRON, AND JOANNE NANCY CORBIN

All children are at risk today. More homes are broken, more are led by single mothers, more have two parents away at work. For children to develop healthily, well-functioning adults must be available and attentive to them at all times. In the SDP school, the adults work creatively and enthusiastically with each other and with the children, setting a powerful model for the children's attitudes toward school, society, and the future.

Schools Have Taken a Mechanistic Turn

Scientific and technological advances are, in Comer's (1989a) words, "increasing the level of development needed to succeed—the highest level ever required in the history of the world" (p. 127). Children need to learn how to integrate the tremendous amount of information that is bombarding them due to the advances in technology, and when to act upon the information (Comer, 1989b, p. 132). When their climate is psychologically nurturing and educationally exemplary, schools can help prepare children to succeed in this complex world.

However, schools have taken a mechanistic turn: "Learning has become very much like the model of the computer, with its input and processing sequences: We assume that a person has learned when he or she is able to make an output" (Comer, 1989b, p. 125). The primary question most schools ask when stating their mission is, "What knowledge and skills do students need to understand?" The current school structure is designed with subject matter as the dominant consideration.

Teachers can be replaced by others with the same certification. Students are scheduled according to subject matter courses. It does not matter who teaches history, as the content and processes have been standardized according to subject area experts. Yet schools organized around content are experiencing difficulties. As knowledge is increasing, the school's curriculum becomes more dense, more concentrated cognitively and academically. The knowledge explosion straps school resources, and we are left with the paradox of an expanding curriculum that actually contracts student options.

In order to counteract the mechanistic tendency of U.S. schools, reform initiatives are looking toward the School Development Program (SDP) for insights. Donald Cohen (1994), director of the Yale Child Study Center, captures the heart of the process when he notes:

> The Comer School Development Program has had an enormous influence in the contemporary view of the role of schools in the lives of children and families. The theoretical perspective of the SDP seems so natural today that we can hardly believe how novel it is and the challenges that its founder faced as he first presented his ideas. The profound influence of social and emotional development in shaping academic success, the role of parents in schools, the concept of school atmosphere as a defining factor in school reform: these, and other concepts which are part of current theory, are all related to the SDP contributions. (p. i)

The SDP school demonstrates three important concepts. The first concept is based on the African proverb, "It takes a whole village to raise a child." "It takes a whole village" of the SDP principal, staff, parents, external change agents such as the SDP facilitators, and community members to facilitate the highest levels of development among the students.

The second concept is that a school with a psychologically nurturing and educationally exemplary climate "permits parents and staff to support the overall development of students in a way that makes academic achievement and desirable social behavior possible" (Haynes, 1993, p. 32). The SDP school is noted for the staff's steadfast efforts to sustain an academic and social climate that promotes students' development. Dimensions of the academic climate of the school, such as staff dedication to student learning, the academic focus of the school, achievement motivation among the students, and high expectations, contribute to the school's academic climate being classified on a range from "educationally appropriate" to "educationally exemplary." The school's social climate can be classified on a continuum from "psychologically adequate" to "nurturing." The social climate has two notable characteristics: (1) the frequency and quality of interactions among parents, teachers, students, the principal, administrators, and adjunct staff; and (2) the feelings of trust and respect that exist within the school community (Emmons, 1992).

Faithful replication of the SDP improves essential dimensions of the climate in the SDP school. As these dimensions improve, students experience significant positive growth along the six developmental pathways and are at reduced risk for negative outcomes while increasing their probability for positive psychosocial behavioral and academic outcomes. A psychologically nurturing and educationally exemplary school is fertile ground for seeding staff professional development and educational reform initiatives aimed at improving *aspects* of the educative process, such as a math program. Grade-level teachers or the teachers of a department that do not work well together cannot come together as a team and implement a new curricular initiative. Individual teachers by themselves are not able to engage in global *preventive* actions on behalf of the students. Poor-quality relationships between staff members and the students interfere with the educative process. Poor interpersonal relationships among the students disrupt the staff's intentions to promote teamwork among them.

Creating the psychologically nurturing and educationally exemplary school climate requires "reinventing" community in the school, tapping the energy of individuals within the school and in the community, and an organizational structure that decreases the friction, the resistance, and the interference to authentic learning. This climate, conducive to learning, is promoted by the daily practice of the three guiding principles—consensus, collaboration, and no-fault—in all aspects of the educative process.

The third foundational SDP concept is that students' behavior, attitude, and achievement levels are to a large extent influenced by the school climate and a strong instructional program rather than by the students' socioeconomic status and ethnic background.

▮▮▮▮ *Children Are Reflections of Their Environments*

Vygotsky argued, in Tudge's words, that "in order to determine the nature and path of development, it becomes essential to examine the social environment in which development occurs and the type of instruction provided" (Tudge, 1990, p. 158). We approach child development with the understanding that the child learns from direct exposure to stimulating and challenging experiences and that the most meaningful learning stems from adult mediation. Comer (1989d) writes:

> Because of the extreme dependency on the child and the important role of the caretaker, the attitudes, values and ways of the caretaker greatly influence those of the young child. This allows the caretaker to mediate the child's experiences—to give them meaning and to establish their relative importance. (p. 353)

The child learns from the interactions that occur in the school setting, including interactions among the adults in the building and the connections between home and school. For example, the treatment of their parents by the school staff, of course, has an impact on how the students perceive the school and education in general. The children's learning process involves the environment in toto, including both the intentional, purposeful interactions and the offhand seemingly inconsequential remark or gesture. Children learn by observing how their peers are disciplined, by overhearing how the adults in the building interact with one another, through contact with written and other cultural products, and especially, through significant adults who take an interest.

With this, we understand, as Vygotsky (1978) discerned, that the higher psychological processes are internalized social relationships. Luria (1976) outlines the higher psychological processes as "the laws of logical thought, active remembering, selective attention, and acts of the will in general which form the basis for the most complex and characteristic higher forms of human activity" (p. 5). Internalization is the process through which the internal plane of consciousness is formed (Wertsch, 1985). In his discussion of the relationship between learning and development, Vygotsky underscored that "static measures assess mental functioning that has already matured, fossilized" while "maturing or developing mental functions must be fostered and assessed through collaborative, not independent or isolated activities" (Moll, 1990, p. 3).

This issue of assessment is at the heart of Vygotsky's theoretical construct of the zone of proximal development: Vygotsky (1978) differentiated between the child's current developmental level and his or her zone of proximal development: "the distance between the actual development level as determined by independent problem solving and the level of potential development as determined through problem solving under adult guidance or in collaboration with more capable peers" (p. 87). The basic message of the zone, according to Valsiner, is the "interdependence of the process of child development and the socially provided resources for that development" (Valsiner, cited in Moll, 1990, p. 4). A school climate that interferes with successful teaching and learning disrupts the emergence of student–teacher relations and the students' interpersonal relations, which are essential for adult mediation and student collaboration.

The school has the power to facilitate the students' attainment of the highest levels of development, that is, "the attainment of the well-managed self that is engendered by the strengthening of linkages among all of the developmental pathways" (Haynes and Ben-Avie, 1994, p. iii). Comer (1994) notes that the acquisition of a reasonably high level of cognitive skills in knowledge is most often made possible through whole child development—physical, cognitive, psychological, language, social, and ethical (p. 11). Content in the SDP school is, therefore, seen through the lens of child development. This is a paradigm shift in thinking about the purpose, function, and structure of schooling.

In the past, educators considered subject area content knowledge to be most worthwhile. Through mastering disciplines such as science and social studies, we would unlock new knowledge, apply existing knowledge to a wider range of situations, and help ensure a better future for our children. Thus, it is not surprising that our schools were organized by subject areas. Our heavily content-oriented school curriculum is a reflection of this belief. As being prepared for school is now a federal goal for the year 2000, we can assume that we have not met this goal yet, and one of the measures of the success of content-oriented education is lacking. Today the content-weighted curriculum is approaching its own demise because there is too much content.

Comer's response has been to urge curriculum designers and teachers to consider children's mastery of developmental milestones in the first round of deliberations of what to include in the curriculum, not the last round. This call rejects the commonplace practice of designing school curricula solely in cognitive and academic terms and regulating developmental or social processes by discipline codes. Staff that promote students' development of higher psychological processes ensure that the students will actually learn and use the curriculum's content. The school, in Comer's view, is the one institution where children's development can be systematically enhanced.

Development and learning are mediated through social processes and not necessarily through the competitive or individual processes that are embedded in our existing model of school. When we focus on social processes, relationships between students and teachers become the vehicle for instruction and are more important than subject area content. In the SDP elementary school, students and teachers may stay together for more than a year, in order to know each other better. As students get older, they may stay together as a group for several "periods" of a day. When development is taken as primary, then epistemologically, the strength of relationship building will take precedence over the mechanics of teaching. Strong relationships build community whether that community is in the classroom or among the teacher, parents, and students in the community of learners we call the school.

Thus, the central question for the School Planning and Management Team (SPMT), the Parent Team (PT), and the Student and Staff Support Team (SSST) is, "How can we build strong relationships that will encourage the development of our children?" This is indeed different from the question with a subject area emphasis, "What knowledge and skills do students need to understand?" The SDP teams help ensure that a community dialogue is created around how to assist in children's healthy development. A theoretical analysis of the SDP process notes:

> The greater the number and heterogeneity of adults endorsing mutual values, goals, and expectancies for a child, the more likely it is that the child will internalize these same goals as part of his or her own sense of identity. (Anson et al., 1991, p. 74)

It is in the service of child development that staff, parents, and elements of the community such as businesses, social service agencies, and volunteer organizations become partners in SDP schools.

▓▓▓ *Reinventing Community Through Parental Involvement*

> I'm the principal of the K–5, with around 700 students. It is a bilingual program. In the morning, I've asked parents to leave so that they could leave the education of children in the hands of teachers. They want to be there; in some instances you have to say very nicely that they're sort of in the way. (Warner, 1994)

The proverbial village that was once small, simple, and nurturing is now very large, complex, and sometimes insensitive. Agencies that serve children and families are often fragmented and unable to adequately address the psychosocial needs that influence how much and how well children learn and perform in school. Industrialization and urbanization have accorded enormous economic and quality-of-life benefits to some children and families, but they have also brought impoverishment and alienation to many. For these children and their families, rebuilding the community and creating a network of services with schools at the center is an urgent need. In addition, Haynes and Ben-Avie (in press) note that some outcomes of parental involvement in schools are less readily discernible:

1. *Teacher outcomes:* When parents are more involved in the school, teachers learn more about the cultural and ethnic communities served by the school. This knowledge base gives teachers greater understanding of the students in realms ranging from speech patterns to the stresses the children encounter in daily life outside school that have an impact on their learning. This knowledge base leads to an improved classroom climate and, thus, teachers' improved efficacy.

2. *Parent outcomes:* Parents who become involved in the school learn ways to help their children and become motivated to further their own education. Those parents who have been alienated from mainstream culture or have had negative school experiences can perceive the school as a bastion of hope for their children and for themselves.

3. *School outcomes:* The key to sustaining educational change, when the new initiatives are no longer "new," is through encouraging the parents to be advocates of their children; the stake that parents have in their children's school success is a powerful change force when the school's structures harness this energy.

4. *Community outcomes:* When these two primary societal institutions—the family and the school—team up, the school becomes a potent force in the community. Schools can be invaluable in spearheading the community's economic advancement, in repairing its social fabric, and in preparing schoolchildren to continue to improve the community in the future. With family involvement, the school becomes a major center of community life.

The principles of parent involvement are based on the three-level approach developed by Comer and his colleagues as part of the SDP and discussed in substantial detail elsewhere (Haynes and Comer, 1990). The levels are shown in Figure 3-1. At the first level, all or most parents support the school's program by attending parent–teacher conferences, reinforcing learning at home, and participating in the school's social programs. At the second level, a significant number of parents are actively engaged in the daily life of the school by being present on-site and constructively involved in supporting the authentic learning activities. At the third level, a group of parents that is truly representative (e.g., socioeconomic levels, race, ethnicity, gender) participates in collaborative decision making with school staff, students, and other identified persons on the SPMT. Parents in the SDP school serve in various capacities in different locations within and outside the school, and of course, at home. Verdell Roberts, formerly principal at Lincoln Bassett School in New Haven and presently on special assignment to the New Haven Public Schools' Central Office, described the difference between parent programs in an SDP school and a non-SDP school:

> The parent program gave structure to what one might want to do in the school. Ordinarily parents come to school to pick up report cards. When parents become a part of the Comer process, they want to be involved in the School Planning and Management Team. Oftentimes, schools say they don't have parents. They assume parents just know what you do in school. You should never assume that they don't care or they don't have time.

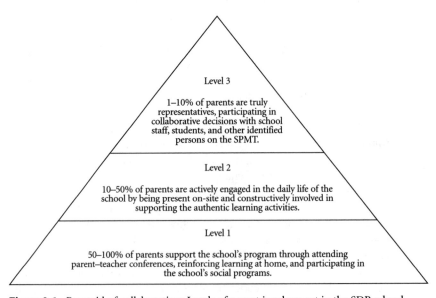

Figure 3-1. Pyramid of collaboration: Levels of parent involvement in the SDP school.

It is up to us to make some connection with people; it's up to us to reach out. The School Development Program gives the parents a framework to work in. There are structures and parent training sessions. Not every parent is expected to do everything, so you also have to know your parents. You start to connect with them: you start to build relationships with them. Those parents become a part of the school.

Parents serve in the libraries as aides; in classrooms as teacher aides; in the hallways as monitors and/or mentors; in the lunchrooms as servers or monitors; in the main office as administrative support personnel; on the playground as mentors, monitors, and coaches; in the music room or computer room as support personnel; and in the parent centers, where they exist, as hosts and guides to new parents, staff, and other guests. Mrs. Ennis, the mother of a former student from a New Haven school, described her involvement:

I would sit in each classroom and see what it was all about and the teachers would come to me and they would tell me what is going on in the school and what they plan on doing, which is good. And most of the time the parents…used to be involved. When [my older children] were going to school, it was not like that. Before the Comer process we would only hear from a teacher when there was a problem with the child, like when they didn't do their homework or something.

In the community at large, parents serve as links to volunteer groups and organizations, service agencies, businesses, and other parents. At home, parents provide the nurturing, support, and reinforcement necessary to strengthen the bond between home and school and to increase the chances of success for their children.

Parental involvement on the teams—the SPMT, SSST, and PT—are the hallmark of the SDP. As Charles Warner, former principal of Jackie Robinson Middle School and Hill Central Elementary School in New Haven and now supervisor for curriculum and instruction for the New Haven Public Schools, noted:

I think as administrators and educators we have a tendency to tell parents what we want rather than having parents with our guidance say what they would like to design for their schools. When you get parents to design programs around your school, plan materials that your classrooms need, and teachers need, then it's something that they want to do—it's not what you want them to do.

Parents bring an understanding of the broader community and of the social development needs and strengths of their children. This understanding contributes to Comprehensive School Plan development and influences the curriculum, instruction, and assessment. Jan Stocklinski, the supervisor of SDP implementation in Prince George's County, Maryland, stated:

We try to think "family involvement" rather than "parent involvement." Getting parents to be partners with us started because parents and families are the most committed and have the greatest interest in their children. In our particular case, it's been our parents and our families that have helped turn around how school people looked at children and our families, and that's pretty much been the history in our county. The administrators come and go, superintendents come and go, sometimes staff come and go, but the parents and the children are always there.

In the SDP school, parents from every socioeconomic, racial, ethnic, and cultural group are involved and empowered to participate and contribute meaningfully. We address the influence imbalances that often arise among parents of different socioeconomic backgrounds and educational experiences. We seek to give equal voice to all parents through openness, respect, full participation, and opportunities for growth. We seek to encourage fathers and mothers to become engaged, tuned in, and turned on to the excitement of teaching, learning, and growing in an SDP school.

Across the country we have found that the majority of school staff and overwhelmingly large numbers of parents are eager to increase the level and enhance the quality of parental involvement in schools. Often, however, the questions are, "How do we do it?" "What are the strategies and the steps?" "Are there some caveats?" The answer to this last question is "Yes" and we discuss these caveats as we address the strategies and steps that follow.

▨▨▨▨▨▨ Build Trust

Basic to any attempt to reach and involve parents—especially the least affluent and educated—is a climate of trust and openness to ideas. Parents sometimes avoid schools because they feel inadequate, unwelcome, threatened, or insecure due to their own past educational experiences and their children's present difficulties. In SDP communities, we seize every opportunity to break down the barriers of distrust by reaching out to parents in their communities through home visits (with appropriate provisions in high-risk neighborhoods); regular and positive telephone calls and memos; and networking through such institutions as churches, synagogues, mosques, community groups, and support services agencies, all of which enjoy some degree of rapport and attachment with many families. Making use of the changing technological environment is important. One SDP elementary school, for example, sent videotapes home with the children to inform parents about school events and activities. The following vignette demonstrates how trust was established between parents in a housing project and the staff at an elementary school in Connecticut.

Northside School is located in an isolated, low-income, drug-infested, and physically decaying section of a midsize urban city. Most of the families live in low-rise projects and are very poor; most are on public assistance. Violent crimes are common and associated with a bustling illegal drug trade in the streets not far from the school. The nascent SPMT at the school included only one parent, who had been recruited by the principal during a friendly conversation. The SPMT decided to embark on a bold course of action to show the parents and children in the community that they really cared. They enlisted the willing and valuable support of the parent to arrange for them to hold some SPMT meetings in the basement of a low-rise project. After some weeks of negotiating and preparation, including some provisions for safety, many meetings were held. Parents' interest soared, as did their visits to the school and volunteer activities. The school now has six parents on the SPMT and has one of the best attended and most successful parent involvement programs in the school district. In addition, student achievement has been consistently high with only minor fluctuations. For the past 2 years, fourth-grade students have won the national Dynamath competition, which involves using the kind of creative, inquisitive, and self-propelled learning and problem-solving skills that the SDP school seeks to nurture.

Plan Well

For parent involvement to be effective and successful it must be carefully planned and coordinated to avoid confusion, anxiety, and disaster. School staff must be adequately represented on the SPMT. Their direct input is often essential, for example, when a parent is paired with a teacher or assigned to work with a staff member. Staff and parents must collaborate with administration in making decisions about which parents serve in what capacities in the school. This process of collaborative planning helps to reduce or obviate tension and creates a climate of mutual respect and support.

Empower Parents

Parents in SDP schools participate fully, including planning and making decisions about the academic and social agenda, through their role on the SPMT and in helping develop the Comprehensive School Plan. They have a voice in deciding how the school shapes the minds and hearts of their children. They also have the opportunity to continually grow and develop and to reform their own habits of mind, heart, and work.

Continually Monitor, Assess, and Modify as Necessary

School communities value informed decisions based on ongoing, careful documentation of processes and activities. This is true as well for our parent involvement activities. We monitor how parents are serving in our schools; we assess the benefits and liabilities to students, staff, and parents themselves related to this involvement; and we modify activities as necessary in response to what we discover.

Parents also benefit from being meaningfully involved. The SDP has documented cases in which parent volunteers who had dropped out of school were motivated and encouraged to return to school. Some obtained their GEDs, and some continued, gaining associate, baccalaureate, and advanced degrees. Some became educators and joined the faculty at their schools. Listen to a former volunteer, now a faculty member in an SDP school on the West Coast:

> It was for me the opportunity of a lifetime to work with a group of people who genuinely cared enough to take the time to encourage me and give me the boost in my self-confidence I needed. Now, here I am trying to do for other parents what my friends did for me.

Even parents who do not pursue more formal education speak of SDP's unquantifiable benefits. One parent explains:

> Every morning I wake up feeling good about being able to come here [to the school] and give something of myself, my time, and wisdom to these precious children. Had it not been for the people here, I mean the staff whom I respect so much, I would not be able to do this.

The SDP school demonstrates that home and school need not be worlds apart. School climate is positive and healthy, children learn and perform well, and staff feel supported and recognized (Haynes, Comer, and Hamilton-Lee, 1988, 1989). When parents are involved, children tend to be more on task in the school, and parents and the school then develop a true camaraderie (Emmons, 1994).

▰▰▰▰▰ Building Community Through Community Involvement

Schools or parents alone, or *together alone,* cannot provide all sustenance, services, and support that children need to thrive and develop well in this increasingly complex society. The entire community of significant others and services must work together to strengthen and prepare our children well for their present and future lives. Nancy Klein (1994), associate dean at Cleveland State University, writes, "According to the African proverb, 'It takes a whole village to raise a child,' we have many outstanding participants in our village who are contributing substantially to the way children in SDP schools in Cleveland are being educated. Truly the Cleveland partnership is a 'village' affair and the partners are enjoying their work together" (p. 8). The Cleveland partnership consists of the Cleveland Public Schools, Cleveland State University (CSU), Cleveland Child Guidance Center, and the Harvard Business School Club. Klein describes the contributions of the latter:

> One unique aspect of the Cleveland Partnership has been the active role played by several members of the Harvard Business School Club (HBSC), an alumni organization. Four members of the HBSC have been associated with each of the four schools, and have worked diligently with businesses surrounding the school to foster interest in, and

support for, the schools. One member, who is retired, has involved a second businessman in the school and is now working with a CSU faculty member on a handbook for productive parental involvement. The specific roles of each person vary from school to school and have included activities such as getting paint and equipment donated so that the community, parents and teachers could paint the school ("It takes a village to paint the school," to paraphrase the African proverb), providing funds for principals and faculty to attend training in New Haven, and raising money from local businesses to provide materials for teachers. They attend SPMT meetings, steering committee meetings and provide support and reflection to the team and principal (p. 6).

The community groups, organizations, and institutions benefit in the short run by becoming more visible to the community. In the long run they benefit by helping to produce healthy, well-educated, intelligent, creative, and productive citizens who become members of the labor force, community leaders, business executives, and responsible heads of households. Indeed, the whole community and entire country benefit from a coordinated and integrated approach of service and education to children and families.

When children, families, educators, and community groups and agencies participate as full partners in the educational enterprise, there are direct and indirect benefits to children. The benefits to students include expanded learning opportunities, a coterie of caring adults, development of leadership skills through internships and apprenticeships, increased motivation to stay in school, and desire and efforts to pursue higher education. The benefits to families include increased access to social services and increased ability to network with child development experts and other parents. Educators benefit by having a network of services and support for children's learning.

One illustration of this network is the Comer-Zigler (CoZi) project, a combination of the SDP school and Edward F. Zigler's "School of the 21st Century" (21C). Zigler, former director of the federal Office of Child Development and currently Sterling Professor of Psychology at Yale and the director of the Yale Bush Center, envisions 21C as:

> a comprehensive set of child care and family support services based or linked to the public school setting which include an outreach program for parents of children ages 0–3, full day care for children ages 3–5, before and after school care for school age children, an information referral service for families, and support for family day care providers in the school neighborhood. (Stern and Flood, 1994, p. 1)

Many 21C schools add other components based on a needs assessment such as health, nutrition, and adult education. In 1991, a program officer at the Carnegie Corporation of New York, a supporter of the SDP and 21C, suggested developing a plan to integrate the SDP and 21C. The integrated project, named CoZi in honor of its founders, "reconceptualizes the school as a base of family support; that is, in addition to its traditional educational mission, the school offers services that children and families need to thrive" (Stern, 1995, p. 1). In March 1992, the Carnegie Corporation awarded a grant to explore the feasibility of combining the two models in Norfolk, Virginia's Bowling Park School, an SDP school located in a public housing community. In this school, more than 75% of the children are considered to be at risk. In 1994, Barbara Stern and Lorraine Flood wrote in their description of Bowling Park School, "The school is considered a beacon of light in the community and the principal and staff enjoy a very positive relationship with the parents of their students" (p. 3). During the summer after the first year of Bowling Park's operation as a CoZi school, the Yale Bush Center conducted a process evaluation. Among the findings, Stern and Flood write:

> Perceived benefits for parents included: less stress related to child care; stronger con-
> nection to the school community; increased knowledge of child development; and
> improved knowledge of services available in the community and in the school ... 81
> percent of the staff said that feelings about their jobs had become more positive since
> CoZi began due to the changes in atmosphere in the school, increase in parent involve-
> ment and the prevailing sense that the school was reaching out to families to promote
> the healthy development of children. (p. 4)

In 1995, Herman D. Clark, Jr., principal of the school for 14 years, and Bowling Park were acclaimed when *Redbook* magazine named Bowling Park one of the top 50 schools in the United States for its overall excellence. In addition, the U.S. Department of Education recognized the school as an exemplary Chapter I school (Savo, 1995, p. 3). In response to the enthusiasm of parents and staff, CoZi has expanded to another site in Norfolk, to sites in Bridgeport and New Haven, Connecticut, and to St. Louis, Missouri (Stern, 1995, p. 5).

Community involvement entails expanding the focus of education beyond the walls of the school building to embrace and include groups and organizations in the community that are willing and able to support the total development of children. This is a two-way process: Community resources are brought into schools, and students and staff in the SDP schools travel into the community to provide services, to learn, and to receive services. Within the SDP framework, the broader community is defined on two levels. The first level includes those community groups, organizations, institutions (such as universities and particularly schools of education), agencies, and businesses in the immediate area. Community resources are relatively easily accessible, and children, school staff, and families interact with them regularly. At the second level, community is defined to include more distant resources that have an impact on the teaching, learning, and assessment processes. For example, large corporations or philanthropic foundations that contribute to SDP's work are members of this extended community. As distance learning and teleconferencing become integrated into the SDP authentic learning environment, other schools and universities in the United States and abroad will also become part of the extended SDP community.

To support the total development of children in SDP communities, the broader communities must be continuously involved. Klein (1994) describes the involvement of the Cleveland Child Guidance Center in the Cleveland partnership:

> In response to the informal survey of principals in the four SDP schools that additional mental health resources were vital in order to fully implement the SDP program, the Cleveland Child Guidance Center (CCGC), which provides mental health services to children and families throughout the greater Cleveland area, was contacted. With support from local foundations, CCGC assigned a clinician to each of the four schools for one day per week. These clinicians provide mental health consultation to teachers, attend the mental health team meetings, and provide direct service to children and families where such intervention is required. In many cases, their discussions with teachers are a professional development experience as the teacher and clinician plan together on behalf of the child. These clinicians have provided excellent services and have contributed markedly to the successful implementation of the SDP in the Cleveland Public Schools through their consultation, training and service. (p. 5)

Some organizations may be called on as needed, such as the Department of Children and Youth Services, whereas others must be involved on a daily basis, such as universities that prepare educators to serve in SDP schools, businesses that provide material and human resources such as mentors, and community health clinics that provide daily health services to children and families, in schools or in the community.

Assembling and Sustaining Community Through the SDP Teams

Comer (1989c) writes: "We observed a direct connection between inadequate organization and management, difficult staff–parent–student relationships, and difficult student behavior" (p. 269). The SDP teams are charged with the responsibility of making the school child centered, which is expressed in the team meetings by: defining the roles of each team member; creating a clear mission statement that guides the tasks; having each team member discuss his or her preferences for how the team should work together on behalf of the children; and creating a strategy for collecting data, solving problems, brainstorming, handling conflicts, making decisions, and assessing the work of the team. On collaborative teams, all members are active. The members control what happens during meetings. Members contribute ideas, insights, opinions, and suggestions, and give feedback about both the tasks (the content of the meetings) and the process (how the team works together).

The SDP facilitator, the SDP change agent in the field, pays attention to the process of the discussion: Who talks? For how long? Who is not so active? Where there are differences or conflicts? Has each side of a conflict been heard completely? The facilitator primarily ensures that the team focuses on the children rather than on the concerns of the adults. In most school districts the facilitators have been experienced and well-regarded employees of the school system (Payne, 1994). The model is flexible: In Chicago, the facilitators are staff members of Youth Guidance, a local social work agency that has been school based since the early 1970s (Payne, 1994). The SDP facilitator's aim is to assist the group in becoming an autonomous cooperative of individuals who can identify their own problems, develop their own solutions, and create their own process for successful problem resolution (Joyner, Haynes, and Comer, 1994, p. 19). In an ethnographic study of the implementation of the SDP, Joyner, Haynes, and Comer (1994) write:

> The successful implementation of the SDP program within a particular school depends on (1) convincing the principal, school staff, and parents that the program will achieve its stated outcomes; (2) developing within the staff an understanding of the model, its key components, structures, and operations; and (3) gaining a commitment from the principal to lead the process in a collaborative, no-fault manner. Much of the responsibility for establishing these pre-conditions for success rests on the shoulders of the facilitators. (p. 18)

The SDP facilitator has multiple roles:

- *Organizational development facilitation on the change process:* A facilitator of a team meeting is part of the team and helps both tasks and processes to move forward. The facilitator must listen, give feedback, clarify issues, and ask questions well, ensuring a balance of participation and, most important, modeling consensus, collaboration, and no-fault.
- *Process consultant for team meetings:* A process consultant is not part of the team but observes the dynamics of the meeting. The focus is exclusively on process and the goal is to give feedback so the team can better understand its own process.
- *Coach:* A coach helps either a team or an individual become better at a particular skill. An SDP facilitator may coach a principal on more collaborative behaviors, coach a team on giving feedback, and coach a teacher on how to see his or her students more in terms of their development than in terms of behavior or grades.
- *"Whatever it takes:"* A key element of good facilitation is the development of strong relationships. Since schools are such busy places, SDP facilitators often pitch in to do the task at hand.

The SDP facilitator is committed to the notion that "As I strengthen people, I empower." To this end, the facilitator takes responsibility along with the team for tasks, relationships, decision making, problem solving, and conflict resolution with the aim of fostering interdependence. As the team evolves, there is less need for clearly delineated roles among the members because all members become responsible, to some degree, for communicating with the group they represent (i.e., the parents, staff, students); asking others continuously for input (and listening!); using the information to help set the agenda and also guide the direction of the team; and communicating and clarifying communication within the team and between team members and the rest of the school population.

The Three Guiding Principles

When community is "reinvented" in the school and when education promotes effective human relations, staff become dedicated to their students' learning and the motivation to achieve. In the SDP "village," whether the adults work on a particular team, focus primarily on the classroom, or are a part of the larger school community, their frame of reference is the three guiding principles: consensus, collaboration, and no-fault. How the student relates to the teacher, how the teacher views the potential of the student, and the expectations the student and teacher bring to each interaction are all guided by this ethos. The way the classroom environment is structured (for example, competitive or collaborative) is a reflection of the way the stakeholders structure their interactions.

No-Fault

The intent of this principle is to focus on problem solving and to operate on the premise that other people's mistakes result from misunderstandings, misinterpretations, or miscommunications and not a deliberate attempt to offend. Accountability is accepted by the team, but time and energy are not wasted in acts of blaming. Individuals need to express their emotions: dissatisfaction, anger over another's behavior, a painful experience. Blaming occurs when individuals feel unsafe or uncomfortable bringing these types of feelings to either a team or another individual. By blaming, the team avoids self-reflection and, thus, the ability of the team to work collaboratively is undermined.

J. Patrick Howley, an SDP project manager and implementation coordinator, offers the following example:

> I was working in a school district that was suffering from the result of much blaming and gossiping. As a result, everyone, especially children in the school, were the losers. Some very fine people who could make significant contributions to school change were paralyzed by the conflict.
>
> To break this cycle of mistrust, I began by individually interviewing the four primary people involved in the conflict. By agreeing to the interview, each person was also agreeing to sit down the following day with me and the other three people directly involved in the conflict in order to talk openly about the issues. In the individual interviews, I focused on several questions: What were they experiencing inwardly? What had they observed? What were they most concerned about? What did they need from the other team members? How did they themselves contribute to this conflict? What did they need to become more open with the other mem-

bers of the team in order to resolve this conflict? My questions were meant to focus the energy within and sustain a no-fault atmosphere.

The following day, the five of us met as a group for most of the day. Our conversation was totally focused on process, on our relationships, on trying to understand one another, on what we were trying to do in behalf of the children. It was a difficult but productive day for all of the parties involved. By addressing the process issues head on, we were able to move to problem solving. By not only acknowledging but also dealing with the conflict and emotions directly, the conflicts could be resolved. Both the individuals and the team were, in fact, transformed.

Three major tensions evolve from the struggle to engage in no-fault behavior. First, the tendency to focus on persons rather than to focus on the work creates tensions. Teams have work that must be done, and spending time on relationships seems to be wasteful. Yet, not to focus on the process issues inevitably results in the content issues becoming increasingly more difficult to resolve. As teams focus on persons, a second tension develops: the tendency to make judgments about persons rather than to give nonjudgmental, descriptive feedback. Teams must be taught to suspend judgment and simply describe the behavior that led to particular emotions. The first two tensions often lead to a third: the tendency to blame others rather than to engage in self-reflection that can result in finding one's own errors or lack of devel-

SDP national staff members J. Patrick Howley and Edna Negron at the SDP Principals' Academy
Photo by Laura Brooks.

opment. At the same time, these tensions allow for enormous potential, if they are channeled by an external change agent such as the SDP facilitator. The process of self-reflection begins by recognizing and naming the tensions being felt. No-fault does not mean that we withhold our honest thoughts and feelings. Rather, no-fault is about providing a safe environment in which we can share our thoughts and feelings directly with the individuals and teams that have provoked the feelings.

Consensus and Collaboration

Another guiding principle, decision making by consensus, is a process in which every stakeholder has input and "winner–loser" feelings are avoided. Energies are invested in achieving consensus rather than in voting. There are four major challenges in trying to achieve consensus:

1. Everyone on the team must be heard.
2. Team members must convey to the speaker that they have fully listened to and respect the viewpoint of the speaker, regardless of what it is.
3. Team members must transcend their own viewpoints so that they can not only live with the decisions that the team makes but also support them.
4. The team must achieve consensus despite time restrictions.

The following vignette, narrated by Howley, illustrates the process of consensus as well as collaboration.

An SDP facilitator was asked to meet with a principal and a professional development committee to help them with the first stages of creating an SPMT. The committee had met for half a year but was paralyzed with fear, indecision, and conflict. Committee members had a high level of trust in the principal and his extensive experience. Now, however, the principal was suggesting that his power be shared among a team of decision makers. The committee perceived the staff as resistant and not ready for this bold move. Each staff member had grown accustomed to his or her independence, and although they worked well with the principal, they could not or would not work together. The principal backed off at first, then slowly prodded his committee to request that an SDP facilitator conduct a workshop with the entire staff of the school.

(Our procedure at the SDP is to work collaboratively *with* a school.) First meeting with the committee, the facilitator developed the theme "Leaders Working Together Collaboratively." The facilitator's design for the workshop was discussed thoroughly with the committee. The committee repeatedly reminded the SDP facilitator that their school staff would need a lot of support. In the first workshop, the school staff had the opportunity to do many unthreatening community-building activities that brought them together in new ways. The design helped them to begin small group discussions of what the school could become. They learned listening skills, and they left the workshop planning to visit each other's classrooms to discuss what teachers were trying to accomplish in other grades. The day ended by looking at and discussing the roles people engage in when working on a collaborative team.

The committee met immediately afterward to debrief and discuss the design for the next workshop. Consensus and collaboration were modeled even as these principles were taught. They slowly made decisions by consensus as the principal and the SDP faciltator worked with the Professional Development Committee, and as the committee worked with the school staff.

Now the committee and the facilitator felt that it was time to take a bold move and design a brief roundtable discussion with the full staff of the school. We wanted to demonstrate how good discussion and dialogue lead to collaboration. Following a brief presentation on SDP research, the facilitator helped the staff members to listen to one another despite their differing viewpoints as they discussed the implications of the research. A number of similar hour-long sessions were held during the next month. As people became committed to listening deeply to one another over the course of the year, they grew to tolerate the tensions stirred by their differences. It was becoming safe to disagree and to learn from one another.

The workshops culminated in the establishment of an SPMT at the school. A representative from each grade level met with the principal and the facilitator. After a 20-minute discussion, the grade-level representatives, the principal, and the facilitator met in a "fishbowl" so that the entire staff could listen to the SPMT discussion. The nascent SPMT decided to charge the representatives with meeting again in grade-level groups to generate a list of the next steps. By experiencing the SPMT process directly and openly, the school staff began to understand, trust, and support a collaborative process. The SPMT that was forged at this school was a diverse team with much potential for conflict. But they also had the potential for creativity and learning from one another. The parents on the SPMT contributed by bringing in their perspectives of the children, gleaned from observing them and teaching them in other settings. The social worker, with her specialized knowledge, and the cafeteria worker, who sees the children in a different social setting, brought additional perspectives.

As this school's implementation of the SDP proceeded over the course of 5 years, with the continued support of the facilitator, the teams emerged and the guiding principles imbued the educative process. The functioning of the teams and the improved climate in the school showed the school staff and the stakeholders that a positive social climate is the primary agent of all educational change (Anson et al., 1991, pp. 56–82), and that the key to sustaining educational change, when the new initiatives are no longer new, is by reinventing community in the school.

▨▨▨▨ *The Student and Staff Support Team*

The Student and Staff Support Team (SSST), formerly known as the Mental Health Team (MHT) in the SDP model, distinguishes the SDP from every other school reform initiative. Joanne Nancy Corbin, an SDP implementation coordinator who focuses on training SSST teams and working with children, parents, and families at the Yale Child Study Center as a social worker, describes the SSST in the following composite vignette.

The SSST of the middle school meets weekly on Tuesdays for 1½ hours. The school principal chairs the team meeting, and the school social worker functions as the facilitator for the meeting. Other members of the team include the guidance counselor, school nurse, school psychologist, and school-based health clinic representative. The team has a standard agenda that is used to ensure that important areas are addressed. The standard agenda includes school climate, global school issues, individual student concerns, and if time remains, a chance for group members to share information pertaining to their work.

This morning an announcement is made over the PA system that the SSST will begin at 10 o'clock, which is in 15 minutes. The principal begins the meeting by discussing the school climate. This gives the team a chance to reflect on the context of the school and how this context affects the students. The guidance counselor begins by discussing concerns over the level of violence that has been occurring in the neighborhood. She says that children are very anxious about traveling to and from school due to the presence of gangs and that some students and teachers are concerned about the presence of gang members within the school. The principal echoes concern and refers to a school survey on students' concerns about violence and safety that has recently been completed. This survey indicates high levels of anxiety among students regarding student conflicts, availability of weapons, domestic violence, and personal safety. The school psychologist indicates that many teachers are hesitant to discuss their concerns about personal safety, although this is a realistic concern. Because the team members are not prepared to discuss the specifics regarding violence in the school, the facilitator suggests that the team members review the summary of the survey and come prepared to discuss the situation further during the next team meeting. The principal suggests that the current school-year data on student suspensions, detentions, and expulsions for violence be reviewed; she will review these statistics herself.

The principal is still addressing global issues on the agenda. She asks if anyone has further concerns. One counselor presents the issue that the fifth and sixth graders are much more immature and younger acting than the seventh and eighth graders and activities that incorporate all students are not well suited for the fifth and sixth graders. She asks if there is anything the school can do about this. Other team members indicate they have noticed the same pattern of behavior. The team members acknowledge the developmental changes that occur as children move into adolescence, and they determine that they need to look at the differences in the developmental stages and change some of the practices in the school to be more developmentally sensitive. One suggestion is that perhaps the fifth and sixth graders should not change classrooms for each period as is currently done, as they appear to be more difficult to settle down after each class change, and it may be more important for the students to develop a relationship with one teacher, rather than trying to relate to a number of teachers. Another suggestion is that since gym classes for the seventh and eighth grades do not consider the developmental needs of adolescents entering puberty, perhaps single-sex gym classes would be more appropriate. This discussion is building increasing interest, and for the sake of time, the facilitator suggests that a subgroup meet to further identify areas of developmental differences with possible resolutions. This global issue will be revisited in 2 weeks. After the SSST has reviewed this issue, the concerns and recommendations will be presented to the School Planning and Management Team.

The psychologist raises the issue of a fire that destroyed an apartment building in the neighborhood overnight. His concern is for the several children attending the school who lived in that building. He asks if anyone on the team has heard from the families or knows whether the children are in school today. No one on the team has additional information about the status of the families. Through a brief discussion it is decided that the team should get more information in order to address the impact of this situation on the children's education. The social worker volunteers to take this lead.

The next item on the agenda is individual student referrals. These referrals are students who are experiencing some difficulties not previously addressed by special education. During this team meeting, five children have been referred by their teachers for discussion. One child is described as a fifth grader from Trinidad whose father has been harshly punishing him for poor schoolwork. The teacher has already mentioned this to the school psychologist. The psychologist's perception is that as punishment continues the child has begun to withdraw in class and is more reluctant to participate in the group work. Input from other team members includes the recent relocation of the family from abroad and no significant contact between the parents and the school. The discussion touches on the cultural differences regarding child discipline. The social worker also raises the concern that if abuse by the parent is suspected, then a referral to the child protective agency is required. It is suggested that someone make the effort to contact the child's parents and talk with them about the school and their concerns about their son's schoolwork. The principal's position of authority and the social worker's knowledge of family functioning make them the best choices to begin this discussion with the parents. The goal of this discussion with the parents will be to build the parents' view of the school as a resource and to identify alternative ways of supporting the child's work in school that are not as harsh.

Another child's situation is presented to the SSST. A seventh grader has been referred by the homeroom teacher because of recent changes in her behavior. She is regularly coming to school late, is pulling away from her usual peer group, and is provoking conflicts with others including the teacher. Her grades are still satisfactory; however, because of her conflicts in the classroom, she has received several detentions. The teacher wants to intervene in a different way before the situation escalates. The team members know the child, but have not been aware of the recent changes. The team suggests that the social worker meet with the classroom teacher to determine the scope of the problem and whether the community mental health counselor can meet with the student.

The facilitator reminds the team that there needs to be an update regarding a student previously discussed. The school-based health clinic representative has taken the lead in this case. She states that she has contacted the student's parents regarding the health concerns of the child. The parents have agreed to let the school-based clinic manage the child's health issues. The team is satisfied with this resolution and decides this student no longer needs to be reviewed by the team.

The final item for the team is to give the SSST members a chance to brief the team on events of various programs. The school nurse indicates that cold and flu season is upon them and that children are usually not feigning sickness but are actually ill. The guidance counselor discusses the upcoming testing that will affect the fifth graders. The social worker discusses the mentoring program for the students, which is sponsored by the school's corporate partners, and encourages the team to seek out other students who might benefit from this program.

The SDP School Focuses on the Academic and Social Climate

The following narrative about the birth of an SDP school, told by the school's first principal, Edna N. Negron, highlights the themes of this chapter. The narrative underscores the collaborative efforts and energy of the staff, parents, and community members to work on behalf of the children. The narrative calls to mind that the SDP is a way of building community since children are dependent on the adults in the community to help them to attain the highest levels of development. Behind the SDP model are deeply committed people employing the model to improve their relationships so that the children will have the finest education that we can provide for them, regardless of their socioeconomic status or family background.

Dr. Ramón Emeterio Betances Elementary School

The Betances school population is approximately 85% Latino (mostly Puerto Rican), 13% African-American, and 2% Asian and Caucasian. It is located in Hartford, Connecticut, the fourth poorest city in the United States. Connecticut, on the other hand, is the richest state in the country, with the highest per capita income in the nation. The area is a port of entry for Puerto Ricans and other Latinos coming to the mainland for the first time; therefore, the school has a comprehensive bilingual/bicultural education program. Eighty-five percent of the students are in bilingual programs, and 85% of the staff in the school (including custodians, secretaries, and professional staff) are bilingual in Spanish and English. The staff includes African-Americans, Puerto Ricans, Central and South Americans, and White/European-Americans. About 15% of the staff are men, a higher percentage than in most other elementary schools in the city.

Almost 100% of the school population qualify for free or reduced lunch. The school district has one of the highest homicide rates in the state. More than 60% of the students come from one-parent homes. The incidence of drugs is staggering. About 50% of the entering kindergarten class suffer from being born of substance-abusing mothers. Although there is a stable core of students, over 50% of the children enter or leave every school year. Most of the city's homeless shelters and soup kitchens are close to the school.

The Dr. Ramón Emeterio Betances School opened its doors in 1985. At first, it was called the "Old Kinsella School" because it had been closed down when the new Kinsella School was built. For 12 years, the building had been allowed to fall into disrepair. The decision to reopen the school was made because an increase in enrollment had reached crisis levels at the new school. The decision was made effective on July 1 for a September school opening. All purchase of furniture, materials, and textbooks, hiring of staff, redistricting, informing parents and community, and making the school presentable and safe for children had to be done in those 2 months.

To make matters worse, I had never been a principal or an assistant principal. It helped that I had been coordinator of bilingual education for the Hartford Public Schools for 9 years and, therefore, had a thorough knowledge of all curricular areas. I had also worked with every department and with every school in the system. I had participated in the hiring and evaluation of staff in most schools, was expert in the budget process, and had been a part of most of the textbook acquisition decisions made in those 9 years at the central office. I did not, however, have any experience in running a school.

The challenge and the opportunity we faced was the ability to create our own school. The new staff came with a clear understanding of the difficulties we faced. Several were seasoned veterans who looked forward to working with me and with each other. Most of them had a track record for dedication and commitment to the involvement of parents and the larger community in the educational process. Many of them had lived or were still living in the school district. For several years, I lived across the street from the school myself. Even before we met Dr. Comer, we were a close-knit family unit. There was a high degree of cultural and linguistic competence among us.

The school itself, however, is in the downtown area buffered by Main Street from the neighborhood where the students reside. Within a four-block radius, the school is surrounded by the State Capitol, the Bushnell Theater, the Wadsworth Atheneum, the Hartford Library, City Hall, the Hartford Federal Court, the Travelers and several other insurance and banking institutions, historic churches of all denominations, the site of the Charter Oak Tree (where the Connecticut Charter precursor to its constitution was hidden), the Charter Oak Culture Center, Hartford Hospital, and most of the Latino social service and advocacy agencies in the city. Some of the staff, myself included, have been members of volunteer boards in those agencies for many years. Two convents are near the school, and one of our third-grade teachers is a nun who resided in one of them. Small businesses in the school district are on an upsurge. There were a lot of *potential* support systems available.

Our first priority was to become an integral part of the community. Since we had had so little preservice time, the staff came together to develop a comprehensive schoolwide discipline plan, including individual classroom objectives. Teams were formed to ensure that the first day of school went smoothly, despite the fact that the students would not know who their teachers were and all new registrations had been deferred until the first day of school due to the massive summer clean-up activities at the school. All students and parents were met outside that day, and the welcoming teams instructed them where to go. Inside the school, the registration team had the flow of registration down to a science. Although our main office and school records were still in boxes, parents did not feel that their new school was not well organized. They were openly welcomed, and the classrooms were brightly decorated and immaculate.

The Parent Team formed almost immediately and included some of the movers in both the Latino and African-American community. The first open house they helped to organize in the third month after the school year opened invited sister schools, all community agencies, and the elected Board of Education to a feast the parents and staff had prepared. More than 400 people attended. Students and staff staged a very professional performance. Elections for PTA officers were held, and we actually established an all-volunteer PTA committee. No one who wished to serve was denied a role. Their first order of business became the renaming of the school.

Both African-American and Latino parents chose Dr. Ramón Emeterio Betances. He was a Puerto Rican patriot, abolitionist, and physician who won the French Legion of Honor in Paris, where he was exiled, for his medical contributions in France. He was a role model of whom everyone could be proud. Our parents carried their request to the Hartford Board of Education. Unlike all other such requests, not only did the resolution pass, but the board made it effective immediately, rather than hold to the 1-year wait usually required. It was a very emotional victory for the school community, reaffirming their need for a strong cultural identity and their power to effect change.

Then La Casa de Puerto Rico, one of the local agencies, launched a fund-raising campaign to commission a bronze relief of Dr. Betances to hang over the portico of the school. The funds were raised and the subsequent year, the bronze—the first piece of public art depicting a Puerto Rican in the state of Connecticut—was installed at our school. Federal Judge Hon. José Cabranes gave the keynote address on that day, and over 300 parents, students, and members of the community were present to celebrate and break bread together. We were no longer the "Old" Kinsella. We were the proud, elegant, new Betances.

The school had undergone massive renovations to bring the magnificent old plant up to the new State of Connecticut building codes. Although we had had to survive the impact of jackhammers inside the school, major demolition, and construction while still trying to teach, the experience had in fact brought all of us closer together and made us even more determined to establish the very best educational programs for our children.

During this time, then Connecticut Senate President Pro-Tem John Larson had launched a series of initiatives to support families and children. One of them was Connecticut's version of Dr. Zigler's School of the 21st Century: the Family Resource Center (FRC). With Senator Larson's help, Betances became the first urban FRC in the nation. It was also the first FRC to provide services in both Spanish and English. With the addition of day care, before- and after-school care, parenting programs, adult education, and family referral services to our school, parents who would otherwise be too overwhelmed to participate fully in their children's education became more and more involved in the school.

It was at this time that I met Dr. James Comer. We were on a panel together. He was explaining the development of SDP, and I was talking about the impact of the FRC in our school community. It seemed like such a natural combination that I immediately presented our staff with the information. Over 85% of the staff at Betances agreed that the principles of the SDP not only validated what they believed in but would enable the school to move forward in a much more cohesive and proactive manner. There *were* those who felt that it would be a lot of work and therefore preferred the status quo, especially since there were active, representative teams already in place and we had a very strong parent component. Nonetheless, Betances parents and staff embraced the SDP in 1990.

As the school had become more known in the Hartford community and more programs and new initiatives were started, the governance and management of the school had become unwieldy and overwhelming for me as the school's sole administrator. Over the next 2 years, as the school's SPMT and SSST developed and became functional, my role changed to one of support. I was no longer the ultimate decision maker for everything. It became clear to all stakeholders that their input was not only welcome but necessary in order to move our school forward.

The school's head custodian is a prime example of the cohesive teamwork that developed. Before becoming a member of the SPMT, he had been reluctant to discipline the children. As he grew more confident, he and his staff established a plan to monitor the lunchroom. They developed a reward system for good behavior that allowed students to help in the maintenance of the school. This same idea was utilized as an alternative to suspensions. Students were required to provide community service to the school under the supervision of the custodial staff. The custodians became our "reality check" to ensure that our plans met with safety requirements and did not interfere with the smooth running of the building.

Additionally, they came in on Saturdays and Sundays so that neighborhood groups could use the school, and they donated their overtime pay for student activities. They worked for free on evenings and weekends when school activities were taking place. They bought uniforms with the school name embroidered on their shirts and jackets, which they proudly displayed on their errands to other schools and departments. They were our best public relations agents. They knew every one of the students by name and were loved and respected.

Since many of our parents were not literate and felt uncomfortable in leadership roles, teachers paired as mentors with the members of the executive committee and played a support role so that effective parental participation would not be impaired. Dr. Comer's emphasis on the importance of meaningful home–school communication was not lost on us. Meetings were held in parents' homes as well as in school. As a matter of fact, a large percentage of the teachers at Betances visited student homes regularly. All our meetings were conducted in Spanish and English, and all school notices were also in both languages. Because of our high rate of mobility, however, every year new parents would come into the process, requiring constant training and support.

As far as I'm concerned, SDP saved my life. Given the linguistic, socioeconomic, cultural, and environmental factors affecting our students, I really needed to be freed to do aggressive outreach for funding, special programs, and additional resources. As our SPMT, SSST, and PT became more and more sophisticated, I was able to spend more time in outreach pursuits. The director of the FRC and the parent trainer already were part of the SPMT, and that integrated those services into the fiber of the school community.

One of the critical issues raised by our SSST was the abysmal health of most of our students. The greatest health problem at Betances was not asthma, although that was astronomical. It was childhood depression. Our students received their health care in emergency rooms. Teachers were battling to infuse students with a sense of hope and to energize them. We had already established a breakfast program to feed all our students in our first year because teachers had noticed extreme lethargy due to hunger. But, how do you teach an unhealthy child effectively?

Then the city moved to another site a community drop-in senior center that was located in the school, opening up three classrooms. Through the combined efforts of Hartford Hospital, the school, and funding from the Travelers, Betances was able to open a beautiful, school-based clinic in those classrooms that provides all preventive and follow-up care for its students and hopes to extend services to the community. The "I Believe in the Children" clinic is open year-round. All Betances students are fully immunized. The clinic provides the services of a child psychiatrist, a developmental pediatrician, a psychiatric social worker to work with families, and full-time nurses, on-site. The partnership with Hartford hospital includes sharing of records and connects care given at the hospital with that being given at the clinic.

The clinic staff visit classrooms, interact with teachers and students, seek and give advice, and influence the classroom curriculum to promote healthy behaviors in students and their families. Ultimately, the goal is to develop a wellness program that will prepare students and parents to engage in healthy behaviors. Members of the clinic staff sit on the SSST and the SPMT.

Prior to the existence of the "I Believe in the Children" clinic, entering kindergarten students lost as much as 2 months of school if they were unable to get the immunizations and physicals required by the State of Connecticut. This was also true of out-of-state students who did not have the necessary health information. If a hospital is unable to verify immunizations, children have to be immunized again. I have often been asked why our parents didn't simply take their children to a doctor. There is a distressing lack of information about the realities poor children face in the United States. Most of the children at Betances did not have a pediatrician. The majority received their care in emergency rooms after their illnesses had become chronic. The existing clinics were overwhelmed and unable to keep up with the need for medical care. Most children only received their immunizations and physical examinations because they would otherwise not be able to enter school, creating a bottleneck at the clinics in September when a huge number of children required services. The health care issue was one of the most emotionally devastating for me as a new principal. With the advent of the clinic, all students were able to begin school immediately upon arrival. All Betances students are fully immunized.

We still had one more critical issue that had not been addressed: dental health. The majority of our students suffered from caries. Some had lost important permanent teeth at a very early age. We were able to get a grant from the Hartford Junior Chamber of Commerce (Jaycees) to establish a beautifully equipped dental clinic with the services of a dentist and a dental hygienist. The efforts of the Betances dental hygienist, who struggled for years to get better dental services for the children, cannot be overstated. Dental hygienists have been a part of the health education program for the Hartford Public Schools for over 50 years. Dental health is an integral part of the curriculum. The additional benefit of full dental treatment was welcomed by parents and staff. It prevented students from having to take a day off from school to visit a dentist. The dentist is scheduled in concert with teachers, thus minimizing the impact on the students' academic program.

What does any of this have to do with schooling? Did we go off on a tangent and develop a social service agency rather than a functioning educational institution? While all these activities were taking place, the SPMT reviewed some very sobering achievement data in our Comprehensive School Plan. It became obvious after gathering information from classroom teachers, special education staff, and parents that the textbook used in the math program, and our English reading program, were actually *interfering* with the learning process!

The curriculum committee launched a search and pilot mission over a 2-year period to look at alternatives and gather information on materials best suited to our children's learning styles and developmental, linguistic, and cultural needs. Members of the staff served on systemwide committees, visited other school systems, and attended staff development activities to enhance their understanding of the problem and to learn new methodologies, and they piloted those materials that appeared best suited to our population.

The year I left Betances—in 1993, after 9 years at the school—the SPMT had received recommendations from the curriculum committee for a new, whole language reading series in the primary grades and for the expansion into the second grade of the literature-based program that one of our sixth-grade teachers had developed over a 5-year period. In addition, the curriculum committee recommended a new math series that had textbooks in Spanish and English for the intermediate grades (the teachers in the primary grades had been trained and were successfully using the "Math Their Way" program in that subject area).

These recommendations were brought before the full staff and were unanimously adopted and fully supported by our PT. The fact that so many of our parents were classroom volunteers greatly aided their understanding of the issues involved. That year, we decided to spend our entire textbook account to implement these initiatives. Because we were the only school in Hartford to purchase the new reading series, the company gave us enough free material to articulate the program through the second grade. They also gave us a substantial amount of science and math supplementary materials for all grades. Since we had bankrupted the textbook account, this was very important.

As I left Betances that year, I had a feeling that my child had grown, gone to college and graduate school, and gotten married and was now in the position to give *me* advice on how to grow and develop! I came to realize that being an SDP principal means being able to cope with the fact that, ultimately, your school doesn't *need you* in order to continue its mission. A successful SDP school develops the ability to renew itself, heal, maintain a high degree of engagement at all levels and in all relationships, and keep the focus on children and their needs while maintaining an unwavering vision for the future.

The ultimate test was the process of choosing a new principal when I retired. The SPMT developed a profile of the qualities they wanted to see in a new principal, with input from all staff. The Hartford Public School Human Resources Department included teachers, parents, and me on the interviewing panel. We were a majority vote, as a matter of fact. The person we unanimously recommended for the principalship had worked at Betances for 6 years as a reading consultant, was SDP trained, and had come in as the top candidate not just in our school's panel but in several other schools as well. She was, in fact, appointed as the new principal of Betances. The process does work!

I miss my school, the community it serves, my children, staff, parents, and above all, the overwhelming feeling of being part of a very special, loving family that faces adversity *every day* and reaffirms *every day* that the next day will be better for all. The hugs, the kisses, the food, the music, the smiles, the tears, the joys, the pain, the disappointments, the successes, the failures, all come together in a magnificent collage that is a tribute to human endurance, to children's amazing resiliency and strength, and to the power that is brought to bear when the whole village is engaged *for children's sake.*

▰▰▰ *References*

Anson, A., Cook, T. D., Habib, F., Grady, M. K., Haynes, N. M., & Comer, J. P. (1991). The Comer School Development Program: A theoretical analysis. *Urban Education, 26* (1), 56–82.

Cohen, D. (1994). Preface. In Norris M. Haynes (ed.), *School Development Program Research Monograph* (pp. i–iii). New Haven, CT: Yale Child Study Center.

Comer, J. P. (1988a). *Maggie's American dream*. New York: New American Library.

Comer, J. P. (1988b). Educating poor minority children. *Scientific American, 259* (5), 42–48.

Comer, J. P. (1989a). Poverty, family and the black experience. In G. Miller (ed.), *Giving children a chance: The case for more effective national policies* (pp. 109–129). Washington, DC: Center for National Policy Press.

Comer, J. P. (1989b). Child development and education. *Journal of Negro Education, 58* (2), 125–139.

Comer, J. P. (1989c). The School Development Program: A psychosocial model of school intervention. In G. L. Berry & J. K. Asamen (eds.), *Black Students: Psychosocial Issues and Academic Achievement* (pp. 264–285). Newbury Park, CA: Sage Publications, Inc.

Comer, J. P. (1989d). Racism and the education of young children. *Teachers College Record, 90* (3), 352–361.

Comer, J. P. (1994). Introduction and problem analysis. In Norris M. Haynes (ed.), *School Development Program Research Monograph* (pp. i–vi). New Haven, CT: Yale Child Study Center.

Comer, J. P., Haynes, N. M., & Hamilton-Lee, M. (1989). School power: A model for improving black student achievement. In W. D. Smith & W. E. Chun (eds.), *Black Education: A quest for equity and excellence* (pp. 87–200). New Brunswick, NJ: Transaction Publishers.

Emmons, C. L. (1992). *School development in an inner city: An analysis of factors selected from Comer's program using latent variable structural equations modeling*. Doctoral dissertation, The University of Connecticut, Storrs.

Emmons, C. L. (1994). Comparison of Comer and non-Comer schools. Presentation at the SDP 25th Anniversary Research Symposium. New Haven, CT: Yale Child Study Center.

Haynes, N. M. (1993). School reform and urban education: A historical perspective. New Haven, CT: Yale Child Study Center.

Haynes, N. M., & Ben-Avie, M. (1994). Foreword. In Norris M. Haynes (ed.), *School Development Program Research Monograph* (pp. i–xiv). New Haven, CT: Yale Child Study Center.

Haynes, N. M., & Ben-Avie, M. (in press). Parents as full partners in the education of their children. To appear in Alan Booth & Judith F. Dunn (eds.), *Family–School Links*. Hillsdale, NJ: Lawrence Erlbaum Publishers.

Haynes, N. M., & Comer, J. P. (1990). The effects of a school development program on self-concept. *Yale Journal of Biology and Medicine, 63* (4), 275–283.

Haynes, N. M., Comer, J. P., & Hamilton-Lee, M. (1988). The School Development Program: A model for school improvement. *Journal of Negro Education, 57* (1), 11–21.

Haynes, N. M., Comer, J. P., & Hamilton-Lee, M. (1989). School climate enhancement through parental involvement. *Journal of School Psychology, 8* (4), 291–299.

Joyner, E., Haynes, N. M., & Comer, J. P. (1994). Implementation of the Yale School Development Program (SDP) in two middle schools: An ethnographic study. In Norris M. Haynes (ed.), *School Development Program Research Monograph* (pp. 1–31). New Haven, CT: Yale Child Study Center.

Klein, N. (1994). The Cleveland Public School/Cleveland State University Partnership: A strategy for successful SDP implementation. Paper prepared for the Yale School Development Program 25th Anniversary Research Symposium. New Haven, CT: Yale Child Study Center.

Luria, A. R. (1976). *Cognitive development: Its cultural and social foundations.* Cambridge, MA: Harvard University Press.

Moll, L. C. (1990). Introduction. In Luis C. Moll (ed.), *Vygotsky and Education: Instructional Implications and Applications of Sociohistorical Psychology.* Cambridge: Cambridge University Press.

Payne, C. (1994). *The Comer school development process in Chicago: An Interim Report.* Evanston, IL: Northwestern University.

Savo, C. (1995). 1995 Patrick Daly awards presented to five outstanding Comer principals. *The School Development Program Newsline, 4* (1), 1, 3.

Stern, B. (1995). The Comer/Zigler Initiative. New Haven, CT: Yale Bush Center.

Stern, B., & Flood, L. (1994). Early findings of the Comer–Zigler collaboration. Paper prepared for the Yale School Development Program 25th Anniversary Research Symposium. New Haven, CT: Yale Child Study Center.

Tudge, J. (1990). Vygotsky, the zone of proximal development, and peer collaboration: Implications for classroom practice. In Luis C. Moll (ed.), *Vygotsky and Education: Instructional implications and applications of sociohistorical psychology* (pp. 152–172). New York: Cambridge University Press.

Vygotsky, L. (1978). *Mind in society: The development of higher psychological processes.* Cambridge, MA: Harvard University Press.

Warner, C. (1994). Parental involvement in SDP schools. Presentation at the SDP 25th Anniversary Research Symposium. New Haven, CT: Yale Child Study Center.

Wertsch, J. V. (1985). *Vygotsky and the social formation of mind.* Cambridge, MA: Harvard University Press.

Chapter 4

University–School Partnership: Reforming Teacher Preparation

DEBORAH B. SMITH
AND LOUISE P. S. KALTENBAUGH

In the past, university schools of education have responded to many theories and philosophies. The SDP is a compelling new influence. The partnership of the SDP, Southern University at New Orleans, and the New Orleans Public Schools offers striking proof that teachers and students from kindergarten through grade 16 can combine forces to teach and learn creatively in the real world. After the formation of the New Orleans partnership, two more partnerships came into being: the SDP, Cleveland Public School District, and Cleveland State University partnership; and the SDP, San Francisco School District, and San Francisco State University partnership. As more universities join SDP schools in this exploration, their unique partnerships will define and solve problems in novel and invigorating ways.

Southern University at New Orleans, the School Development Program, and the New Orleans Public Schools partnership, known as the Comer Project or "the partnership," was initiated as a result of the reform climate of the 1980s. The partnership utilizes action research and praxis—a combination of direct practice and reflection of one's own teaching and its effect on learners—as a basis for change.

In the 1960s through the early 1980s, universities were above criticism when the question of "What's wrong with our education system?" was being posed in the K–12 setting. Then in the 1980s, universities in general and schools or colleges of education in particular were being challenged to rethink the way teachers were being prepared and the impact that the prevailing teacher preparation practices had on the K–12 educational system. During that time, the Holmes and Carnegie reports (1986) assessed the professional development programs for preservice teachers and found them lacking, particularly regarding the need to strengthen linkages with school districts.

In response to the call for reform, the new chancellor at Southern University at New Orleans (SUNO) determined that the College of Education would be one of the colleges that would engage in renewal. The questions of "how" and "with whom" became pivotal since we would have to go beyond our traditional boundaries and begin earnest dialogue with a school system. Since SUNO is a historically black institution whose primary constituents are from the New Orleans Public School (NOPS) system, itself a predominately urban, African-American school district, a partnership idea evolved as a natural outcome. We had three issues that we knew would be essential to a partnership arrangement. One was *trust*. For years, university–school relationships were based on authority–receiver roles. Thus, to begin dialogue with a school system and talk about partners in the preparation of preservice teachers required key stakeholders to be willing to work together with no hidden agendas and to rethink the current modus operandi. The second was *team building*. Key stakeholders had to be willing to work together through turf issues, such as placement of SUNO students at the school sites, willingness of classroom teachers to serve as mentors and nurturers of SUNO preservice teachers assigned to their classrooms, and the overall structure and requirement of SUNO clinical field experiences. The third issue was *change*. Each partner had to recognize that change would be inclusive and indeed necessary.

These initial dialogues paved the way for not only recognizing the need for reform but also the beginning basis for a K–16 partnership. It was at this juncture that persons, roles, responsibilities, and activities were discussed, identified, and defined. Three significant outcomes resulted based on these dialogues. One was the role of the SUNO/NOPS university coordinator as a change agent for teacher preparation.

The second outcome was the intensive breadth of communication across schools and university via the schools' School Planning and Management Teams (SPMTs). The SUNO/NOPS coordinator, Deborah B. Smith, or the SUNO/NOPS administrator, Louise P. S. Kaltenbaugh, participated in SPMT meetings at the schools. In addition, the administrator observed the SUNO students as they worked in the schools and, upon returning to the university, met with the students to discuss their reaction to their experiences. As part of the K–16 partnership collaboration, university services were identified based on recommendations garnered from the SPMTs. The SPMTs were determined to be the primary linkages between the schools and the university. During the SPMT meetings, the key stakeholders identified the needs while the university coordinator recommended possible resource options. These options were discussed and negotiated at the meetings as part of a collaborative framework.

The third outcome was the number of university students involved in the K–16 partnership. In the first year, 1991–1992, approximately 152 students were involved in the K–16 partnership as mathematics tutors, reading assistants, speech and hear-

Dr. Deborah Smith (foreground, seated at far right) and Dr. Louise Kaltenbaugh (standing center) with students from Southern University at New Orleans.

ing diagnosticians, art enrichment assistants, and social work interns in the SDP schools. In 1992–1993, approximately 362 university students reported to the SDP partnership schools and delivered similar services, with the addition of health and nutrition assistance. In the third year, 1993–1994, services were maintained with a cadre of 288 university students. While providing services to the schools, the university students themselves gained invaluable experience. As will be discussed in depth in this chapter, prior to the partnership, the teacher preparation program was conducted primarily in isolation from the schools with minimal field experiences required before the preservice students' senior year. Now field experiences in the Comer Project are mandated in professional core courses beginning as early as the students' sophomore year. Under the guidance of their university professors, these preservice teachers have the opportunity to reflect on their ongoing experiences and learn from them during the course of their years at SUNO. With these structures in place, and the immersion of preservice teachers in schools, the partnership's interactions affirmed the need for ongoing reform.

▚▚▞ *The Need for Reform*

For more than a decade, educators have been involved in continual dialogue about America's schools and how to improve them. Although opinions vary about what is wrong with our schools, there is agreement that schools must undergo structural change to address issues pertinent to the needs of today's youngsters.

This dialogue began in earnest in 1983, when the National Commission on Excellence in Education published the results of its 18-month study of our schools and colleges. Comparing our system of education with that of the rest of the industrialized world, the commission labeled us a "nation at risk." The study reported that our educational system is steeped in mediocrity and is failing to produce a population capable of competition in the global market. Although this came as confirmation to many who had earlier advocated change movements in our schools, it surprised many others who were distanced from education. The *Nation at Risk* report served to spark the initiation of various academic, business, and political coalitions that sought to respond with varied reform and restructuring configurations. These configurations targeted several starting points within our system of education: administrative postures, teacher accountability, learner accountability, parental involvement, state appropriations, federal policies and regulations, and corporate/private-sector involvement, to name a few. And many of the far-reaching reforms identified teacher preparation programs as a crucial component for change implementation.

The emerging national consensus on the need to change the way teaching and learning occurs in the United States confronts educational institutions as an indictment and leaves no sector unaffected: elementary, secondary, vocational and technical schools, and higher education. The reasons for this indictment include social conditions such as the collapse of the family, the negative influence of television on the school-age population, teenage parenthood, increased violence, the rise in drug involvement and related crimes, gender/age/sex discrimination, and the abject failure of local and national leadership. It is suggested that these are results, not causes, of a failing educational system (Roberts, 1991). Although the United States is recognized as having a successful system of higher education (Kantrowitz and Wingert, 1991), that, too, has come under attack, from outside and from within the academy. Teacher education colleges and instructors are being forced to rethink their curricula and their instructional techniques as more school districts begin to demand that their teachers incorporate contemporary issues that relate to growing, racially diverse, urban populations (Nicklin, 1991).

Amid this struggle, institutions of higher education have joined with political, business, and community groups to create programs that will restructure, redesign, or reform curricular content, instructional practices, administrative management, school and community relations, and the interaction between content and pedagogy. However, the reality is that there is no one simple solution to address the current situation.

Two important organizations responded to the national call for reform with reports that included recommendations to link colleges and universities closer to schools. The first report was prepared by the Carnegie Forum on Education and the Economy in 1986. *A Nation Prepared: Teachers for the 21st Century* focused on the vital connection between national economic growth and an intellectually competitive population. It targeted the teaching profession as the starting point for reform, and identified strategies for redefining essential standards for the preparation and practice of the profession. A major theme contained throughout the report is the link between teacher training programs, educational excellence, and the economic growth of our country.

Similar connections were discussed in a critical report published by the Holmes Group in 1986. The Holmes report sought to retain and to give visibility to efforts to strengthen teacher education programs by creating new lines of communication and cooperation between universities and schools. *Tomorrow's Teachers* is a two-phase plan that calls for the development and implementation of rigorous new standards for teachers' education. These standards are designed to make the education of teachers intellectually more rigorous through broader curricular and graduation requirements. Colleges of education are called upon to recognize differences in teachers' knowledge, skills, commitment, and educational backgrounds. To improve teacher preparation programs, colleges of education are asked to connect with schools and practicing teachers in order to systematically inquire into practice and, thus, to give student teachers training that reflects reality (Holmes Group, 1986).

▣▦▦ *Intellectual Foundations of Teacher Training Programs*

Both the Carnegie and Holmes reports have been highly influential in setting a national agenda for the establishment of partnerships between universities and schools. The disconnectedness between schools and universities in the 20th century reflects the manner and historical context in which American teacher training programs evolved, as well as persistent disagreement about what is best for schools, teachers, and students.

Historically, teacher preparation curricula has had no master plan, and no consistency between philosophy, ideology, and practice. The "why" and "how" of education can be traced to several philosophical and ideological foundations: idealism, realism, humanism, experimentalism, and existentialism.

▦▦▦ Philosophical and Ideological Foundations

Idealism stresses subject matter and emphasizes literature, religion, and intellectual history. It is steeped in the liberal arts for content and validates its worth in terms of "pure knowledge." The preferred teaching methods are lecture, discussion, recitation, and understanding the connectedness of ideas. The scope of the curriculum emphasizes the past, is stable, and is predetermined by some authority (Orzmon and Craver, 1981).

By contrast, *realism* stresses the sciences and mathematics. It is primarily concerned with the physical world of things that are measurable, definite, and precise. Two preferred teaching methods include demonstrations and drill for accuracy and precision. Acceptable behavior is stated in terms of expectations and objectives. The curriculum has a quantitative structure and is steeped in the scientific process (Orzmon and Craver, 1981).

Humanism bridges idealism and realism and is concerned with the interests and ideals of people rather than with religion or the natural world. Curricula focus on concerns and problems that are germane to all people and stress the study of the humanities for the discipline of the mind and the development of analytic thinking skills. The spirit of the individual and the improvement of the intellect are the primary forces. Great ideas from the past and present are used to shed light on the human predicament. Language, mathematics, and the classics are also stressed. Once again, lecture, formal drill, and recitation are the preferred teaching methods. Group decision making and collaboration are stressed to promote belonging, individual worth, and cooperation. The ultimate goal is total learning (Henderson, 1978).

Experimentalism emphasizes human experiences, scientific problems, and social dilemmas. Betterment of society through involvement is a key issue. The preferred teaching methods are analysis, problem solving, criticism, evaluation, collaboration, group consensus, and discovery. Curricula relate to the past for informed decision making, emphasize the present to apply the agreed-upon decisions, analyze the consequences or results, and respond to the future through an evaluative process. Experimentalism can be seen in strategic planning activities and in programs that have community involvement at their core (Henderson, 1978).

Although there are more, the final philosophy discussed here is *existentialism.* Individuality is stressed most in this philosophy—the role of the individual as a being who chooses and makes commitments. Individuals are allowed to pursue their own choices. Existentialists oppose any single mode of education and are very critical of modern education methodologies because they believe that not enough room is provided for individual thinking and criticism (Orzmon and Craver, 1981). Curricula are based on individual change through considering past actions, present responses, and ultimately, future responses.

Theoretical Foundations

Practices within and among colleges of education also vary based on the diversity of theories that exist in education. Perennialism, essentialism, reconstructionism, and progressivism are four theories of education that have influenced the development of the American school. Each theory can be seen in organizational structure in terms of curricula and in response to students.

Perennialism closely aligns with idealism and classical humanism. It is a recent term in educational thought, but its roots can be traced back to the belief in classical antiquity that human nature does not change. Therefore, "good" education must develop the intellect of the child, and the proper goal is to discipline students' rational powers (Henderson, 1978).

Essentialism is similar to perennialism. It defines an educated person in terms of the fundamentals of knowledge—reading, writing, and arithmetic. Essentialists deemphasize a strictly rational approach to knowledge and favor one that emphasizes observational or empirical data as equal or superior to rational thought.

"Back to Basics" movements are the leading advocates of this theory. The controversies within this theory relate to the extent and depth of those basics (Orzmon and Craver, 1981).

The prevailing theme in *reconstructionism* is that education should be the principal means for reconstructing a better social order. Reconstructionists feel that the seriousness of today's problems cannot wait for long-term solutions. They advocate an educational format with international scope that contains a great deal of practical experience. Consensus, values, and motivation are all stressed as critical components to support the development of a harmonious world civilization (Orzmon and Craver, 1981).

Last, *progressivism* includes several components and brings together three major commitments in a new relationship that should be the major concern of all schools: (1) commitment to equal educational opportunity for all children to reach their potential; (2) commitment to the dominant ideals of our democratic society to embrace the enhancement of the individual, society, and the community; and (3) commitment to the mental and physical health of the child. Progressivists promote an interdisciplinary approach in education and believe that learning should involve a cooperative interchange between the individual, the school, and the larger society, with emphasis on the individual's learning potential. Here is the theoretical basis for the programs developed by James P. Comer (1980) and Henry Levin (1989), which emphasize the health and intellectual growth of the child as being crucial to the parent–school–community relationship (Henderson, 1978).

Prior to the 1980s, higher education was relatively free of society's criticisms, which had plagued public education from kindergarten through 12th grade. However, in the early 1980s the focus shifted, and the competency and commitment of teachers came under scrutiny. The inextricable links between philosophy and theory, theory and practice, and philosophy and practice have resulted in multiple views regarding the purpose of education, the way to educate, and the way to prepare educators. In the elementary curriculum, preservice teachers take a series of methods courses; at the secondary level, the preservice teachers take courses in the content-of-teaching area, with one or two methods courses. After completing the coursework and passing a standardized teacher examination, the preservice teacher begins student teaching. Most of the interaction that preservice teachers have in the schools is incidental to the required curriculum. Schools began to find fault with the way teachers were being prepared. Inservice teachers were questioning the validity of the college theory courses. Student teachers were experiencing the trauma of the dichotomy between the reality of the public school classrooms and the training they received at the university. The university was not particularly interested in what the schools thought regarding the preparedness of the student teachers.

Thus, throughout the entire preparation process, there was no mutually beneficial interaction between university and school. The interfacing usually occurred during the preservice teachers' last semester, and the schools merely provided the sites so that the preservice teachers could fulfill the legislative requirement of completing a student teaching process. Clearly, the way teachers were being prepared required redirection and restructuring. The isolation of the teacher preparation process, the disparity between theory and actual practice, and the lack of what some reformers referred to as the "depth and breadth" of the liberal arts, science, and mathematics courses became major aspects of the call for reform. According to Murphy (1990), an analysis revealed that administrators and teachers represented the bottom of the intellectual barrel and were poorly trained for their respective roles. Although this may have been the perception of some, individuals directly involved in the milieu surrounding education recognized that there were underlying societal problems and that the source of the problems could not be specifically attributed to teacher preparation. Nonetheless, the educational attainment of our youngsters clearly indicated that something was awry. It was recognized that educational systems, particularly teacher preparation programs, were inadequately preparing teachers to meet the demands of the 21st century. There were tensions involving theory and actual classroom experiences and university practices.

It is this very nature of the teacher preparation curriculum that is now under attack. The 1990s have been a critical decade, spent researching and reporting on the social context in which education has been determined a failing system. Admitting that educational reform is no substitute for the radical social reform needs that are indicated by existing demographic projections (Hodgkinson, 1991), what seems certain is that an opportunity confronts us to demonstrate a new commitment to children and their future in society.

The SDP Model Formed the Basis for the Partnership

This self-study has led the entire educational community to accept the need to reform. It has also given the greater society the chance to help select the criteria to address many of our nation's growing social ills through new educational programs and methodologies. Among the possibilities is one educational reform model that has gained national attention, the School Development Program. It is this educational reform model that formed the basis for the partnership described later in this chapter between Southern University at New Orleans (SUNO) and the New Orleans Public Schools (NOPS) involving students from kindergarten through college.

In the School Development Program's model, school climate is improved through an applied understanding of child development, through a process of participatory management, and the promotion of increased parental presence in schools. These principles support the model's child-centered concept that virtually all students can be successful and that low-achieving students are simply "underdeveloped" (Comer, 1980).

Trained in the application of the model's principles and appropriate implementation techniques, support teams made up of university faculty act as change agents within the school district and at the participating university in that they link appropriate resources within the university to the schools, train school site faculties and monitor their progress, and assist in preparing formative and summative status reports for the school district. Also, paramount to the support team's overall responsibility as change agent is its mandate not only to improve teaching and learning within the schools, but to improve teacher preparation within the university. These teams "use the knowledge gained from working in schools to drive change in the curriculum and the methodology used to prepare prospective teachers for positions in school systems" (Comer et al., 1990).

It is in this new relationship (university–school partnership) that teacher preparation will and must emerge. Schools and universities will form partnerships in a symbiotic relationship. The new relationships must explore governance and incorporate school-based management. Roles of teachers, administrators, central office, and school boards must be redefined. Universities must also be involved in this redefinition process. In fact, the redefinition must include society in general to affect institutionalization, at least at state levels. Although the term *joint steering* has been in use, it must be redefined and the definition agreed upon.

Kuhn (1976) discusses the importance of language in the emergence of a paradigm. He states that the language, research, and concepts become so specialized and technical that only another practitioner within that paradigm can understand the schematic discussion. Although that posture can work in the pure sciences, it has its limitations for education. According to Muller (1960), "The meaning of a term cannot be grasped without learning how to use the term as part of the whole language structure in which it plays its part. In general, being able to use the term correctly is necessary to having the particular concept associated with that term." Although new paradigms incorporate much of the vocabulary of old paradigms, the vocabulary must assume different nuances.

An example is collaboration. Collaboration has been a buzzword since the 1980s. Collaborative learning was hailed as the way to provide maximum learning for all students. However, if one were to ask 10 teachers to define collaborative learning, most likely there would be 10 different responses. Thus, Kuhn and Muller's comments regarding language, concepts, and terms need to be heeded.

As schools and universities join in teacher preparation, the redefinition of the concept of partnerships and the process of partnerships must become specific. According to Pitsch (1991), the early school–college partnerships were initiated to provide prospective teachers with a site to develop their teaching skills. Since the 1980s, university–school partnerships have been developed to provide an infrastructure for improvement in the ways in which preservice teachers are trained. In *Linking America's Schools and Colleges,* Franklin Wilbur and Leo Lambert (1991) describe four types of partnerships:

- Programs and services for students, including programs for at-risk students, college courses for high school students, and programs of accelerated study for gifted students
- Programs and services for educators, including inservice training and staff development, teacher education centers, school–college faculty exchanges, leadership programs for teachers, and management programs for teachers and administrators
- Curriculum development and assessment projects
- Programs to promote sharing of educational resources, such as the use of tutors and adopt-a-school programs

Wilbur and Lambert identified the necessity of collaboration between university and schools in the preparation of preservice teachers. Based on the historical and current implications, the comprehensiveness of the reform, the necessary connectedness to society, and the diverse teacher preparation programs, various questions needed to be addressed in the establishment of a partnership:

- What will the structure of the partnership be?
- How should we connect with the schools?
- What theory and/or philosophy should we embrace?
- What model should we use: K–12 or K–16?
- How should the relationship be structured?
- Which school(s) should be selected?

Without deep structural change, the partnership would result in rhetoric, some cosmetic changes, and then, business as usual.

Deep structural changes were made by our partnership in New Orleans. Through our evaluations of these changes, we have concluded that teacher preparation reform becomes most effective when it is strategically and comprehensively connected with the day-to-day operations of schools. This is essential because it can provide preservice teachers with real experiences as early as the sophomore year. These experiences should begin with simple tasks and become more complex as the preservice teachers become acclimated to the school environment and progress to and through student teaching and graduation.

SUNO/NOPS *Partnership*

Through the initiative of the vice chancellor of academic affairs and the dean of the College of Education at Southern University at New Orleans (SUNO), preliminary discussions were held with representatives from Yale University and the Rockefeller Foundation to explore the feasibility of a university–school partnership and the likely direction of the partnership. Taking into account the urgent needs of urban and inner-city schools, of students who attend these schools, of teachers who teach in these schools, and of the university (which provides the major corps of minority teachers for the school system), a partnership arrangement appeared to provide a process and framework for bringing about lasting and significant change.

On March 1, 1990, SUNO and the New Orleans Public Schools (NOPS) received a planning grant to enable SUNO and NOPS to talk and work together. The key activities supported by the planning grant were:

- Selecting a planning committee
- Determining goals and objectives
- Reviewing current practices
- Conducting needs assessments
- Identifying training needs
- Developing a statement of work
- Establishing an evaluation system
- Identifying supplementary funding sources
- Developing an application package for submission

Based on the success of the planning grant, a partnership between Yale, SUNO, and NOPS was established, known as the Comer Project or the partnership. The partnership's goal is twofold: to enhance the preservice elementary and secondary teacher education program at SUNO in order to address more effectively the needs of inner-city teachers and students, and to implement the School Development Program in the identified target schools. It was decided to systematically reassess and modify the goals at the end of each project year.

The partnership represents a philosophical collaboration and a cooperative effort to replicate the School Development Program (SDP). In addition, it maintains and supports the student teacher feeder mechanism already established; that is, most of the elementary school students involved—the students of the SDP schools—move up to the same middle school and the same high school, and they are likely to continue their education at SUNO. Thus, the College of Education joins in a K–16 partnership.

The above goals are to be accomplished through the assistance, training, and direction of consultants from the Yale Child Study Center and educational consultants from other universities. The specific objectives of the program are as follows:

1. Continue the process of collaboration, cooperation, and communication between SUNO and NOPS.
2. Coordinate and enhance the many educational and social activities already in place at SUNO and NOPS.
3. Improve the school climate of the target schools and SUNO.
4. Improve teaching and learning aspects of the educational process including an emphasis on child development.

5. Initiate collaborative sharing of professional expertise and dialogue among the teachers of the target schools and the SUNO faculty.
6. Revise and strengthen the preservice education program at SUNO to include:
   (a) a mentor program for "at-risk" education majors
   (b) a "classroom assistant" program beginning in the sophomore year for education majors for early practicum experiences
   (c) a series of training sessions by educational consultants to inform, update, and motivate the university faculty to incorporate current educational pedagogy
   (d) curricula enhancement to include cultural diversity with an African/African-American emphasis
   (e) revision and/or development of curricula and instructional materials that address the needs of prospective urban educators
7. Revise and strengthen SUNO's inservice training of elementary and secondary school faculty and staff both at SUNO and at the target schools.
8. Enhance and strengthen the education program at the target schools to include:
   (a) improving basic skills, particularly reading and math
   (b) developing patterns of shared responsibility and decision making among parents and staff
   (c) increasing motivation for learning, achievement, and ultimately mastery in a way that will increase academic achievement for each child
   (d) reducing social distance and distrust among parents, teachers, and administrators
   (e) fostering a climate of sharing, honesty, and trust in order to reduce the number of behavior problems

Revising Preservice Teacher Preparation

The major focus of the partnership's activities at SUNO was the preservice preparation of teachers who intended to serve in urban and inner-city schools. The proposed program differed from existing programs in theoretical emphasis, working relationships, and preservice field experiences.

SUNO's teacher preparation program had emphasized pedagogical methods and content knowledge of specific curricular areas, but had no systematic or uniform plan for school-site activities emphasizing practical child development knowledge and interpersonal skills. The supervised classroom components were limited to directed observation with mandatory participation for one semester and then student teaching. Some professors did include school-site visits and/or tutorial experiences as course requirements. However, there was no consistent approach that all instructors could use. The partnership's coordinator and the NOPS facilitator collaborated with school-based faculty and college faculty to address these issues.

▨▨▨▨▨▨ Year One (1991–1992)

The goals of the first year of the partnership included the following components:

- Immediate modification of the preservice preparation of teachers at SUNO to include early intervention for tutorial and/or school-site experiences in the target schools
- Establishing a climate for change at the target schools, which included coordination of resources and establishing SDP teams
- Beginning to train principals, designated faculty, support staff, and parents in the skills needed to implement the SDP model

In the first year of the partnership, administrative start-up details included selecting key personnel from SUNO and NOPS. Bimonthly meetings were held to:

- Plan inservice training for school faculty who would be involved
- Identify methods courses to be included
- Identify professors who desired to become involved
- Coordinate field experiences for education majors and their professors (this continued into year 2)

Two other very important aspects during year 1 were "selling" the university–school partnership as a viable framework for restructuring a teacher preparation program and working through territorial issues at both the university and the participating schools.

▨▨▨▨▨▨ Year Two (1992–1993)

Based on the recommendations of the SUNO/NOPS team and on the activities in year 1, it was decided that preservice activities for education majors should and must be coordinated and planned by university faculty whose students were actively engaged in fieldwork at the SDP schools. Clinical experiences were stipulated with expectations clearly delineated in the course syllabi by participating faculty.

In addition, based on recommendations by participating preservice education majors and teachers in the SDP schools, an Upper Elementary Program was designed and implemented. It was during this time that preservice education majors were included in school planning meetings, school–community involvement workshops, and parental training.

▨▨▨▨▨▨ Year Three (1993–1994)

When sophomores have the chance to work in classrooms, they have an early opportunity to test their desire to become teachers in an urban or any other school district. Their involvement becomes more complex as they progress to various levels of skill and preparedness. It is because of this progression that the faculty and staff of SUNO's College of Education began to rethink all aspects of the existing teacher preparation program. The SUNO/NOPS partnership has served as the catalyst for changes that are now occurring in year 4.

Formative Evaluations

In keeping with the partnership's goals and the action research model, formative evaluations came from a variety of methods, multiple sources, and different time frames. Based on the fluid, reflective practice posture, the partnership provided opportunities for dialogue between and among key players, such as School Planning and Management Teams, other school contacts, university professors, and preservice teachers. Specifically, teachers in the field provided feedback in areas of preservice preparation in meeting the demands of the day-to-day operations of the classroom and in content knowledge. Preservice teachers provided feedback regarding their preparedness in areas of course content and classroom management. These responses were documented through interviews, informal discussions, surveys, and noted modifications in course syllabi.

For the purpose of this chapter, we have elected to report on the findings from the preservice teachers' surveys that address teacher preparation issues. (Chapter 6 shows the impact of the partnership on the SDP schools in New Orleans). In all, four surveys were administered: 1993–1994 survey (year 3) that was administered during final examination week of the Spring 1994 semester; two student teacher surveys (identical) administered during final examination week of the Spring 1994 and Fall 1994 semesters; and the 1994 Fall survey (beginning year 4) that was administered during the last class prior to final examination week of the Fall 1994 semester. Data are presented in table form for the 1993–1994 survey (year 3) and in narrative form for the student teacher surveys and the Fall 1994 survey (year 4).

Overall, the results of the surveys were very positive about the program. The SUNO students involved in preservice field experiences felt that they had gained substantially from their participation, that they had become sensitized to the skills required for effective urban education, and that they had improved their knowledge of the schools, their interactions with students and teachers, and their preparation for teaching as a profession.

1993–1994 Survey (Year 3)

In the 1994 Spring semester, the 1993–1994 survey was administered to 200 preservice students. Fifty-seven surveys were then randomly selected to be evaluated. Not every item was answered on all 57 surveys. Therefore, the *N* response may vary from item to item. The student survey consisted of five separate sections: "Background Information," designed to collect basic demographic information about the university students involved in the field experience; "Preparation for Field Experience"; "Field Experience"; "School Climate"; and "Impact of Field Experience."

Since the school climate data focused on the schools—and not on teacher preparation—the topic of school climate will not be discussed in this chapter.

▨ Findings

BACKGROUND INFORMATION

The background information results of the 1993–1994 survey are presented in Table 4-1. The majority of the respondents were female (87.2%), African-American (93.0%), and Louisiana residents (94.5%).

Most students who responded to the survey were primarily full-time students (96.5%); this group was almost evenly split between daytime (57.9%) and both daytime and evening (42.1%) attendance. Almost 70% of the students said that they aspired to get a master's degree or higher. Slightly more than 80% of the students were enrolled in the program during the Spring of 1994. The students also indicated a reasonable level of exposure to education courses: Almost 75% had completed two or more.

THE STUDENTS' PREPARATION FOR FIELD EXPERIENCE

Table 4-2 shows the respondents' preparation for field experience. Slightly more than 80% of the responding students either agreed or strongly agreed that they

Table 4-1. *Student Characteristics*

	Number	Percent
FULL OR PART-TIME ATTENDANCE ($N = 57$)		
Full-time	55	96.5
Part-time	2	3.5
DAY OR DAY AND EVENING ATTENDANCE ($N = 57$)		
Daytime	33	57.9
Daytime and Evening	24	42.1
HIGHEST DEGREE PLANNED ($N = 56$)		
Certificate (teaching, etc.)	3	5.4
Associate's Degree	1	1.8
Bachelor's Degree	13	23.2
Master's Degree	18	32.1
Doctorate	21	37.5
SEMESTER OF PARTICIPATION IN COMER PROJECT ($N = 56$)		
Fall 1993	9	16.1
Spring 1994	47	83.9
EDUCATION METHOD COURSES COMPLETED ($N = 56$)		
1 or less	15	26.8
2–5	27	48.2
6 or more	14	25.0

received ample information about the field experience, referred to as the Comer Project. More than 73% of the students agreed that they were adequately prepared for their activities in the schools; however, it is important to note that more than a quarter of the respondents did not feel adequately prepared.

More than 75% of the students agreed that the college provided ample support for their activities. Slightly more than 20% felt that the support from the college could be better. In spite of minor reservations about the support provided, more than 90% agreed that the preparation was challenging. Finally, the logistics of scheduling the field experience proved to be problematic for some students, almost 24% of them indicating a conflict with their regular class schedule. Fortunately, almost 66% of the students disagreed that there was a schedule conflict.

FIELD EXPERIENCE

Table 4-3 presents responses about the field experience. Although the majority of the students (69.7%) felt that the teachers in the school were aware of their activities, more than a fourth did not agree. Almost 90% indicated that they received ample assistance in the school. The students also felt that there was no substantial gap between theory and practice in the field.

More than 80% said that their materials were developmentally appropriate and appropriate for the classroom conditions. Some students felt pressed for time: More than 30% of the preservice teachers (the students) felt that there was not enough time to complete their activity. However, the preservice teachers felt that they were encouraged to participate (96.4%), received adequate assistance from school staff

Table 4-2. *Preparation for Field Experience (in percent)*

	Strongly Agree	Agree	Disagree	Strongly Disagree	Not Applicable
I received ample information on the Comer Project. (N = 56)	30.4	50.0	10.7	5.4	3.6
I was adequately prepared to execute the assigned activity. (N = 56)	25.0	48.2	23.2	3.6	0
The faculty and staff of the College of Education provided ample assistance. (N = 56)	32.1	44.6	16.1	5.4	1.8
Preparation for the field experience was academically challenging for me. (N = 56)	33.9	57.1	7.1	1.8	0
There was a conflict with my class schedule and the school site experience. (N = 55)	5.4	18.2	38.2	27.3	10.9

Table 4-3. *Field Experience (in percent)*

	Strongly Agree	Agree	Disagree	Strongly Disagree	Not Applicable
Teachers at the school site were fully aware of my proposed activity. (N = 56)	16.1	53.6	25.0	3.6	1.8
I received adequate assistance from teachers and staff at the school site. (N = 56)	21.4	66.1	10.7	0	1.8
There was no substantial gap between theory and practice. (N = 56)	8.9	64.3	16.1	5.4	5.4
My materials were developmentally appropriate for the assigned students. (N = 54)	16.7	68.5	7.4	3.7	3.7
My materials were appropriate for classroom conditions. (N = 56)	16.1	71.4	7.1	3.6	1.8
I had ample time to complete my activity. (N = 55)	18.2	49.1	25.5	7.3	0
Students were encouraged to actively participate. (N = 56)	37.5	58.9	1.8	0	1.8
Student involvement met my expectations. (N = 55)	38.2	56.4	3.6	0	1.8
Teacher participation was encouraging. (N = 56)	30.4	57.1	8.9	0	3.6
The experience was enjoyable and fulfilling. (N = 56)	57.1	37.5	5.4	0	0
I learned from the experience. (N = 56)	53.6	44.6	1.8	0	0

(94.6%), and were encouraged by teacher participation in the partnership arrangement (87.5%). In the partnership arrangement, the classroom teachers served as mentors and enabled preservice teachers to test theory and methodology. Preservice teachers gained experiences in classroom management and instructional techniques. More than 94% felt that the experience was enjoyable and fulfilling. Almost all students (98.2%) felt that they learned from the experience.

IMPACT OF FIELD EXPERIENCE

Table 4-4 shows the impact of the field experience. Almost 95% of the students indicated an improvement in their knowledge of teaching as a profession, and

Table 4-4. *Impact of Field Experience (in percent)*

	Strongly Agree	Agree	Disagree	Strongly Disagree	Not Applicable
This program has improved my knowledge of teaching as a profession. (N = 54)	51.9	42.6	3.7	0	1.9
This program has improved my knowledge of social work as a profession. (N = 53)	18.9	41.5	11.3	1.9	26.4
This program has improved my knowledge of counseling as it relates to education. (N = 52)	23.1	42.3	11.5	0	23.1
This program has improved my knowledge of elementary schools. (N = 53)	39.6	49.1	1.9	1.9	7.5
This program has improved my knowledge of elementary school students. (N = 53)	43.4	45.3	1.9	1.9	7.5
This program has improved my opinion of teaching as a profession. (N = 53)	44.4	46.3	5.6	1.9	1.9
This program has improved my opinion of social work as a profession. (N = 54)	20.4	38.9	11.1	1.9	27.8
This program has improved my opinion of counseling as it relates to education. (N = 53)	22.6	47.2	7.5	0	22.6
This program has improved my opinion of elementary schools. (N = 54)	31.5	53.7	5.6	1.9	7.4
This program has improved my opinion of elementary school students. (N = 53)	43.4	45.3	3.8	0	7.5
My involvement in this program has been a great benefit to the teachers in the school. (N = 56)	37.5	60.7	1.8	0	0
My involvement in this program has been a great benefit to the students in the school. (N = 55).	47.3	50.9	1.8	0	0
My involvement in this program has been a great benefit to the parents of children. (N = 56)	28.6	46.4	5.4	3.6	16.1

60.4% and 65.4%, respectively, reported increased knowledge of social work and counseling as professions. Equal proportions reported improved knowledge of elementary schools (88.7%) and elementary school students (88.7%).

About 91% of the students said that their opinion of teaching as a profession improved as a result of their involvement in the program. The students' opinions of social work (59.3%) and counseling (69.8%) as professions also improved, as did their opinions of elementary schools (85.2%) and elementary school students (88.7%).

Slightly more than 98% of the students felt that their involvement in the program was a great benefit to the teachers in the school; the same percentage felt they had benefited the students in the schools; and 75% felt that they had benefited the children's parents.

▨▨▨▨ *1994 Student Teacher Surveys*

During the Fall and Spring semester of 1994, 110 SUNO students who were enrolled in student teacher courses (elementary and secondary) were asked to complete the student teacher survey. Of the 110 student teachers, 83 were female and 27 were male. The survey asked the students to identify their student teaching school and indicate the extent of their involvement with the Comer Project during their coursework at SUNO. The open-ended survey was designed to ascertain how involvement with the Comer Project affected their student teaching experiences.

▨▨▨▨ Findings

The analysis of their responses clustered around three major themes. The responding students indicated that their experiences in the Comer Project improved their knowledge of the schools, their interactions with students and teachers, and their preparation for teaching as a profession.

KNOWLEDGE OF THE SCHOOLS
As a result of experience in the Comer Project, the student teachers felt they knew more about the operation of elementary schools in particular. Although they recognized that schools differ, there are enough similarities so that exposure to any school improved the knowledge base about all schools. Improved knowledge of the schools also made the students more genuinely appreciative of the challenges faced by teachers. One student said:

> I know the limitations of these schools; the materials that are available makes the teachers' work a bit more challenging. I was never threatened, but I understood that the areas most of these Comer schools were located in were difficult areas. It made my stay more challenging, especially in the discipline area.

INTERACTIONS WITH STUDENTS AND TEACHERS

Several students felt that the Comer experience helped improve their interactions with students and teachers:

> It has made me aware of what to look for when I begin my student teaching.

> The experience involving the Comer Project helped me to realize how important it is to have one-on-one interaction with the student. You can really observe the program as it is taking place.

> I was involved in the math tutoring program.... I helped three children, whom I enjoyed very much. It sort of helped me get ready to deal with children in the inner-city schools.

PREPARATION FOR TEACHING AS A PROFESSION

Several students indicated that the Comer Project served as a good preparation for the profession of teaching:

> I enjoyed the program very much. I feel safe in saying that my time spent with the students was appreciated and needed.

> The experience that I had with the Comer Project has been most beneficial. I attended and participated in several areas with [the Project], and it has helped prepare me for the real world in classroom curriculum.

> The students were eager and enthusiastic that I chose an SDP site to do my student teaching.

1994 Fall Survey

SUNO students who were enrolled in selected elementary and secondary methods courses during the Fall semester of 1994 were asked to complete the Informed Responses for Restructuring Preservice Teacher Education (IRRPTE) survey during the last class prior to final examination week. This survey asked 55 students to identify their school placements and indicate the extent of their involvement with the field experience known as the Comer Project during their course work at SUNO. Of the 55 students, 51 were female and 4 were male. The IRRPTE asked the students to discuss how adequately they were prepared (1) to meet the demands of their field experiences and (2) on issues relevant to urban education. The survey consisted of five separate sections. "Comer Experiences" collected information on the number of Comer experiences, the schools, grade levels, and discipline areas. "Adequate Preparation" asked the students to assess their overall preparation in content, instructional strategy, planning, discipline, classroom management, individual differences, and assessment. "Relevant Issues for Urban Education" allowed students to identify and discuss specific issues. "School Setting" allowed students to assess school climate, student–teacher interactions, student morale/self-concept/esteem, principal–student interactions, and principal–teacher interactions. "Impact of Field Experience" attempted to determine personal reactions. The next section presents the analysis of responses to questions of adequate preparation.

Findings

The analysis of the preservice teacher responses addresses the implications of teacher preparation in seven major areas. The students indicated that their experiences in the Comer Project affirmed certain areas of preparation and identified areas to be considered during the restructuring of the teacher preparation program. The responses to preservice activities suggest that these activities do indeed contribute to a comprehensive understanding of schooling and the demands that are thrust upon the key stakeholders in the school environment. Moreover, not only did the preservice experiences crystallize the demands of the teaching profession for education majors, the activities were also undergirded by the reality that students lack certain knowledge and/or competencies in theory and praxis. This was especially evidenced in the areas of classroom management, planning, discipline, assessment, and individual differences. On the other hand, students generally believed that they were adequately prepared to meet the demands of most field experiences. They felt particularly equipped in the areas of instructional strategy and content.

ADEQUATE PREPARATION: CONTENT

As a result of field experiences in the Comer Project, the preservice teachers believed that they were adequately prepared to meet the demands of their field experiences. Several students commented:

> I was a bit apprehensive at first. Getting to meet students and work on reading skills was actually a pleasant experience.

> Initially, I was skeptical. I didn't think I was prepared enough to teach reading until I got there and worked with the students. Once I got started, my experiences with school [came into] focus.

> My general studies as well as professional studies gave me the abilities needed to be successful in tutoring.

> I believe that I should have focused more on English because I can see now how important it is to be able to communicate well and write well.

ADEQUATE PREPARATION: INSTRUCTIONAL STRATEGY

Several students noted that the field experiences afforded them the opportunity to bridge theory and praxis in actual classroom environments. Although some felt that their strategies were somewhat limited, they believed that they had learned ample strategies to be successful in their field experiences:

> This is my very first semester so I am still learning many strategies. As time progresses, I feel more confident because situations that are discussed in class [at SUNO] actually come up in the classroom so I am better prepared to handle them.

> I centered on student individual instruction by trying to access their previous knowledge and asking questions dealing with the present topics.

> All my instructors gave me plenty of examples and research on how to instruct a class.

ADEQUATE PREPARATION: PLANNING

Several students indicated that their involvement in the university–school partnership proved the need for thorough comprehensive planning. Some, however, believed that they were not adequately prepared in this area but that they had managed to learn from ongoing contact with the experienced teacher and students:

> My planning was coordinated with the teacher in attempts to develop a sequence of learning experiences built on past learning(s) of the students and realistic expectations from current readings.

> [It] became easier after each visit with the students; knowledge of students was the key.

> Originally I didn't know how to plan, so the class time went too fast without me accomplishing much. Now I plan at night before I go to class and am actually accomplishing goals that I set out to accomplish.

> After the first day, I was able to prepare myself because then I knew what kinds of questions to expect and what was expected of me.

> I learned how to make plans for all the courses being taught.
> My instructors taught me how to plan and anticipate the unexpected.

ADEQUATE PREPARATION: CLASSROOM MANAGEMENT

The students gained from the experience by learning that effective classroom management techniques are essential for quality teaching and authentic student learning:

I found that as long as the class was on task with the given assignment, the teacher had no problem with her class.

Since there was control already established through discipline, classroom management became easier to manipulate and control. There seemed to be a voluntary spirit of cooperation from students.

Principles of Secondary Education [class] was very helpful because I learned how to manage the time in the classroom. I tried to manage the time so that almost all of the time is dedicated to teaching what I wanted to teach and not things like taking roll.

I spent very little time in learning classroom management [in college]. The SDP teachers were helpful in passing on tips.

ADEQUATE PREPARATION: INDIVIDUAL DIFFERENCES

Some students identified courses that specifically helped them to meet the individual needs of the students in the classroom:

There were obvious differences [between] the students in behavior and personality, but I noticed that my reacting to each "type," individually, showing care and concern for each encouraged participation.

Educational Psychology [class] proved very useful. I can tell what each student is interested in, and I try to incorporate all of the students' interests within the lesson plan.

Each student is different and requires different amounts of time, but I see that a positive attitude helps the kids. It seems like a way of getting the best performance out of the kids.

[My college preparation was] very adequate. I believe that only actual practice could enrich this area.

ADEQUATE PREPARATION: ASSESSMENT

Several students indicated that they were somewhat prepared for informal assessment but inadequately prepared for formal assessments. Students also stated that additional classroom instruction on assessment was needed:

I feel more comfortable with informal assessment. I really don't have much experience with formal assessment yet.

I was prepared to assess my students through on-task reviews as well as encouraging them to practice reading outside of the classroom and on their own time.

I didn't actually administer any kind of test, but I did try to ensure that they grasped the concept that I was trying to convey.

I expect to grow as I observe and get more experience in working with students.

REACTION TO PRAXIS

Given the students' responses and the professors' reactions to their perceptions, the teacher preparation program has incorporated significant changes. Before the university–school partnership was implemented, the teacher preparation program was conducted primarily in isolation from the schools with minimal field experiences required prior to the senior year. It also stressed methodology and theory rather than praxis. With the implementation of the university–school partnership, course content, pedagogy, and course design were adjusted in field experiences and in identifying issues relevant for urban education. As the university–school partnership evolved, this redirection became restructuring. Hence, there was gradual movement from a symbiotic relationship to a more synergistic one.

In the synergistic phase a new concept emerged in the philosophy of teacher preparation. This concept embodies the notion that teacher preparation must be fluid and allow for reflection and praxis. The restructured teacher preparation program now includes:

- Mandated field experiences in professional core courses beginning as early as the sophomore year
- A reduction in professional methodology courses with an intense concentration on effective instructional strategies
- Courses that address issues pertinent to urban education and a multicultural society
- Deletion of dated courses
- An upper elementary curriculum that specifically addresses social, emotional, psychological, and academic needs of youngsters in grades 5–8
- An increase in specialized academic education courses

Discussion

A viable university–school partnership does indeed provide structure and stability through administrative changes, program restructuring, and philosophical postures. In addition, issues of turf and power become negotiable when the focus remains on what is needed to prepare preservice teachers to educate our youngsters for the future. This may be attributed to the basic principles of collaboration, consensus, and no-fault inherent in the School Development Program. Because of the philosophical precepts, a nonthreatening posture is at the core of the K–16 model. Key stakeholders are ultimately in a win-win position, and each entity is allowed to move from a posture of disconnectedness to interrelatedness to a synergistic relationship.

Based on the findings of the SUNO/NOPS partnership, it has become clear that time for dialogue between and among university professors, classroom teachers, and preservice students must be included as an essential component within course requirements. These dialogues provide the basis for the informed and collaborative decision making that is at the core of SDP and must become the foundation of teacher preparation.

As students progress in their studies, their focus shifts from routine operations to the complex relationships between teaching and learning. They gain the understanding, knowledge, and expertise to respond to the diverse personalities, skills, abilities, and psychological issues of their students and can validate educational theory through practice. These actual experiences provide the framework for reflective, fluid, and responsive informed decisions about pedagogy and practice.

Thus, any college of education considering teacher reform should strongly consider a partnership arrangement with the local system. Additionally, the partnership must recognize that a crucial component in teacher preparation is the involvement of either a local mental health agency or a school of social work. This is essential because preservice students need to acquire the skills necessary to identify and cope with the psychological, social, and emotional issues that affect our youngsters.

☐☐☐☐ *Vision*

University schools and colleges of education must dispel the myth of their being the only entity that can prepare preservice teachers for entering the teaching profession. At the same time, public and private schools must move from a passive posture to actual participation and claim ownership in the teacher preparation process. This redirecting allows for shared ownership—an equal partnership—in teacher preparation. Each entity will no longer be an autonomous unit but will be a stakeholder in a collaborative team that prepares teachers based on the recommendations of academicians, master teachers, and master practitioners through processes of negotiation and consensus.

All too often the teacher preparation curriculum tends to emphasize only three of the six developmental pathways: cognitive, physical, and language. However, in school settings, preservice teachers encounter children who need daily adult support and guidance along the social, ethical, and psychological pathways because they have to cope with drugs, violence, and issues related to changing values and family structures. A shared ownership arrangement will encourage both a viable and a vital holistic process needed to reform teacher preparation for life in the real world of schools.

▨▨ *References*

The Carnegie Forum on Education & the Economy (1986). *A nation prepared: Teachers for the 21st century.* New York: Carnegie Corporation of New York.

Comer, J. P. (1980). *School power.* New York: The Free Press.

Comer, James P., Joyner, Edward T., et al. (1990). The Yale University Child Study Center School Development Program–University/Public School Partnership: A Guide to School Improvement. New Haven, CT: Yale University.

A Report of the Commission on the Education of Teachers into the 21st Century (1991). *Restructuring the Education of Teachers.* Reston, VA: Association of Teacher Educators.

Henderson, George (1978). *Introduction to American education: A human relations approach.* Norman, OK: University of Oklahoma Press.

Hodgkinson, H. (1991). Reform versus reality. *Phi Delta Kappan, 73,* 9–16.

Holmes Group (1986). *Tomorrow's teachers.* East Lansing, MI: The Holmes Group, Inc.

Kantrowitz, Barbara, & Wingert, Pat (1991, December 2). The best schools in the world. *Newsweek,* pp. 51–52.

Kuhn, Thomas S. (1976). *The structure of scientific revolutions* (2nd ed.). Chicago, IL: University of Chicago Press.

Levin, Henry M. (1989). Accelerated schools: A new strategy for at-risk students. *Policy Bulletin, 6.* Bloomington, IN: Consortium of Educational Policy Studies, School of Education, Indiana University.

Muller, Herman J. (1960). The international role of evolutionary approach through education. *Educational Theory,* pp. 51–56.

Murphy, Joseph (1990). *The educational reform movement of the 1980s.* Berkeley, CA: McCutchan Publishing Company.

National Commission on Excellence in Education (1983). *A nation at risk: The imperative of educational reform.* Washington, DC: U.S. Government Printing Office.

Nicklin, Julie (1991). Teacher-education programs face pressure to provide multicultural training. *The Chronicle of Higher Education, 38* (14), A1: A16-17.

Orzmon, Howard, & Craver, Samuel M. (1981). *Philosophical foundations of education.* Columbus, OH: Charles E. Merrill Publishing Company.

Pitsch, Mark (1991, September). School–college links seen as fundamental to education reform. *Education Week,* p. 12.

Roberts, Thomas B. (1991). When the drug war hits the fan. *Phi Delta Kappan, 73* (1), 58–61.

Wilbur, Franklin, & Lambert, Leo (eds.) (1991). *Linking America's schools and colleges: Guide to partnerships and national directory.* Washington, DC: American Association for Higher Education.

Chapter 5

Time and Alignment: Potent Tools for Improving Achievement

DAVID A. SQUIRES AND EDWARD T. JOYNER

The SDP process requires and facilitates clear-eyed looks at content and at the way time is spent in the classroom. In a series of straightforward explanations and exercises, the authors offer concepts and procedures for improving the fit between aims and practice in everything from the largest content areas to the smallest time spans in the school day.

The School Planning and Management Team (SPMT) is charged with developing and coordinating a comprehensive school plan that systematically addresses the students' development including academic achievement. The team wrestles with such questions as: What is important in addressing academics? What data do we collect? How can we be confident that our changes will make a difference? This chapter introduces three concepts, drawn from research, to help SPMTs answer the all-encompassing question of how to improve academic achievement. The three areas discussed are use of time, alignment and coverage, and student success. These concepts, taken together, define school level academic challenges as well as academic learning time, which is a powerful indicator of student performance on standardized tests. Before tackling these ideas, we examine the definition and importance of academic achievement.

Academic Achievement

In the broadest sense, academic achievement encompasses learning the concepts, skills, and attitudes necessary to become a productive citizen, a lifelong learner, a person who understands the history and cultures of the past and present, and a person who works successfully on teams. Unfortunately, academic achievement is measured much more narrowly, through standardized testing once a year, focusing on discrete skills in reading, language arts, and math. *The SPMT must wrestle with the ambiguities of trying to improve academic achievement in the broad sense, while also improving scores on the relatively narrow measure used in standardized tests.*

Although standardized tests do not measure the full range of academics, they do give an insight into a school's performance in some important areas of reading, language arts, and mathematics. There are other ways to measure academic achievement, such as grades on report cards and criterion reference instruments embedded in the curriculum. Our focus narrows in this chapter to the two developmental pathways that directly enhance performance on standardized tests—the cognitive and language pathways—because standardized tests are usually designed to measure these two areas.

To be fair to students, we think the school's curriculum should be designed and implemented to ensure that they do well on standardized tests. Indeed, if the students do poorly on standardized tests, this performance indicates a failure somewhere in the school or school system. Standardized test results receive wide publicity, and the public judges schools partially on the results of these tests. Given the importance of these tests to students' futures and the public at large, improving standardized test scores remains a primary target for the SPMT. This must be accomplished, however, without compromising the development of academic competencies in the broader sense. It is important to note that the SDP process of school improvement has resulted in increased student achievement (Haynes, 1991).

Use of time, alignment and coverage, and student success are three areas where investigation and change may lead to improved standardized test scores. For each area, we briefly describe some research findings, review the rationale for using the area for investigation, and show how an SPMT might investigate and suggest changes. (For more detailed information, please consult the references.)

Use of Time

What teacher or administrator wouldn't like to have more time to cover all of those important topics to which students should be exposed in school? But we all know that there is lots of competition for time as schools meet some of the other developmental needs of students. Schools are called on to serve students lunch, transport students to school, provide remedial instruction, screen for health concerns, and provide a well-rounded academic program. Time is a fixed quantity; the school day is defined. But how we use the time within the school day will be an important variable in helping to improve academic outcomes. Thus, the first area the SPMT should discuss is the amount of time set aside specifically for instruction.

How Much Time Is Available for Instruction?

Not all of a school day is available for instruction. Students need to eat, go to the restroom, participate in recess, sharpen pencils, put away materials, move from one place to another, and get ready to go home. The worksheet in Appendix A could be filled out by the faculty or the SPMT to estimate time available for instruction. This exercise will highlight the data needed to make decisions about increasing or rearranging instructional time. We suggest that the SPMT complete this exercise again once consensus is reached to determine how many minutes per year are gained from the decisions, and then explain to the rest of the faculty so they will understand the rationale for decisions. Central office staff may also need to make modifications to existing procedures.

Can Time Allocated for Instruction Be Increased?

The SPMT's job is to look at the school schedule and find ways to increase the time allocated for instruction. Obviously, some field trips and assemblies are important experiences and should not be removed. Health screening is mandated and cannot be eliminated. (Besides, health screenings provide a possible data source for the Student and Staff Support Team.) The following examples explain how schools have increased instructional time.

One school looked at its dismissal process and shortened the time needed from 15 to 10 minutes. Time savings amounted to $5 \times 180 = 900$ minutes of instructional time per year, or 15 hours—the equivalent of 2.5 days of instruction.

Another school found that teachers were using 8 minutes to return their children from lunch. The SPMT decided they could do better. The principal rang the bell on the playground 2 minutes early to signify the end of the lunch period so the students would be in their lines when the teachers arrived. The principal and SPMT saw a real need to have teachers be on time to pick up their lines, and the teachers' on-time performance improved. The teachers also decided that students would enter the classroom and begin by taking out a book and reading for 10 minutes. Teachers enforced a rule of no talking after entering the classroom. Now it took 3 minutes to get back from lunch and down to work instead of 8—another 2.5 days of instruction gained each year.

In another school, the principal started screening morning announcements done over the intercom. She only read the ones considered important and put the rest on an announcement page that was dropped off in teachers' mailboxes. Teachers only read the announcements that pertained to their students. Teachers estimated that 2 minutes a day were saved.

In a secondary school, the SPMT decided to eliminate the 10-minute homeroom by increasing the first period by 5 minutes. Four minutes of passing time were saved, and a minute of instruction was added to each period.

Many of these changes, although small, can add up to significant time savings for the instructional program over the course of a year. The more time available for the instructional program, the more likely it is that students will perform well on standardized tests. That is, providing they are paying attention.

▰▰▰ *Student Engagement*

Not all students pay attention—"are engaged"—during the time allocated for instruction. Indeed, the research suggests a range of 30% to 90% of students engaged in learning at any given point in time in different classrooms. Researchers determined this range by going into classrooms while teachers taught and making inferences about whether students were engaged. Students who were fighting, sleeping, or out of the room obviously were not engaged. Those who were answering questions, raising their hands, or looking at the teacher were determined to be engaged. The range of engagement rates is wide, which suggests the SPMT might look for improvement in this area.

We suggest that members of the SPMT take a look in their classrooms to get an estimate of engagement rate. (A process is suggested in Appendix B.) This is important because whether students are engaged has a profound effect on student learning. A small improvement in this measure can yield more learning time for instruction during the school year.

Let's take a look at how engagement rate affects the amount of instructional time. Research suggests that an engagement rate between 80% and 85% is good (see Karweit, 1988; Squires, Huitt, and Segars, 1983; Walberg, 1988, for a more detailed account of the research).

▨▨▨ Example 1

Let's assume we have 300 minutes a day allocated for instruction and an engagement rate of 80%—an example from an effective classroom.

ENGAGEMENT RATE × AVERAGE DAILY ALLOCATED TIME = ENGAGED TIME

80% × 300 minutes = 240 minutes

▨▨▨ Example 2

The same 300 minutes a day in the classroom with only a 60% engagement rate yields a strikingly different result:

ENGAGEMENT RATE × AVERAGE DAILY ALLOCATED TIME = ENGAGED TIME

60% × 300 minutes = 180 minutes

The two examples demonstrate that an increase of 20% more students (that is, 6 students in a class of 30) paying attention yields an average of 60 more minutes per day of instruction. Multiply this amount by 180, and you find more than 26 additional days for instruction in the school year.

▧▧▧▧▧ Can Student Engagement Be Increased?

Strategies can be developed that encourage students to pay attention. One teacher found that by allowing 5 minutes for a nutritious snack in mid-morning the engagement rate of his class went up before lunch. He was able to make up in engaged time the time lost during the snack. In a middle school, one teacher appointed a "Simon Sez" student to conduct a 3-minute game after 25 minutes of instruction. Those lost 3 minutes enabled her to get a 15% gain in engagement rate during the last 10 minutes of instruction.

Another school found that students who participated in cooperative learning spent more time engaged than when the teacher was lecturing. Although the teacher did not give up lecturing completely, he did use cooperative learning more frequently. Another school found that discipline was interfering with students' paying attention. The SPMT planned a schoolwide program following the tenets of a popular schoolwide discipline approach. Effectiveness of that program was measured by how much the engagement rate increased.

One district decided that student engagement should be placed on the teacher observation form so that when administrators did observations, this important dimension of the classroom would be systematically sampled. Secretaries then collated the data across observations to determine one measure of the engagement rate of the school. These data, without teachers' names, were shared with the SPMT as they assessed staff development needs for the coming year.

▧▧▧▧ *Alignment and Coverage*

If time is available for instruction, and students are engaged and paying attention, our next question becomes:

> Do students have the opportunity to learn the concepts and skills covered by the standardized assessment?

One study (Brady et al., 1977) showed that the range of content taught that was covered on the standardized assessment was between 4% and 94%. That means that in some classrooms, only 4% of what was on the standardized test was addressed during classroom instruction. The range is wide, and that is bad news.

Texts should help. Teachers have traditionally relied on texts to help them determine what to cover. However, studies suggest that by just following the text, coverage of standardized test topics may not be assured. For example, Freeman et al. (1983) suggest that coverage in mathematics between standardized test topics and textbook topics ranged from 22% to 50%. Although we would expect textbooks to cover a broader range of topics than those tested on the standardized test, the fact that 50% of topics covered on the standardized test were not addressed by at least 20 problems in the text is a matter of concern. Goodman et al. (1988)

make similar points when evaluating the effectiveness of basal textbooks in reading. Additionally, coverage in a text may be accomplished in a page, whereas more emphasis may be needed in the instructional program if most students are to master a particular concept. Texts may help, but they also may hinder high student achievement on standardized tests.

The good news is that it is relatively easy to determine whether topics on the standardized tests are covered in instruction. This information on coverage is essential information for the SPMT to have if coverage is a concern. Although there are many ways of gathering information about coverage, one is suggested in Appendix C.

The exercise begins with teachers' lesson plans and texts to create a description of what is taught. Lesson plans are usually completed once per week, so they are the best way to compare what was covered in each classroom with what was planned. These plans can also be used to provide data on school improvement initiatives since they indicate that the content on the standardized test is actually taught. The exercise also shows whether the texts cover the content of the standardized test. The following questions can then be answered from these data:

- Are lesson plans covering topics on the standardized test?
- Are textbooks covering topics tested by standardized tests?
- Have the gaps been identified and instructional time and material found to teach topics covered on standardized tests?
- Have areas of improvement been identified for each teacher and grade level?

The SPMT needs to weave the answers to these questions into the staff development plans. For example, in one school a need was found to cover number sentences more thoroughly because teachers did not place great emphasis on number sentences in their lesson plans, and students had poor results on the three questions dealing with number sentences on standardized tests. The school team requested the district mathematics supervisor to prepare a 1-hour faculty meeting on number sentences. They specified that it should include a rationale of why it is important to teach number sentences, as well as a number of suggested teaching strategies.

Similarly, faculty need to understand that not all topics in a text are of equal importance. Indeed, most teachers, if pressed for time, will not teach the last chapters of the text. Assisting faculty to make decisions about what is important, ensuring mastery of skills necessary for success at the next grade level, and covering topics tested on standardized instruments may mean leaving bits and pieces out of a number of chapters in the text or spending less time on review at the beginning of the year.

Coverage is important enough that administrators in a school need to keep track of whether what we plan to teach actually gets taught. One school solved this problem by asking teachers to agree across each grade level and in each subject area when the unit test would be given. A standard form was developed for the beginning of the year (see Figure 5-1). The principal asked each teacher to submit a copy of the form to the office upon unit test completion. A secretary or instructional assistant then updated the master list of units completed. The principal reviewed the master list once every 2 weeks to determine if everyone was keeping up with their projected pace through the curriculum.

When teachers fell behind, the principal and teachers met to make decisions about what to deemphasize or what not to cover for the year. In one school, for example, the teacher who was behind was assigned an instructional assistant for 3 weeks to help move the class along at a quicker pace.

Grade _____	Subject Area _____	
	PROJECTED DATE OF COMPLETION	**ACTUAL DATE OF COMPLETION**
Unit Title _____	_____	_____
Unit Title _____	_____	_____
Unit Title _____	_____	_____
Unit Title _____	_____	_____
Unit Title _____	_____	_____
Unit Title _____	_____	_____
Unit Title _____	_____	_____
Unit Title _____	_____	_____
Unit Title _____	_____	_____
Unit Title _____	_____	_____
Unit Title _____	_____	_____

Figure 5-1. Beginning of year projection of unit completion.

▰▰▰ Student Success

Student success in this context refers to the extent to which students accurately complete assignments they have been given (Squires, Huitt, and Segars, 1983). Students experience a wide range of success in school. Some students complete assignments quite easily and well with few errors; others experience high error rates. Crawford (1978) suggests that students with low motivation and high fear of failure learn best when their success on assignments or during class participation is high, around 90%. Students with high motivation and low fear of failure appear to need challenges in their schoolwork and opportunities to make mistakes. What levels of student success on assignments are appropriate? Most classrooms are set up so that students who are least motivated and highly fearful of failure work at low levels of success. Variable assignments may help to have students working at success rates that produce optimal learning: challenging assignments for the highly motivated and students with low fear of failure, and assignments that are designed to ensure success for students with low motivation and high fear of failure. As a first step toward increasing motivation and decreasing fear of failure, students should be offered both types of assignments, receiving equal credit for either one completed. The SPMT may want to discuss this issue as part of their drive for improved academic achievement, especially since current practice is counter to what research suggests is most effective.

Schools as organizations have a difficult time generating information about students' success, especially over long periods of time. This is a puzzling state of affairs. Yes, grades are given, report cards are issued, and permanent record cards are updated. But usually this information is not used to improve programs. And there are reasons. An "A" in one class means something different from an "A" in another class. Teachers factor in different amounts for homework, class participation, tests, and quizzes. It is difficult to know what grades mean in terms of what students actually have learned. Although grades may combine all of the different pathways to learning (physical, cognitive, psychological, language, social, and ethical), they give us little information of use to improve programs.

One way to begin to generate information that is useful in program improvement (at least for the cognitive pathway) is to have teachers agree on the same unit assessments and report results so the SPMT has information to make decisions about the school plan and the staff development plan.

For example, one middle school found that students were having difficulty in the area of fractions on the standardized test. The SPMT knew that the fraction units were covered because everyone had completed a unit on fractions at each grade level from fifth to eighth grade. Because the SPMT gathered information about student success on unit tests, they knew that the grade-level average for passing the unit tests decreased each year. Students scored worse in seventh grade than they did in sixth. This also paralleled the results from the item analysis of the standardized test. The SPMT appointed a committee of interested teachers to study the problem and come back with recommendations in 1 month. The committee found:

1. The unit tests did a good job in predicting scores on the standardized test.
2. Not enough time was given to instruction in fractions starting in sixth grade.
3. Students received relatively little instruction in fractions before fifth grade.

Based on the findings, the committee recommended:

1. Increased amounts of time should be spent on fractions above and below fifth grade.
2. An additional unit on subtraction of fractions should be developed in the fifth grade to ensure the prerequisite skills for success in sixth grade.
3. The school committee should meet with the mathematics supervisor to determine how fractions could be taught with more hands-on material and how extra time for fractions could be gained in the curriculum structure of the district.

Appendix D presents a structured way for an SPMT to look at student success using unit test results.

Academic Learning Time

Academic learning time combines all that we have discussed into one measure that has been correlated with improved scores on standardized achievement tests. Academic learning time is defined as the amount of time students spend actively working on criterion-related content at high success rates. Let's work through this definition in parts.

We have discussed the amount of time available for instruction in a school day and the amount of time students spend actively working. These are reduced when students are not engaged—not paying attention. Criterion-related content is the match between what is taught and what is tested on the standardized test. (We discussed this subject in the "Alignment and Coverage" section.) A high rate of success appears to be desirable in producing good results on achievement tests. We suggested that success rate could be determined through reports of unit tests.

Not surprisingly, researchers found that different students and different classes vary widely in academic learning time. For example, Brady et al. (1977) found that fifth-grade students had an average of 14 minutes of academic learning time a day in math and 35 minutes in reading. This suggests that looking into academic learning time's components is one way to improve student achievement.

Let's see why those figures may be so low:

- If the time allocated for math is 45 minutes, and 5 minutes are spent in transition activities, then that leaves 40 minutes for instruction.
- The average engagement rate for the class may be 75%, meaning that there are only 30 minutes of engaged time.
- But not all instruction is on topics covered by the standardized test. In this case, only two-thirds of the topics presented for instruction are on the standardized test (2/3 × 30 minutes = **20 minutes of student engaged time on** topics tested by standardized achievement tests).

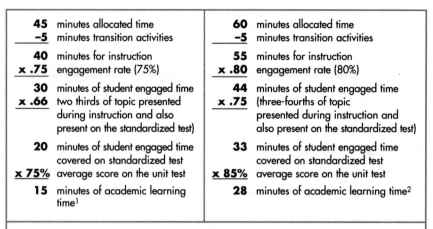

45	minutes allocated time	60	minutes allocated time
−5	minutes transition activities	**−5**	minutes transition activities
40	minutes for instruction	**55**	minutes for instruction
x .75	engagement rate (75%)	**x .80**	engagement rate (80%)
30	minutes of student engaged time	**44**	minutes of student engaged time
x .66	two thirds of topic presented during instruction and also present on the standardized test)	**x .75**	(three-fourths of topic presented during instruction and also present on the standardized test)
20	minutes of student engaged time covered on standardized test	**33**	minutes of student engaged time covered on standardized test
x 75%	average score on the unit test	**x 85%**	average score on the unit test
15	minutes of academic learning time[1]	**28**	minutes of academic learning time[2]

[1]The studies on academic learning time quoted in this chapter did not measure academic learning time in this fashion. We are using the example because it provides one way to understand the ideas behind academic learning time in the context of school. The data collection instruments and procedures here are not designed to replicate the way the data was collected in the original studies (Fisher, et al., 1978)

[2]Ibid.

Figure 5-2. Altering academic learning time.

- On average, students scored 75% on the unit test, which yields 15 minutes of academic learning time (20 minutes × 75% = 15 minutes of academic learning time). These results are shown in the left-hand column of Figure 5-2.

A teacher can significantly alter these figures by a few changes. Allocated time for math can be increased from 45 to 60 minutes. By structuring lessons differently, the engagement rate can be raised to 80%. With more time, more reteaching is possible, so students' scores on the unit tests increase to an average of 85%. The results are shown in the right-hand column of Figure 5-2.

By making these changes, academic learning time is almost doubled, which means that 1 year of instruction under this new system is almost equal to 2 years of instruction in the first example. Small yet significant changes can yield significant results.

In working through the data collection suggested here, the staff will need to make some value decisions, as they probably will not have enough time to complete everything suggested by texts, tests, and district curriculum guides. Questions will arise about whether the school should be driven by standardized tests; some will argue that the textbook authors knew what they were talking about and so the instruction should follow the text, and not the test. These are good and healthy discussions to have as the SPMT and the school staff approach consensus on improving the academic program for students.

We strongly suggest that the SPMT examine and collect data on all four aspects of academic learning time (a blank form is given in Appendix E). When these factors are considered as a whole, and if there is commitment on the part of the professionals and parents of the school, then improvement in academic achievement on standardized tests may come within 1 to 2 years.

■■■■ *References*

Ben-Reretz, M., & Bromme, R. (eds.) (1990). *The nature of time in schools.* New York: Teachers College Press, Columbia University.

Brady, M. E., Clinton, D., Sweeney, J. M., Peterson, M., & Poynor, H. (1977). *Instructional dimensions study.* Washington, DC: Kirschner Associates, Inc.

Crawford, J. (1978). Interactions of learner characteristics with the difficulty level of instruction. *Journal of Educational Psychology, 70* (4), 523–531.

Cuban, L. (May 1984). Transforming the frog into a prince: Effective schools research, policy and practice at the district level. *Harvard Education Review, 54,* pp. 131–132.

Fisher, C. W., Filby, N. N., Marliave, R. S., Chaen, L. S., Dishaw, M. M., Moore, J. E., & Berliner, D. C. (1978). *Teaching behaviors, academic learning time, and student achievement: Final report of Phase II-B, Beginning Teacher Evaluation Study.* San Francisco: Far West Laboratory for Educational Research and Development.

Freeman, D., Kuhs, T., Porter, A., Floden, R., Schmidt, W., & Schwille, J. (1983). Do textbooks and tests define a national curriculum in elementary school mathematics? *The Elementary School Journal, 83,* 501–513.

Goodman, K. S., Shannon, P., Freeman, Y. S., & Murphy, S. (1988). *Report card on basal readers.* Katonah, NY: Richard C. Owen Publishers, Inc.

Haynes, N. (1991). *Summary of school development program documentation and research.* New Haven, CT: Yale Child Study Center, School Development Program.

Karweit, N. (1988). Time on task: The second time around. *NASSP Bulletin,* February.

Squires, D. A., Huitt, W. G., & Segars, J. K. (1983). *Effective schools and classrooms: A research-based perspective.* Alexandria, Virginia: Association for Supervision and Curriculum Development.

Walberg, H. J. (1988, March). Synthesis of research on time and learning. *Educational Leadership,* pp. 76–84.

APPENDIX A

Worksheet for Determining Allocated Time for Instruction

1. Length of school day for students

   _____   _____   _____
   Begin   End   Total Minutes
                                in School Day

2. Minutes in school day _____

3. Minutes used in getting to class _____

4. Minutes used in opening exercises _____

5. Minutes used in transition between subjects _____

6. Minutes used in getting ready for and coming back from lunch _____

7. Minutes used for student lunches _____

8. Minutes spent on announcements _____

9. **TOTAL OF LINES 3–8** _____

10. To derive **ALLOCATED DAILY INSTRUCTIONAL TIME,** subtract
    line 9 from line 2 _____

11. Health screenings per year   _____ × _____   minutes =   _____

12. Fire drills per year   _____ × _____   minutes =   _____

13. Assemblies per year   _____ × _____   minutes =   _____

14. Shortened days per year   _____ × _____   minutes =   _____

15. Field trips per year   _____ × _____   minutes =   _____

16. Snow days per year   _____ × _____   minutes =   _____

17. Total Other _____   _____ × _____   minutes =   _____

18. To derive **YEARLY ESTIMATE OF INTERRUPTIONS IN MINUTES**
    add lines 10–17 _____

19. Allocated Daily Instructional Time (from line 10) _____

20. Student days per year (the average daily attendance
    for students x student days/yr)   × _____

21. Minutes/year allocated for instruction
    (multiply line 19 by line 20) _____

22. Subtract Total of Interruptions (from line 18)   − _____

    TOTAL MINUTES PER YEAR ALLOCATED FOR INSTRUCTION _____

23. Divide line 22 (total minutes/year) by line 20
    (student days per year) to get the average number
    of instructional minutes per day _____

▰▰ APPENDIX B

Worksheet and Instructions for Determining Training Process and Engagement Rate

Engagement rate data are best collected by someone other than the classroom teacher, such as another teacher, an instructional assistant, a parent volunteer, an administrator, a supervisor, or a high school student.

The School Planning and Management Team (SPMT) should complete steps 1–8 (discussed below) before using the data to make decisions.

▬▬▬ Step 1

THE SPMT NEEDS TO AGREE ON A LIST OF BEHAVIORS THAT INDICATE ENGAGEMENT OR NONENGAGEMENT (SEE FIGURE B-1).

Nonengaged Behaviors	**Engaged Behaviors**
MANAGEMENT/TRANSITION ACTIVITIES Getting ready for instruction Waiting Listening to nonacademic directions Changing activities	Reading Writing Speaking about topic at hand Listening to comments related to instruction Raising hands Answering questions
SOCIALIZING Interacting socially Watching others socialize	Writing on the chalk board Working on homework Completing worksheets Working on projects
DISCIPLINE Being reprimanded by an adult Being punished Watching others being scolded	Working in groups if the group is on task
UNOCCUPIED/OBSERVING Wandering about with no evident purpose or goal Watching other people Playing with materials Doodling	
OUT OF ROOM Student leaves the classroom	

Figure B-1. Student behaviors that indicate engagement and nonengagement.

▨▨▨▨▨ Step 2

THE SPMT NEEDS TO APPOINT A TRAINER AND DECIDE WHO WILL COLLECT THE INFORMATION ON ENGAGEMENT.

▨▨▨▨▨ Step 3

THE TRAINER SHOULD PRACTICE COLLECTING INFORMATION IN A FEW CLASSROOMS.

When collecting the data in classrooms, the person collecting the information should listen to what the teacher is saying. Look at an individual student for approximately 2–3 seconds. The person will decide whether the student is not engaged, mark the form (see Figure B-2), and go on to the next student. In a few minutes, the person collecting the information will have looked individually at each student in the classroom. This cycle should be repeated 5 to 10 times per classroom per instructional period.

RULES FOR STEP 3
The person collecting the information should use the following rules when deciding whether the student is engaged or not. The decision rests on what the student is doing (paying attention or not) and what the teacher is doing (presenting academic content, helping students, or involved in other necessary classroom activities).

Date _____   Grade _____

Teacher _____   Subject _____

Data Collector _____

	Time	Time	Time	Time	Time	Time	Time	Time	Time	Total
	10:00	10:10	10:20	10:30	10:40					
Number of Students	19	19	19	19	19					
Not Engaged	////	////	₮₮₮₮ ₮₮₮₮ ///	₮₮₮₮ //	₮₮₮₮					

1. Total number of students not engaged
   (Add all the marks in all the time periods) _____

2. Total number of students observed
   (Add all the numbers in the "Number of Students" line) _____

Divide line 1 by line 2 and subtract it from 100 for Engagement Rate _____

Figure B-2. Worksheet for calculating engagement rate.

1. If the teacher is presenting academic information and the student is engaged (paying attention), then no mark is made on the coding form. The person collecting the information moves on to the next student.
2. If the teacher is presenting academic information and the student is, for example, talking to a fellow student or sharpening a pencil, then the student is not engaged. The person collecting the information makes one mark on the coding form and moves on to the next student.
3. If the teacher is directing transition activities (e.g., "Now students, get out your books and turn to page 67"), and the student is paying attention, the person collecting the information puts a mark on the worksheet. Transition activities are not part of engagement. Therefore, the student is not engaged in instructional activities and a mark goes on the form indicating that the student is not engaged in academic activities.

When the first student is observed, the person collecting the information records the time. Marks for unengaged students then are placed under this time period. When the person collecting the information looks at the first student again, the time is recorded for the second set of observations. Figure B-3 below is an engagement rate form that has been filled out.

Date _10/16/95_					Grade _4_					
Teacher _Mrs. Smith_					Subject _Math_					
Data Collector _Suzanne_										

	Time	Time	Time	Time	Time	Time	Time	Time	Time	Total
Number of Students	23	23	23	23	23	23	23	23	23	207
Not Engaged	///	///	++++	++++ /	//	0	//	///	////	27

1. Total number of students not engaged
    (Add all the marks in all the time periods) _27_

2. Total number of students observed
    (Add all the numbers in the "Number of Students" line) _207_

Divide line 1 by line 2 and subtract it from 100 for Engagement Rate _86.96%_

Figure B-3. Example of completed worksheet for calculating engagement rate.

▭▭▭▭ Step 4

TRAIN OTHERS WHO HAVE BEEN DESIGNATED TO USE THE FORM AND FOLLOW THE RULES
FOR COLLECTING INFORMATION.

The trainer should go into the classroom with the others who will be collecting the information and fill out the form for practice. After leaving the classroom, the trainer and trainees will then compare forms to see if the engagement rate is within 5% of the trainer's engagement rate. For example, if the trainer came up with an engagement rate of 70%, trainees who had between 65% and 75% would have an acceptable score. They would then be ready to observe on their own.

▭▭▭▭ Step 5

SET UP AND PUBLISH A SCHEDULE OF INFORMATION-COLLECTING SESSIONS FOR ALL FACULTY.

This will help to relieve anxiety because teachers will know when information collectors will be in the classrooms. Naturally, some teachers will prepare especially for this and will probably do better than "normal." This is a desired situation because it will show the faculty and the SPMT what the school can do at its best. There should also be agreement within the SPMT, as part of the no-fault provision of the SDP process, that this information will not be used in the formal teacher evaluation process.

▭▭▭▭ Step 6

CONDUCT THE INFORMATION-COLLECTING SESSIONS.

Leave a copy of the completed form with the faculty member.

▭▭▭▭ Step 7

COLLATE THE DATA ON ENGAGEMENT RATES.

Set up a database so that information can be aggregated in a number of different ways, such as by subject area and by grade level. Publish this information in summary form. Do not publish individual results, as this is a "no-fault" process.

▭▭▭▭ Step 8

ONCE THE INFORMATION IS COLLATED, SHARE THE INFORMATION IN AGGREGATE WITH THE
SPMT.

This process should be completed at least twice a year so the SPMT will know if their changes yielded results. Use this information to create the Staff Development Plan and make suggestions for curriculum improvement.

▨▨ APPENDIX C

Worksheet and Instructions for Determining Alignment and Coverage

Year _____ Subject _____ Teacher _____ Grade _____

Unit titles and objectives	Standardized test objectives	Standardized test results	Texts of other material	District curriculum	Time estimate	Comments

Figure C-1. Worksheet to determine coverage overlap of lesson plans, units, curriculum, texts, and tests.

Determining alignment and coverage requires the SPMT to take a number of steps before teachers and administrators can make decisions. First, unit titles and 3–7 unit objectives for each title are generated using lesson plans and text material. As much as possible, this should represent the instructional program that is actually taught. Next, the description of the curriculum as taught is aligned to the objectives tested by the standardized test. Then the specific text material that is used to teach the units is listed. Finally, the item analysis from standardized test results is indexed according to the units.

▨▨▨ Step 1

USE LAST YEAR'S LESSON PLANS AND TEXTS TO DETERMINE A LIST OF UNIT TITLES AND A LIST OF 3–7 OBJECTIVES THAT SUPPORT EACH UNIT.

While this exercise can be done individually, it works best if done in groups of teachers who teach the same subject or course.

1. Determine unit titles. Using the textbook and lesson plans, develop a list of unit titles. A unit is a sequence of lessons that comes between major tests and typically lasts 2–4 weeks. The unit titles might be exactly what

the text has for chapter headings. Do not list any unit titles that were not taught last year. This is important because this may point out gaps in coverage. Make sure that the list of unit titles can be taught in one school year. To do this, get a school calendar and put the beginning and ending dates for each unit. Remember to leave some time for all those "interruptions," such as holidays.

2. Under each unit title list the major objectives that you cover in that unit. Again, you may be able to take these directly from your lesson plans, or you might get them from the teacher edition of the textbook. No more than seven objectives should be listed. This will help pinpoint the primary focus of instruction. List objectives you can promise teachers of the next grade level that most students have mastered.

3. (Optional) Share the results across grade levels and see if any duplication can be eliminated or any prerequisite skills have not been addressed. Finalize your list of objectives.

Step 2

DETERMINE THE OVERLAP BETWEEN UNIT OBJECTIVES AND STANDARDIZED TESTS.

To determine the overlap between unit objectives and standardized tests, two steps must be completed: (1) list the standardized test objectives that address the unit objectives, and (2) make some decisions about the data and discuss decisions as a group.

1. Use the worksheet at the beginning of this appendix. To complete this task, you will need a detailed list of objectives from the standardized test. (A one-page sample from the California Achievement Test is found at the end of this appendix in Figure C-2.) For each unit, list the standardized test objectives that address the unit objectives. You may address standardized test objectives in more than one unit; if you do, write the standardized test objective as many times as is necessary. If you believe you address a standardized test objective in a unit, but did not list this as a major objective for the unit, then consider revising the unit objectives. Use the same language in the unit objectives as in the standardized test objectives, thus facilitating the process of determining coverage and also giving teachers a standard vocabulary to discuss content. This shared vocabulary should be used in lesson planning, as well.

2. Share the results with colleagues. This process will help everyone know the focus of particular courses. Although individual teachers completing this exercise will come to their own conclusions on where improvements can be made, efforts to share trends within the same grade level or course should be made. Team recommendations should be shared with the School Planning and Management Team (SPMT).

▮▮▮▮▮▮▮ Step 3

CHECK THE ALIGNMENT BETWEEN THE STANDARDIZED TEST, THE UNIT DESCRIPTIONS, AND THE TEXTBOOK.

Record the pages that cover the unit objectives. Often there is a handy reference or index in the teacher's edition that will assist you in this task. If you use this index, please check the pages referenced since the textbook editor's judgment may not be the same as yours. As textbooks are often the primary resource for instruction, this gives everyone a good idea of how much emphasis the textbook places on standardized test objectives and the unit descriptions.

Textbooks are designed, and should be designed, to cover a broad range of objectives, some of which are not on the standardized test. Usually these need to receive coverage as well, and should be listed in your unit objectives.

▮▮▮▮▮▮▮ Step 4

INTERPRET THE DATA.

Look at the item analysis for the most recent standardized scores for a particular grade-level. Then decide for a grade-level what needs to have more emphasis, less emphasis, more time, less time. Are there areas in which the grade-level did not do well and the teachers would like to have more inservice training? Should areas be addressed during schoolwide inservice training? These recommendations should be reported back to the SPMT, which should encourage grade-level groups of teachers to work together on this exercise to build consensus.

▮▮▮▮▮▮▮ Step 5

ALIGN THE UNIT OBJECTIVE TO THE DISTRICT CURRICULUM.

Using the district curriculum guide, indicate by a "Y" or an "N" if the unit objectives reflect the contents of the district curriculum guide. If there are more than a few "not sures," then the subject area supervisor or district curriculum person will need to be informed.

▮▮▮▮▮▮▮ Step 6

USE THE INFORMATION.

At the end of the exercise, teachers and administrators should know specifically where each grade-level or course stands in terms of coverage and alignment between and among the unit objectives, the standardized test content and objectives, the results of the standardized test, the textbook and other materials, and the district curriculum.

The SPMT will need to develop plans and time lines to address the gaps in alignment and coverage. The faculty may decide to use the language of unit and test objectives in their lesson planning, so alignment is more apparent and the amount of time spent on a topic can be tallied. One principal gave the faculty a copy of the standardized test objectives, reduced to one page, to keep in their plan books as a reference when writing lesson plans. Some teachers developed numbering systems so that they did not have to write out the objective "Identifying Main Idea" each time it was the major focus of the lesson.

To implement these ideas, the SPMT may want to try out a variety of ways of recording this information in lesson plans before deciding on a format that may be appropriate for the whole faculty. Teachers of subjects other than reading, language arts, and math may need assistance to understand how their work supports student achievement on standardized assessments and how they can use the standardized test objectives as part of their lesson planning descriptions.

(Appendix C continues on overleaf)

Figure C-2. Test objectives from the California Achievement Test: Item Classification for CAT E and F, Level 15.

Test	Category Objective Subskill	Recall and Recognition		Inference		Evaluation	
		Form E	*Form F*	Form E	Form F	Form E	Form F
Test 6 Mathematics Computation	65 MULTIPLICATION OF WHOLE NUMBERS	7, 17–19, 27–29, 37, 46	7, 17–19, 27, 28, 37, 39, 46				
Test 7 Mathematics Concepts and Applications	73 NUMERATION						
	fractional parts	4	24	41	43		
	recognize numbers	39	52				
	expanded notation	2, 31	4,11				
	place value	12	25				
	rounding	34	39				
	estimation			23,29	26,31		
	word names	55	14				
	Roman numerals	36	44				
	number lines			5,26	23,36		
	74 NUMBER SENTENCES						
	identify sentence			13	5		
	missing elements	10	7	3,18,20	1,13,37		
	ratio and proportion		16				
	75 NUMBER THEORY						
	odds, evens						
	properties	33	3,18				
	divisibility	1	30				
	factors		32	24			42
	equivalent forms						

Objective						
76 PROBLEM SOLVING						
pre-solution						
one-step	37,46	45,47	14,16	21,29	11,15	12,19
multistep			22,27,32,35	17,20		
graphs			40	34,35,48–51		
77 MEASUREMENT						
time	6,8,47,49,50	8-10,33	17	41		
length, metric		2	7,9,48	22	38	
mass, metric			21	15		
capacity, metric			28	46	45	

Source: Class Management: CAT 4th Edition. CTB MacMillian/McGraw-Hill. Monterey, CA., 1987.

▮▮▮ APPENDIX D

Worksheet and Instructions for Using Unit Test Results to Gain Information About Student Success

▮▮▮▮▮ Step 1
DEVELOPING CONSENSUS

In most school districts, unit test results are not collected or analyzed. In fact, there may be more than a few teachers who do not think that using unit test results will foster school improvement. The SPMT needs to develop strategies to allow these objections to surface, so that a consensus can arise.

The SPMT may want to devote a series of faculty meetings to taking a look at the idea of collecting information on unit tests. One school decided to begin with mathematics. Another school decided to begin with the ninth grade in major subjects. Another school decided just to use volunteers and bring others on board as the procedures were refined.

▮▮▮▮▮ Step 2
GENERATING UNIT TESTS

After the faculty decides to try out the idea, unit tests need to be the same for each unit at a particular grade level. Generating tests needs to be written into the Staff Development Plan.

In one school, staff decided that they would meet over the summer and develop the unit tests. Another school's staff agreed to appoint the "best test maker" for the subject area to design tests for the school, with peer review. Yet another school's staff decided that the faculty as a whole needed to consider more completely the varieties of unit assessment. A staff development program then looked at different forms of assessment—from essays, to multiple choice, to holistic scoring of writing samples and portfolios. Groups were appointed to refine the existing unit tests. Indeed, staff found that the unit tests they used revealed their ideas about what was most important to teach.

▮▮▮▮▮ Step 3
DECIDING ON RULES AND FORMS FOR COLLECTION AND USING UNIT TEST INFORMATION

The SPMT will need to decide how to collect the information and generate consensus about how the information will be used so that people feel safe. One way to collect the information is by using a form similar to the one in Figure D-1.

Teachers can then copy the students' identification numbers and scores in their roll book and duplicate the form for the number of units in that subject area. At the end of each unit, the teacher fills in the unit title, the date, and each student's score and returns the form to a central collection point.

Deciding how the data will be aggregated and used is important to providing a no-fault environment. One school decided that no individual teacher averages

Subject _____	Teacher _____
Unit _____	Date _____

Student ID# _____	Score _____
Student ID# _____	Score _____
Student ID# _____	Score _____
Student ID# _____	Score _____
Student ID# _____	Score _____
Student ID# _____	Score _____
Student ID# _____	Score _____
Student ID# _____	Score _____
Student ID# _____	Score _____
Student ID# _____	Score _____
Student ID# _____	Score _____

Figure D-1. Worksheet for using unit test results to gain information about student success.

would be shared with the SPMT but that the grade-level averages for each unit would be. However, individual teachers were urged to compare their classroom averages with that of the grade-level. Another school district analyzed results from certain parts of the unit tests to make sure the students were learning the concepts. Then they reported the results of their analysis to the SPMT. Another school set the goal that the test average would improve by a point or two from last year. Teachers had copies of their last year's results, so they could determine if the goal had been met.

▨▨ APPENDIX E

Worksheet for Examining Effects of Decisions on Academic Learning Time

```
    _____   minutes of allocated time per day in a subject
 − _____   minutes for transition activities

    _____   minutes for instruction
 × _____   student engagement rate

    _____   minutes of student engaged time
 × _____   estimated % of topics covered on standardized test

    _____   minutes of student engaged time covering test topics
 × _____   average score on the unit test

    _____   minutes of academic learning time
```

Larry Cuban (1984) noted several years ago that improving test scores is not enough:

> To conclude that a school is effective once it demonstrates test score gains is implicitly to conclude that students need to develop no other capacity than to answer multiple-choice items correctly. The concern that drives many schools today—that of improving student performance on achievement tests—is a short term, useful but constricting one...To evaluate the effectiveness of complex organizations as schools solely on the basis of percentile rank is little better than to judge a car's quality solely on the basis of its miles-per-gallon or a hospital's effectiveness solely be the number of its vacant beds. (pp. 131–132)

We ask our schools to frame their work around optimizing students' physical, cognitive, psychological, language, social, and ethical development. Emphasis on high levels of cognitive and language development should allow a student to perform at levels beyond that measured by standardized testing.

We are not suggesting that schools teach to the test. We are suggesting that students be taught the skills and content that they need in order to perform well on any reasonable measure of what they should know and be able to do at their respective grade levels. In effect, we are asking schools to teach beyond any standardized test by having a clear instructional focus that is developmentally oriented and that maximizes use of time and resources.

Performing well on standardized tests as well as other measures of learning is only one of our many objectives for children. Our collective experiences as educators suggest that doing well on standardized measures is also a reflection of good attendance, orderly behavior, focused instruction, and a well-planned academic program. In the twelve years since Dr. Cuban made his observations, standardized tests have moved well beyond multiple-choice items into areas that require original writing and higher-order thinking skills. Reasonable educators would agree that standardized testing measures skills that are certainly worth teaching. We are suggesting that schools teach those skills and more.

Chapter 6

The School Development Program Evaluation Process

NORRIS M. HAYNES, CHRISTINE L. EMMONS,
SARA GEBREYESUS, AND MICHAEL BEN-AVIE

Most educational change initiatives implement a program and claim results on the basis of test scores alone. By contrast, the SDP conducts research and evaluation in the real-life situation of the school. In addition to evaluating test scores, SDP staff members calibrate school climate and children's self-concept, behavior, and social competence, and then measure these elements against the level of program implementation. To offer timely and useful information, the SDP's national research and evaluation staff has built the capacity to visit schools, collect data, conduct data analysis, and report findings to the schools and the school districts within a timely manner.

From the start, a key feature of the School Development Program (SDP) has been that it is a data-driven school improvement process. Consistent, careful, and clear documentation of the *process* of SDP implementation in schools and of the *impact* of implementation provides us with a continued sense of purposeful direction. Norris M. Haynes, director of the SDP Research and Evaluation Unit, states in the Epilogue of this book, "Measuring program outcomes, such as improved student performance on standardized tests, is meaningless unless there is a commensurate assessment of the level and quality of program implementation." The documentation of the SDP process and of its impact is regarded as a collaborative effort between schools and SDP staff at the Yale Child Study Center.

The purpose of documentation is threefold: (1) to provide formative process data to improve and strengthen program implementation; (2) to provide measures of program impact on salient outcome variables, including those identified in Comprehensive School Plan goal statements; (3) to contribute to the theory on how schools change and how students succeed.

Included in the formative process is the *needs assessment,* the purpose of which is to show the current state of the school and to collect baseline data that become the comparison points for future changes. *Formative assessment* provides continuous feedback for improvement and takes place at several levels: school, district, and SDP national office at the Yale Child Study Center. *Summative assessments* serve as benchmarks of progress and do not imply finality.

Theory building, although not the primary purpose of the SDP evaluation process, is an important aspect of it. Although the SDP has a strong theoretical base, that theoretical base must be regularly tested for its continued validity, and for refinement and enhancement. Knowledge is not static. As we study school reform through implementation, we increase our knowledge of how change takes place and is sustained, about the nature and development of human beings, and about the role of relationships in human development and organizational change. The weaving of this information into the fabric of a coherent theory allows for its application in fields beyond school reform. For example, the principle of no-fault can be applied to problem solving in any situation.

▨▧▨ *SDP Research and Evaluation Framework and History*

▨▨▨▨ Theoretical Framework

The theoretical framework for the SDP evaluation process is consonant with the theoretical underpinnings of the program. The school is viewed as a system in which change in any part affects all the other parts. Therefore, the research design allows for data to be gathered from all stakeholders: the students, parents, school staff including teachers, administrators, janitorial, secretarial, professional, and nonprofessional support staff. As the views of all are sought in decision making, the opinions and responses of all are sought during the evaluation process. The SDP evaluation process is conducted with the philosophy that all stakeholders should be involved, that the responsibility and decision making should be shared, and that whatever is done should be in the best interest of children.

The SDP is a process that creates a healthy, positive, and supportive school climate through its nine-element design: three teams (the School Planning and Management Team or SPMT, the Student and Staff Support Team or SSST, and the Parent Team or PT); three operations (Comprehensive School Plan, staff development, monitoring and assessment); three guiding principles (consensus, collaboration, and no-fault). See Figure 1-1 in Chapter One.

Through these nine elements, and specifically with the implementation of the three teams, the SDP improves essential dimensions of school climate. As these dimensions improve, students experience significant positive growth along the six critical developmental pathways and are at reduced risk for negative outcomes. The probability of positive psychosocial behavioral and academic outcomes is also

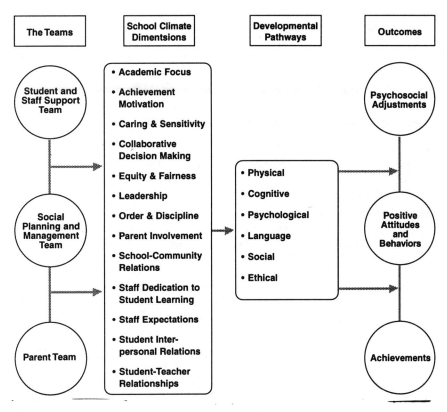

Figure 6-1. The School Development Program (SDP) model of effects.

increased when appropriate programmatic and instructional activities are implemented as part of the school's comprehensive planning process.

Figure 6-1 shows that the three SDP teams help to create essential positive school climate dimensions that support and nurture total student development along the six developmental pathways, through well-planned and focused activities, resulting in increased likelihood of positive outcomes.

The three SDP guiding principles—consensus, collaboration, and no-fault—apply as much to documentation as they do to implementation.

CONSENSUS
It is important that decisions about what data to collect and how to collect them be made through the consensus process. This process involves the brainstorming of ideas, the consideration of pluses and minuses of each idea, and the general agreement to try one or two ideas first, and then to try other ideas as alternatives.

At the school level, working through the Comprehensive School Plan as a guide, the school community reaches consensus on the what and how of documentation. This process requires an informed school community, a mechanism for optimum input by constituents, and a procedure for feedback and review of decisions on documentation. At the district level, there should be a committee or team approach to documentation involving the SDP facilitator, research and evaluation specialist, as well as other key program coordinators and staff.

COLLABORATION
As with implementation, the best approach to documentation must be built on a commitment to the principles of true collaboration and inclusion. At the school level, staff, parents, and students serve as sources of information and participate in the documentation process. At the district level, through the committee or team approach mentioned above, all key personnel in various departments work together to produce the needed data in an integrated way.

NO-FAULT
There is collective responsibility for identifying data needs and gathering the necessary information to meet these needs. The Comprehensive School Plan process at the school level allows everyone in the school, through representatives, to identify needed data and ways to collect them. Instead of holding one person liable when needed information does not exist, there is shared accountability, since the identification and acquisition of important information is a system responsibility.

Operating with mutual respect requires that the results of the evaluation be shared with the schools from which the data were collected. Each school receives from the SDP Research and Evaluation Unit copies of all school-level reports produced about that school, and copies of all district-level reports that include data collected from that school. The sharing of reports is important also because the intent is that the information contained in the reports will assist the SPMT, SSST, and PT in making decisions that would improve the quality of life for the children.

▓▓▓▓▓▓ History of SDP Evaluation

James P. Comer's work began in two individual schools in New Haven. Comer and his staff worked closely with these two schools and monitored their activities regularly. As the work expanded and his team intervention slowly grew into national program implementation, close relations with school staff that allowed for individual dialogue, evaluation through regular observation, and immediate feedback and modification changed to a more distant, less frequent interaction with SDP national office staff. The inclusion of a large number of schools into the SDP's network meant that the SDP staff could no longer easily do both implementation and research work. This necessitated the employment of research and evaluation staff to undertake the evaluation of the program implementation and its impact on school climate and student outcomes including self-concept, attendance, and achievement. This has been the major focus of our research and evaluation activities during the past 9 years. Our studies have been cross-sectional quasi-experimental studies designed to assess SDP efforts. We have just begun a 6-year longitudinal study to assess the long-term effects of SDP. We are now in a position to do this assessment due to committed support for a more longitudinal study and demonstrated need. This issue is further discussed in a later section in this chapter.

The research and evaluation staff developed a variety of questionnaires including school climate surveys and implementation questionnaires. Gradually, the climate instruments were revised and psychometrically tested, and additional protocols for interviews and documentation of the implementation process were developed.

Several cross-sectional quasi-experimental studies comparing SDP and non-SDP schools on school climate, student self-concept, student attendance, and student achievement favored the SDP schools. Follow-up studies on middle school students who had attended SDP and non-SDP schools indicated a long-term positive effect in terms of adjustment and achievement that favored students who had attended the SDP schools. However, the results, not always consistent, suggested that in-depth understanding of the SDP implementation process in the field was needed. There needed to be a triangulation of theory, quantitative, and qualitative research to deepen understanding of the change phenomenon.

Committed to a multimethod assessment and modification plan that was designed to best document and capture the process of implementation and the contextual factors in the schools, we conducted selected semiethnographic studies and administered school implementation questionnaires in select districts. In this documentation process we used our interview protocols and observation logs, examined school archives, and engaged in individual and group dialogue. These selected case studies provided us with important preliminary results and laid the foundation for conducting further research on a number of issues.

The results of both the quantitative and qualitative studies, in conjunction with SDP implementation field experiences, have led to a change in focus from the implementation of SDP in individual schools to its implementation at a systemic level, meaning the commitment of the district central office, the school board, and the school building staff to the process. Our research has shown that the individual school needs the support of the district central office and the school board if the process is to be fully successful. This change in focus from individual school to systemic implementation has also shifted the focus of the Research and Evaluation Unit from individual school to the documentation of systemic implementation and its outcomes. As a result, we have developed a 6-year longitudinal plan to monitor the implementation of SDP in the three systemic districts: New York Community School District #13, Washington, D.C., and New Haven (which is in transition).

As the number of schools involved in the SDP grew, so did the need for additional personnel in the field who understood the School Development Program and could assist with its implementation at the school and district level. The Comer

Process for Change in Education (CPCE), the implementation unit within SDP, developed leadership programs to train school personnel to facilitate the implementation of the SDP in their district. Consistent with SDP policy of continuous assessment and modification of all aspects of the program, the SDP Research and Evaluation Unit in collaboration with CPCE developed procedures for the evaluation of both the leadership programs and the quality of implementation in the schools. Both quantitative and qualitative methods are used for this evaluation.

To document the growth of the SDP across the United States, and now internationally, the Research and Evaluation Unit has developed a national database that lists the schools implementing SDP, the demographics of the students, and selected school-level outcome data, for example, attendance and achievement.

As shown from this brief description, the SDP evaluation process has both affected the implementation of SDP and has been affected by it. This symbiotic relationship has resulted in a widening upward spiral that expands the breadth and complexity of SDP implementation, and the depth, scope, and difficulty or intricacy of evaluation and research.

Previous Research on SDP Process and Outcomes

Academic Effects

School-level aggregated data analyses provide evidence of significant SDP effects on achievement. In 1986, an analysis of achievement data in the Benton Harbor Michigan Area Schools showed significant average 4-year gains, between 7.5 and 11.0 percentile points, in reading and mathematics, at the second, fourth, fifth, and sixth grades for SDP schools, exceeding gains reported for the school district as a whole. Program schools also registered higher gains in mathematics and reading than the district as a whole, with regard to the percentage of students obtaining 75% and above of the objectives on the Michigan Educational Assessment Program (Haynes, Comer, and Hamilton-Lee, 1988a). These data are presented in Table 6-1.

An assessment of SDP effects conducted by the research office of the Prince George's County Public Schools in 1987 revealed that average percentile gains on the California Achievement Test between 1985 and 1987 were significantly greater for Milliken schools that used the SDP than for the district as a whole. At the third-grade level, program schools gained about 18 percentile points in mathematics, 9 percentile points in reading, and 17 percentile points in language. The district as a whole registered gains of 11, 4, and 9 percentile points respectively in mathematics, reading, and language. At the fifth-grade level, program schools recorded gains of 21, 7, and 12 percentile points in mathematics, reading, and language compared to gains of 11, 4, and 7 percentile points for the district as a whole (Comer, 1988b, p. 47). Further analysis also revealed that academic gains were linked to the degree and quality of implementation of the SDP. These data are summarized in Figures 6-2 and 6-3.

Table 6-1. *Four-Year Average Gains at Each Grade Level on the California Achievement Test*

Grade levels	1	2	3	4	5	6
			SDP Schools			
Reading	9.3	9.8*	7.5	7.0	7.5**	11.0**
Math	12.5	10.5**	11.5	9.5**	7.8	10.5
Total Battery	11.0	9.8	10.3	7.5	7.5	9.8
			District			
Reading	11.0	9.8	8.5	7.5	6.0	10.0
Math	13.3	9.3	12.0	9.0	11.5	11.5
Total Battery	11.5	10.0	11.5	9.0	9.0	13.3

*Equals District Gain.
**Exceeds District Gain.

Source: Haynes, N. M., Comer, J. P., Hamilton-Lee, M. (1988). The School Development Program: A model for school improvement. *Journal of Negro Education, 57* (1), pp. 11–21.

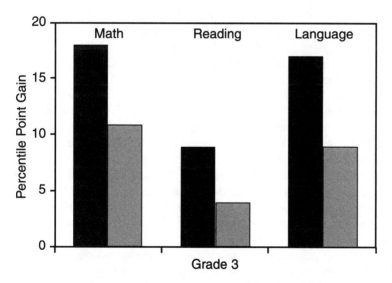

Figure 6-2. Grade 3 average percentile gains, 1985–1987, California Achievement Test scores. *Solid bars:* SDP schools; *hatched bars:* district. (*Source:* Comer, J. P. [1988]. Educating poor minority children. *Scientific American, 259* [5], 42–48.)

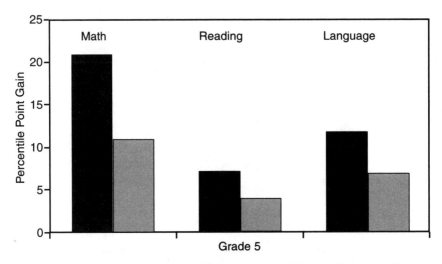

Figure 6-3. Grade 5 average percentile gains, 1985–1987, California Achievement Test. *Solid bars:* SDP schools; *hatched bars:* district. *(Source:* Comer, J. P. [1988]. Educating poor minority children. *Scientific American, 259* [5], 42–48.)

A trend analysis of achievement data among fourth graders in the two pioneer SDP schools in New Haven conducted by our SDP research team based on objective archival data provided by the school system indicated steady gains in mathematics and reading between 1969 and 1984. The grade equivalent scores for the two schools increased from about 3.0 in reading and mathematics in 1969 to 6.0 in reading and 5.0 in mathematics in 1984 (Comer, 1988b).

Several experimental control group studies involving randomly selected students in carefully matched schools reported significant differences in academic achievement between students in SDP schools and students in non-SDP control schools. A study by Cauce, Comer, and Schwartz (1987) reported that seventh-grade students from SDP schools had significantly higher averages in language, work study, and mathematics, and an overall higher mean grade equivalent than students from non-SDP schools. These data are summarized in Table 6-2.

In a restropective follow-up study conducted at a New Haven middle school (Haynes, Comer, and Hamilton-Lee, 1994), 92 sixth and eighth grade students were studied. Forty-seven (51%) were from a non-SDP elementary school and 45 (49%) were from a program elementary school prior to entering the middle schools. The academic achievement of these students was measured by report-card grades and by percentile scores on the Metropolitan Achievement Test. Significant differences in favor of the SDP students were found for sixth graders in mathematics, language, and total battery on the Metropolitan Achievement Test. SDP students obtained consistently higher scores on all other achievement measures. Recent data from Lincoln

Table 6-2. *Long-term Effects Related to Attendance at an SDP Elementary School: Mean Grade-Equivalents for Seventh-Grade SDP and Non-SDP Students on the Iowa Test of Basic Skills, 1985*

Skill	SDP students (n = 24)	Non-SDP students (n = 24)	F-Statistic
Language			
Vocabulary	6.18	5.12	20.22***
Reading	7.80	5.60	9.67**
Spelling	7.20	5.38	14.95***
Capitalization	7.00	5.02	17.26***
Punctuation	7.50	5.80	20.83***
Usage	7.00	5.18	24.12***
Total	7.00	5.34	27.52***
Work-Study			
Visual Materials	6.58	4.96	9.08**
Reference Materials	7.28	5.97	9.46**
Total	6.95	5.46	13.01***
Mathematics			
Concepts	7.25	5.94	9.93**
Problem-Solving	7.12	5.73	9.53**
Computation	7.28	6.49	6.46*
Total	7.22	6.05	9.55**
Composite	6.90	5.56	9.65***

*$p < .05$
**$p < .01$
***$p < .001$

Source: Cauce, A. M., Comer, J. P., Schwartz, B. A. (1987). Long term effects of a systems-oriented school prevention program. *American J. Orthopsychiatry, 57* (1), pp. 127–131.

Bassett School in New Haven, one of the best implementing SDP schools which is located in one of the poorest and most troubled areas in the city, indicated significant achievement gains for third graders on mathematics and language following adoption and implementation of the program in 1987; these data are presented in Figure 6-4.

In New Orleans, which is a district with a university and school district partnership for implementing the SDP described in Chapter 4, a strong effort is made to harness the resources of the "whole village" for the benefit of the students. In addition to the SDP facilitator, Southern University of New Orleans staff with their students work closely with the schools. An examination of achievement for the

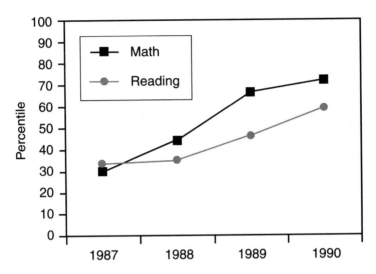

Figure 6-4. MAT-6 results 1987–1990, grade 3, Lincoln Bassett Elementary School. *(Source: SDP National Database.)*

first four SDP schools, three of which began implementing the program in 1991–1992, and one of which began implementing SDP in 1992–1993, shows a general positive trend. Figures 6-5 and 6-6 illustrate the trend in reading and math achievement scores for grade 3 for the years 1991–1992 to 1993–1994.

The upward trend seems to indicate that the SDP is having a positive effect. Our ethnographic work indicates that a rigorous system of monitoring student performance and growth was in place in some schools as a result of the SDP. This may have accounted for the significant improvement observed in student performance.

▭▭▭▭▭ Behavior and School Adjustment Effects

Experimental control studies conducted by Haynes, Comer, and Hamilton-Lee (1988b, 1994) indicated that SDP students experienced significantly greater positive changes in attendance, and teacher ratings of classroom behavior, attitude toward authority, and group participation, when compared to non-SDP students. A study by Cauce, Comer, and Schwartz (1987) found that SDP students reported significantly better perceived school competence and self-competence compared to a control group of non-SDP students.

▭▭▭▭▭ Self-Concept

In a recent study (Haynes and Comer, 1990) SDP students in the fourth and sixth grades were compared with non-SDP students on six self-concept dimensions on

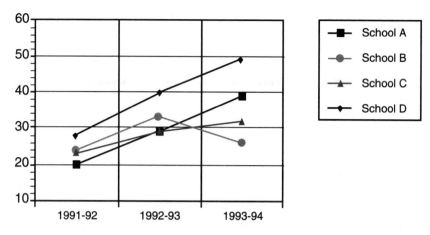

Figure 6-5. CAT/E: median percentile score, grade 3, reading, 1991–1994. (*Source:* SDP National Database.)

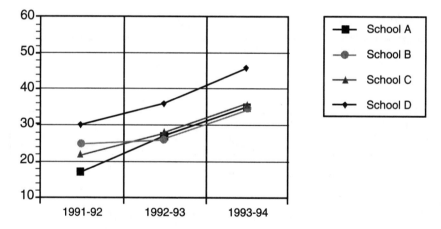

Figure 6-6. CAT/E: median percentile score, grade 3, mathematics, 1991–1994. (*Source:* SDP National Database.)

the Piers Harris Self-Concept Scale. Both groups of students were also compared with the national normative sample on total self-concept. Analysis of covariance was used to control for pretest differences that existed between SDP and non-SDP students. On the post-test measures, SDP students scored significantly higher than the control group of non-SDP students on all six self-concept dimensions and significantly higher than the normative group on total self-concept (see Table 6-3 and Figures 6-7 and 6-8).

Table 6-3. *Means and Standard Deviations (SD)on Piers-Harris Self-Concept Dimensions for SDP and Non-SDP Students, 1988–1989*

Self-Concept Dimensions (highest possible score)	Pre-Test Means (SD) September 1988		Post-Test Means (SD) April 1989	
	SDP Students *n* = 87	Non-SDP Students *n* = 87	SDP Students *n* = 87	Non-SDP Students *n* = 87
Behavior (16)	6.9 (1.8)	7.6 (2.6)	12.2* (1.7)	8.1 (2.5)
Intellectual and School Status (17)	7.9 (1.6)	8.7 (2.4)	13.2* (1.5)	8.9 (2.3)
Physical (14)	8.4 (1.7)	8.7 (1.8)	10.0* (1.4)	9.0 (1.7)
Anxiety (14)	8.0 (1.8)	8.6 (1.9)	10.1* (1.9)	8.7 (2.1)
Popularity (12)	7.9 (1.9)	8.1 (1.6)	9.4* (1.5)	8.4 (1.6)
Happiness and Satisfaction (10)	6.0 (1.5)	7.1 (1.6)	9.0* (.87)	6.9 (1.7)
Total Score (89)	45.1 (6.3)	48.8 (7.6)	63.9* (4.9)	50.0 (7.4)

*Significant post-test mean differences ($p < .001$).

Source: Haynes, N.M. and Comer, J.P. (1990). The effects of a school development program on self-concept. *Yale Journal of Biology and Medicine, 63,* 275–283.

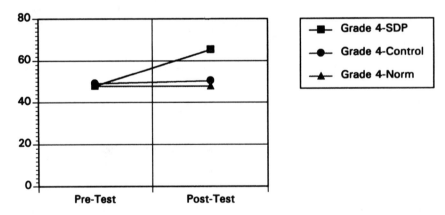

Figure 6-7. Comparison of mean total self-concept scores for fourth grade SDP students, non-SDP students, and normative group, 1990. *Note:* Highest possible score is 80. *(Source:* Haynes, N. M., and Comer, J. P. [1990]. The effects of a school development program on self-concept. *The Yale Journal of Biology and Medicine, 63,* 275–283.)

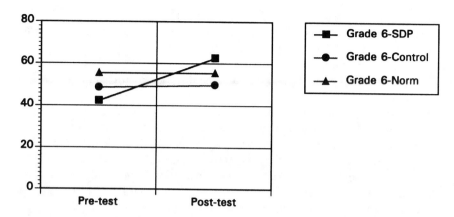

Figure 6-8. Comparison of mean total self-concept scores for sixth-grade SDP students, non-SDP students, and normative group, 1990. *Note:* Highest possible score is 80. *(Source: Haynes, N. M., and Comer, J. P. [1990]. The effects of a school development program on self-concept. The Yale Journal of Biology and Medicine, 63, 275–283.)*

Classroom and School Climate

In a quasi-experimental study (Comer, Haynes, & Hamilton-Lee, 1989b) designed to examine the effects of the SDP on climate and other variables over the period of an academic year, students in the SDP schools reported significant improvement along five of the nine Trickett and Moos (1974) *Classroom Environment Scale* (CES) subscales, and on the total CES. Students in the four control schools reported significant improvement on two of the subscales. Parents' assessment of school climate as measured by the School Climate Survey (SCS), 1985 version, showed significant positive change for the SDP schools. Parents of non-SDP schools reported significant negative changes in their assessment of the climate in those schools.

Qualitative/Ethnographic Findings

As noted earlier, qualitative studies formed an important and integral part of SDP's evaluation of its implementation process. Ten sites were selected for study in 1992–1993. Our investigation in each of the 10 selected sites began in Spring 1993. In our effort to learn about how schools instituted the nine SDP elements, we sought to understand what if any conditions already existed in the various districts that facilitated or hindered the processes of establishing the nine elements, and how the schools overcame the hindrances. Our aim was to understand the processes by which the SDP structures were built in each of these schools.

FACILITATING CONDITIONS

The conditions that facilitated the establishment of the nine elements in the schools included (1) direct SDP and district-level collaboration, (2) positive interpersonal relationships, (3) facilitators' knowledge and use of preexisting change mechanisms in the schools, and (4) parent and student participation.

(1) Direct and formal collaboration between the School Development Program and the school districts greatly helped the restructuring process. This collaboration was secured through a contractual agreement with the central office. The superintendents appointed district-level facilitators, most of whom dedicated more than 50% of their time to ensure the implementation of the SDP. The facilitator attended SDP professional leadership development sessions to enhance facilitation skills. The principals and school staff also obtained training in the philosophy of the SDP. Once trained, the facilitators provided the school administrators and staff members with formal SDP orientations and training to help initiate the establishment of the SPMT, SSST, and PT.

(2) Most facilitators identified the quality of the relationship they created with principals, parents, and school staff as a crucial element in their initial efforts to introduce the nine elements of the SDP to the schools. Good relationships are built when the facilitator honors commitments made to the school, assists with school functions, and takes the time to describe the nine elements of the SDP to individual staff members as needed. Such collaboration with and accessibility to school and community staff helped the facilitators to strengthen their relationships and build trust among parents and school staff.

(3) Facilitators' knowledge and use of preexisting structures that are similar to the SDP teams have proved useful in their initial implementation efforts. Preliminary assessment helped the facilitators to customize their formal orientation to the knowledge level they found in the schools. Restructuring and reorganizing existing teams in these sites facilitated the introduction of the School Development Program in schools.

(4) The other common characteristic shared by all 10 schools was that these schools had some form of parental participation, student referral team, or management team.

Thus, we learned that the role of the district facilitators in the selected sites was crucial in shaping and directing the initiation of the SDP in the schools, and that changing existing mechanisms worked to the advantage of these schools. The willingness of the principals and the school staff to implement the program was key to the success of the facilitators' work in this implementation process.

CONDITIONS THAT HINDERED

Conditions that hindered the implementation of the SDP in schools included (1) staff members' negative experiences with previous school reform programs, (2) staff members' lack of desire to change, (3) low interaction comfort level between parents and staff, and (4) teachers' resistance to parent involvement.

(1) Although most of the school staff members supported the efforts of the SDP to change the schools positively, some lacked faith in SDP's ability to do so. Past experience with other school reform programs showed them to be ineffective and short-lived. They expected the same of the SDP. Thus, at the initial stages of implementation, these schools resisted changes in school management. The existence of other school reform initiatives concurrent with the School Development Program also created confusion among school staff, who assumed that the SDP process would simply mean additional teams and management structures.

(2) Another reason for slow implementation of the team leadership was some staff members' wish to adhere to traditional ways of management and avoid any kind of change in general. Our interviews with the district facilitators revealed that some school staff members felt comfortable having the principal assume the authority and responsibility for managing school affairs. These staff members were not interested in assisting with the management and decision-making process in their schools.

(3) A low parent–staff interaction comfort level proved to be another hindrance to the smooth implementation of the SDP, especially for the Parent Team component. Parents feared that they might be rejected by the staff at their children's school. Some parents felt incompetent and as a result were inhibited in approaching school staff. Parents who spoke other languages and were of different cultures from the predominant language and culture of the schools felt too shy or inhibited to interact with school staff beyond attendance at teacher and parent conferences when needed. Most parents lacked time to manage their family affairs and attend parent activity meetings in the schools, and some parents lacked transportation to attend school events and volunteer in school activities.

(4) Teachers' resistance to parent involvement formed a further barrier to SDP implementation. Some teachers believed that active parental involvement would permit overbearing parents to unfairly criticize them and monitor their work so as to hinder their role as teachers. Some staff members mistrusted parents' motives, interests in, and concern for their children's educational well-being, and many teachers believed that parents would have little to offer by engaging actively in the schools because of their limited knowledge and skills about the schools.

PROBLEM SOLUTIONS

This was the context in which most of the principals operated when they began implementing the principles of the SDP. In their efforts to solve the challenges they encountered and advance the implementation of the SDP, the principals drew from their leadership training they obtained at the Yale Child Study Center. They sought to alleviate some of the conceptual misunderstandings that some of their staff members espoused about school reform organizations in general. They promoted team leadership and made efforts to increase parental involvement through various mechanisms.

The principals worked synergistically with the district facilitators and school staff to identify solutions for the problems they faced. As the first step toward the initial implementation, selected groups of teaching and nonteaching staff and parent volunteers were sent for SDP training at the Yale Child Study Center. Workshops on SDP, and school and community-building training, were given on site by the SDP facilitators. School staff also benefited from the ways in which the principals demonstrated their efforts to change their administrative and leadership styles as they promoted the principles of consensus, collaboration, and no-fault. The principals encouraged broad participation of the school staff in the decision-making process of the schools' academic and social affairs. For example, school staff regularly participated in preparing comprehensive school plans and assessing staff development needs.

Although the implementation process was slow, the principals, facilitators, and school staff members in these schools were able to reap the fruits of their collective work as they progressed through the various implementation levels. The ability of staff to appreciate team leadership and increased parental involvement in the schools were reasons to celebrate. Collaborative decision making not only required courage and foresightedness on the part of the principals who shared their authority, but also necessitated that staff adapt to team leadership styles.

The formation of the SPMT and SSST in the schools helped to reinforce parental involvement. We found that it was an old tradition in all of the schools that we visited to have periodical social evenings for parents (Haynes, Gebreyesus, and Comer, 1993). However, with the introduction of the SDP, concerted efforts were being made to encourage parents to be more meaningful members of the school community. Thus, parents were trained to develop the skills they needed to participate in the schooling process. For example, experts were invited to conduct workshops around the issues such as parent–school staff communication, parenting skills for younger mothers, and computer literacy. Parents participated in the school's process of decision making through their attendance at SPMT and Parent Team meetings. Parents contributed to their children's social and academic skills by serving as teachers' aides, participated in organizing social evenings, solicited other parents to get more involved and interested in their children's school, and assisted in grading papers and posting items on bulletin boards (Haynes, Gebreyesus, and Comer, 1993). Additional steps taken to increase parental involvement included (1) holding meetings in the community where access was easier for parents, (2) arranging with employers for release time for parents to attend meetings as the employers' contribution to the educational change process, (3) asking volunteer parents to reach other parents in the community at large and in social agencies, such as churches and health centers, and (4) establishing carpools to transport parents to meetings and other events.

The struggle to implement the nine elements and the changes that occur during such implementation can perhaps be summarized in this respondent's words:

Traditionally in any school you have decisions that are being made, usually by the principal and what have you, and I think for a lot of us it was uncomfortable when introducing the Comer process that we found ourselves in the position of being a part of that decision-making process.... I think I can honestly and truly say that we are moving to a point that I can envision that no ... pertinent decisions will be made without ... parental input, as well as the management team's input for the coming years.

Current SDP Agenda

The responsibility of the SDP Research and Evaluation Unit is to conduct formative and summative assessments of the work of the School Development Program. This involves the monitoring of work at the SDP national office and in the field, and includes an action research component. The major SDP research activities are (1) implementation assessment, (2) assessment of SDP impact, (3) development of the national SDP database, and (4) evaluation of SDP leadership development programs.

Implementation Assessment

The purposes of this assessment are to document the implementation process itself, to validate the SDP life cycle, and to examine the degree and quality of implementation in various schools and how this is related to the school climate, student attendance, and student achievement.

The life cycle (see Figure 6-9) of the SDP refers to the particular sequence in which the implementation of the program seems to occur. There are five phases in this sequence called the life cycle: (1) *planning and preorientation,* which is the preparation at the district level for the implementation of the SDP; (2) *orientation,* during which information about the SDP is disseminated, and individuals become acquainted with the mission, goals, philosophy, and nine elements of the program; (3) *transition,* involving the establishment and refinement of the nine SDP elements; (4) *operation,* during which the nine elements are in place and working efficiently; and (5) *institutionalization,* which reflects the infusion and saturation of the philosophy and elements of the SDP throughout the school.

The implementation evaluation consists of two main parts. The first part is qualitative research on the process of implementation, including the in-depth documentation of the process of systemic reform. Currently, the research is concentrated on one systemic district and takes the form of attendance at and documentation of district-level team meetings: interviews with the superintendent and district-level staff involved in the district-level implementation of the SDP, with the SDP staff responsible for systemic implementation in the district, and with representatives from the funding agency. As systemic reform is implemented in schools, interviews will be extended to include principals, staff, parents, and students of selected schools. The interviews can be considered semistructured in that an interview protocol, developed by the SDP staff, is followed. However, because

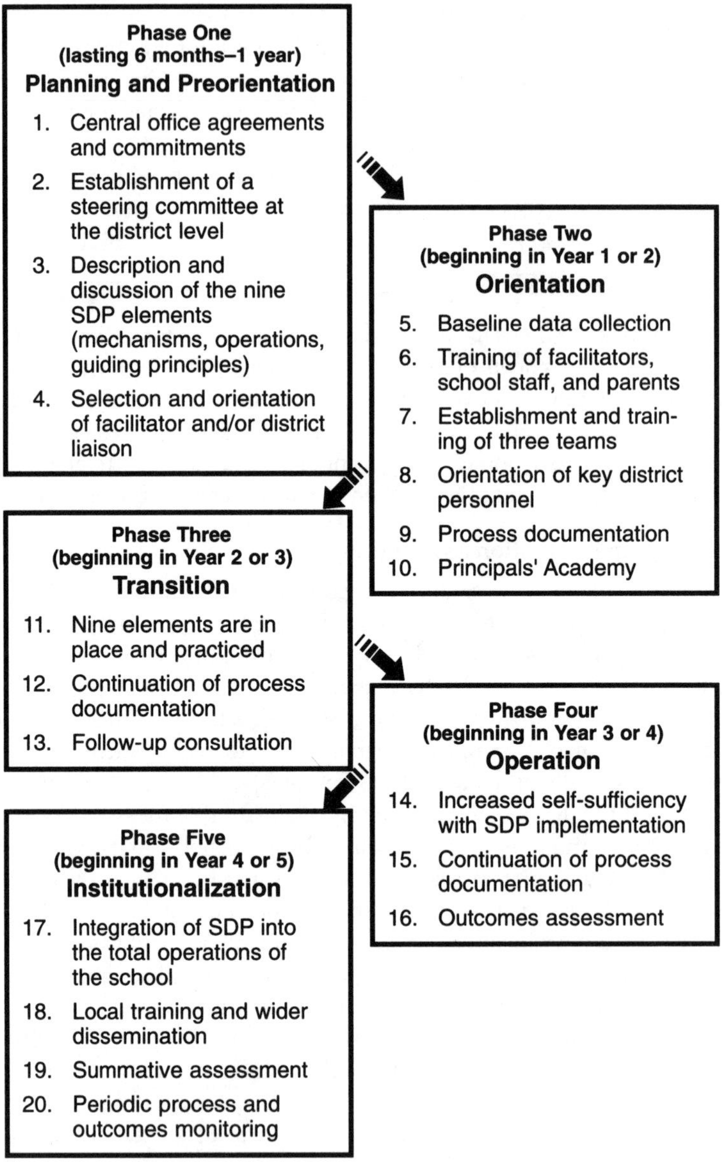

Phase One
(lasting 6 months–1 year)
Planning and Preorientation

1. Central office agreements and commitments
2. Establishment of a steering committee at the district level
3. Description and discussion of the nine SDP elements (mechanisms, operations, guiding principles)
4. Selection and orientation of facilitator and/or district liaison

Phase Two
(beginning in Year 1 or 2)
Orientation

5. Baseline data collection
6. Training of facilitators, school staff, and parents
7. Establishment and training of three teams
8. Orientation of key district personnel
9. Process documentation
10. Principals' Academy

Phase Three
(beginning in Year 2 or 3)
Transition

11. Nine elements are in place and practiced
12. Continuation of process documentation
13. Follow-up consultation

Phase Four
(beginning in Year 3 or 4)
Operation

14. Increased self-sufficiency with SDP implementation
15. Continuation of process documentation
16. Outcomes assessment

Phase Five
(beginning in Year 4 or 5)
Institutionalization

17. Integration of SDP into the total operations of the school
18. Local training and wider dissemination
19. Summative assessment
20. Periodic process and outcomes monitoring

Figure 6-9. Phases in the implementation of the SDP life cycle.

the questions are open-ended, the researcher can pursue an area of interest or ask for elaboration. Further interviews will also pursue the topic of specific programs, activities, and changes in attitudes that have occurred in the school because of the implementation of the SDP.

The documentation of the meetings and retreats involves not so much what is being said or what decisions are made (this is already reflected in the minutes), but the type and quality of interaction that occurs and the role that each person is playing. Such observation allows for the examination of the growth and practice of consensus, collaboration, and no-fault at the district-level.

Archival records such as minutes of meetings, district plans, agendas, mission statements, and staff development materials form part of the resources used for documentation. It is noteworthy that systemic implementation of SDP came as a result of qualitative research on optimal conditions for the faithful replication of SDP.

The second part of the implementation evaluation is the quantitative aspect involving the distribution of the *School Implementation Questionnaire—Revised* (SIQ-R) and the gathering of school-level outcome data. The SIQ-R is being administered to staff and SPMT, SSST, and PT members in more than 110 selected schools. In our current research plan, the SIQ-Rs are being distributed in all the SDP schools in the three systemic districts yearly over a period of 6 years. Concurrent school-level attendance, achievement, and, in selected cases, school climate data are also being collected.

Previous qualitative research on degree of implementation sparked the need to perform this type of systematic, longitudinal research on degree of implementation and its relationship to outcomes. Through observation in the field and especially through interviews and focus groups, the SDP staff found that the degree of implementation varied widely across schools, even among schools that began the program at the same time. Outcome results also varied, with the tendency for schools with high levels of implementation to manifest better climate, improved attendance, and, in some cases, increased achievement. We expect the longitudinal implementation study to clarify issues around the pattern of implementation termed the life cycle, the variability of the SDP implementation, and the impact of the SDP implementation on school-level outcomes.

Assessment of SDP Impact

EFFECT ON SCHOOL CLIMATE

The reason for assessing school climate is to examine the extent to which relationships among adults and between adults and the youth have changed as a result of the implementation of the SDP. Because positive relationships are crucial for the establishment of a caring climate and are the foundation on which meaningful change is built, it is essential that changes in relationships be monitored. We have found that change in climate is the first signal that the process is in place and working.

Our previous research on school climate has been mainly quasi-experimental in that schools were not randomly assigned to SDP or non-SDP conditions, but were selected with these preexisting conditions. In other words, schools implementing the School Development Program in a selected district were compared to schools with similar demographics from that same district on student, staff, and/or parent perceptions of the school climate. Studies showed that the SDP schools tended to have significantly better climate than non-SDP schools.

In our current study, we focus on change over time in 21 schools across two systemic districts. This study began in 1994–1995 and will conclude in 1999–2000. School climate data will be collected every other year beginning in 1994–1995. We have already collected the first wave of data for this study.

The School Climate Survey (Haynes, Emmons, and Comer, 1994), parent, student, and staff versions, developed by SDP staff, will be administered in each of the 21 schools. The sample is comprised of students from grades 3 and higher, their parents, and all members of the school staff. We hope to answer two main questions:

1. Do successive cohorts of students view the climate of the school significantly differently from one another, e.g., as increasingly more positive?
2. Is level of SDP implementation related to perceptions of school climate?

Because the 21 schools involved in this study are also involved with the implementation study, we will be able to examine the relationship between degree of implementation and quality of school climate.

Sharing the School Climate Reports with the school principals permits their use as information input into the decision-making process regarding what activities should be included in the Comprehensive School Plan for the purpose of improving the conditions at the school.

EFFECT ON STUDENT OUTCOMES
The first steps in this research are to examine what changes in programs and activities are taking place because of the school's involvement with the SDP, and to measure the extent to which changes in the degree of implementation are related to changes in school climate. The reason for this approach is for us to be able to make strong causal attributions regarding the SDP's role in changing the climate of the school. The next step is to examine the relationship between students' perceptions of the climate of their school and their attendance, behavior, social competence, and achievement.

Research in the area of school climate has shown significant relationships with student self-concept, attendance, behavior, dropout rate, and achievement. Our own research supports these findings. Because the SDP is built on the theory that positive relationships are essential to creating the type of environment in which the whole child can be developed, it is important for us to understand to what extent changes in these relationships are related to changes in student outcomes. More recent research (Kuperminc and Kamensky, 1995) indicates that a significant amount of variance in students' internalizing (e.g., depression, withdrawn behavior) and externalizing behavior (e.g., aggression, disruptive and acting-out behavior) can be explained by students' perceptions of the school climate as measured by the SDP School Climate Survey—Elementary and Middle School Version. The notion that school climate is related to students' mental health is one that Comer refers to early in his work (1980) but one that we are just beginning to explore from a clinical viewpoint. We have done extensive work linking school climate to self-concept, but not to clinical manifestations of poor school adjustment and behavioral problems.

This longitudinal cohort study began in 1994–1995 and will conclude in 1999–2000. School climate, social competence, attendance, behavior, and achievement data will be collected every other year beginning in 1994–1995. We have already collected part of the first wave of data for this study, which is being conducted in the same 21 schools as the climate study. However, only one set of climate data is collected from the students for use in both studies. The sample is comprised of students from grades 3 and higher. At each wave, data will be collected from all students, grade 3 and higher, for whom we receive parental permission. Data collected are:

- Student perceptions of the climate of the school measured by the School Climate Scale—Student Versions, mentioned above
- Students' self-perceptions of their social competence measured by the SDP Behavior Assessment Scale for Students
- Student attendance, achievement, and, where available, behavior referral and dropout data from archival sources
- Classroom climate data to be collected in the second and third wave of data collection
- Self-concept data to be collected in the second and third wave of data collection

We hope to answer the following questions:

1. How has implementation of the SDP contributed to changes in school climate?
2. Are students' perceptions of school climate related to their perceptions of social competence, self-concept, behavior, attendance, and achievement?
3. Are changes in students' perceptions of climate related to changes in their perceptions of their social competence, self-concept, behavior, attendance, and achievement? (Because this is a longitudinal study, we expect to have some of the same students in each round of data gathering.)

Because the 21 schools involved in the cohort study are also involved with the implementation study, we will be able to examine the relationship between degree of implementation, quality of school climate, and student outcomes.

MODELING THE FLOW OF CAUSE AND EFFECT

Because the SDP is a school reform program, the aim of which is the optimal development of each child through positive change in the relationships among individuals, it is important for the SDP Research and Evaluation Unit to test the causal relationships among the SDP process, school climate, developmental pathways, and student outcomes (see Figure 6-1). Previous SDP research (Emmons et al., 1992) has supported the hypothesis that school climate influences student achievement through self-concept and behavior. In our current research we hope to answer the following questions:

1. Does level of SDP implementation influence student attendance, behavior, and achievement?
2. Does level of SDP implementation affect student social competence, attendance, behavior, and achievement through school climate?
3. Do students' perceptions of school climate affect their attendance and achievement through self-perceptions of social competence?

▰▰▰ DEVELOPMENT OF THE NATIONAL SDP DATABASE

This database, still in the process of development, contains information on initial year of SDP implementation, student demographics, student attendance and achievement, and socioeconomic index of the school. Level of SDP implementation and school climate perceptions will be included for selected schools. The purposes of this database are overall program reporting and monitoring, and tracking changes over time as part of longitudinal research efforts.

▰▰▰ EVALUATION OF THE LEADERSHIP DEVELOPMENT PROGRAMS

Week-long professional development programs are offered annually for SDP facilitators, selected parents, selected school staff, and other stakeholders as the school or district deems necessary; and the Principals' Academy is held for principals whose schools are in the initial stages of implementing the SDP. Evaluation of these programs consists of daily feedback forms completed by the participants to assess the adequacy of the models presented each day. The forms are reviewed at the end of each day and modifications are made as needed.

Evaluation also consists of a focus group meeting at the end of each day with the national faculty brought to assist with the training. During these meetings, presenters and national faculty reflect on the program for that day, concentrating on what did and did not go well, and making adjustments for the next day. This is an illustration of the assessment and modification process in action at the SDP national office level.

Another evaluation component is the distribution of the ASK (attitude, skills, and knowledge) inventory to Principals' Academy participants 6 months after the completion of the professional development sessions. The purpose of this inventory is to assess the relevance and effectiveness of the sessions in assisting the participants to implement the SDP in their schools and districts. We want to know if the attitudes, skills, and knowledge that the presenters intended to impart were received by the participants. Comments from participants on this instrument serve as input in the planning of sessions for the next year. Reports are prepared from the data collected from responses to the ASK, and shared with the relevant participants.

Conclusion

The four current activities of the SDP Research and Evaluation Unit are interrelated. The leadership programs provide training for building the knowledge base and skills necessary to implement the SDP in schools and districts. It is important to monitor and assess how effective the training is in preparing leaders and facilitators in the field. The implementation study provides the starting point from which we can make causal attributions with respect to the impact of SDP. The data collected through the impact study complement data contained in the national database. This serves both to expand the context in which implementation takes place and to provide us with school-level outcome measures such as attendance, suspensions, achievement, and, in some cases, referrals.

The interrelation among these activities is especially clear when modeling the flow of cause and effect. Preliminary analysis of the first wave of data collected this past year shows strong relationships between level of implementation and perceptions of school climate at the school level. It is especially interesting to note that student and parent perceptions of climate as well as those of staff were strongly related to perceived levels of implementation. Previous research studies (Emmons et al., 1992) have shown links between students' perceptions of school climate and student behavior and achievement. We expect in our modeling of cause and effect to establish the relationship between implementation, climate, student development, and student outcomes. It is clear from our research that where the program is implemented well, strong positive school-level and student-level outcomes result.

References

Cauce, A. M., Comer, J. P., & Schwartz, B. A. (1987). Long-term effects of a system-oriented school prevention program. *American Journal of Orthopsychiatry, 57* (1), 127–131.

Comer, J. P. (1980). *School power.* New York: Free Press.

Comer, J. P. (1988a). *Maggie's American dream.* New York: New American Library.

Comer, J. P. (1988b). Educating poor minority children. *Scientific American, 259* (5), 42–48.

Comer, J. P., Haynes, N. M., & Hamilton-Lee, M. (1989b). School power: A model for improving black student achievement. In W. D. Smith & E. W. Chun (eds.), *Black education: A quest for equity and excellence* (pp. 187–200). New Brunswick, NJ: Transaction Publishers.

Emmons, C., Owen, S., Haynes, N., & Comer, J. P. (1992). A causal model of the effects of school climate, classroom climate, academic self-concept, suspension, and absenteeism on academic achievement. Paper presented at the 1992 conference of the Eastern Educational Research Association.

Haynes, N. M., & Comer, J. P. (1990). The effects of a school development program on self-concept. *The Yale Journal of Biology and Medicine, 63,* 275–283.

Haynes, N. M., Comer, J. P., & Hamilton-Lee, M. (1988a). The School Development Program: A model for school improvement. *Journal of Negro Education, 57* (l), 11–21.

Haynes, N. M., Comer, J. P., & Hamilton-Lee, M. (1988b). The effects of parental involvement on student performance. *Educational and Psychological Research, 8* (4), 291–299.

Haynes, N. M., Comer, J. P., & Hamilton-Lee, M. (1989). School climate enhancement through parental involvement. *Journal of School Psychology, 27,* 87–90.

Haynes, N. M., Comer, J. P., & Hamilton-Lee, M. (1994). School development effect: Two follow-up studies. In Norris M. Haynes (ed.), *School Development Program Research Monograph* (pp. 1–26). New Haven, CT: Yale Child Study Center.

Haynes, N. M., Gebreyesus, S., & Comer, J. P. (1993). *Selected case studies of national implementation of the School Development Program.* New Haven, CT: Yale Child Study Center.

Kuperminc, G. P., & Kamensky, M. S. (1995, October). Associations of middle school social emotional climate with student competences and mental health: Questions for future research. Paper presented at the 12th Annual South Eastern Eco-Community Conference at Division 27 of APA. Smith Mountain Lake, Virginia.

Trickett, E. J. and Moos, R. H. (1974). The classroom scale. *American Journal of Community Psychology* 2(1), pp. 1–12.

Acknowledgment. We extend our grateful acknowledgment to Maloke Efimba, M.P.H., and Beverly Crowther, Research Associate, for their contribution to the review of literature, charts, and proofing of the data for this chapter. We would also like to acknowledge Ms. Crowther's participation in the proofreading team that reviewed the entire text of the book.

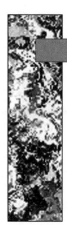

Chapter 7

Changing American Schools: Insights from the School Development Program

JONATHON H. GILLETTE AND ROBERT D. KRANYIK

> *The number of schools participating in the SDP has exploded in recent years from two in 1968, to 70 in 1990, to 267 in 1993, and to more than 550 in 1995. Reviewing the SDP's evolution, and mindful that as programs grow they can stray from their original mission, the authors describe their vision of entire school districts enthusiastically engaged—and supported—in meaningful educational reform.*

As the School Development Program (SDP) moves into its next 25 years, it is fitting to reflect on the process that has touched the lives of so many children and adults. Since its modest beginning in two elementary schools in New Haven, the SDP has been expanded, tested, refined, and implemented in more than 550 schools in more than 80 school districts across the nation. The SDP staff has been deeply involved in both research and implementation aspects of the program in these schools and school districts. Through this work in the field, we have gained a number of insights. The insights are sorted into three main categories: specific lessons about the SDP design at work in individual school contexts; general lessons about planning and directing the implementation of the SDP; and finally, insights about sustaining change and "going to scale."

These insights emerged from conversations with SDP staff, local educators implementing the SDP, and parents and students participating in the process. Despite such a diverse group, with such diverse experiences, the insights emerged with considerable consensus. It is a tribute to James P. Comer's original work that his process remains intact. It has provided both his staff and practitioners in the field with a means not only to change schools, but also to gain profound knowledge about the change process.

▓▓▓ *The SDP Design*

When he first entered the school world, Comer brought a perspective that was outside education: He was a trained child psychiatrist. His questions, problem-solving skills, and form of inquiry were based on training that began with the child. This sophisticated understanding of children differed from the way most educators viewed schools and the process of schooling. Their focus was often on curriculum, instruction, testing, managing, organizing, and even just plain surviving. The school world perspective was not wrong—it raised important, even critical questions. But that perspective was not sufficient in that it was missing understandings—theories—that were fundamental to promoting healthy human development.

The SDP design was a means of moving those theories into practice. An early challenge of the SDP was to see the impact of many of these "outside" theories in practice. Although there was a lot of success in the first New Haven schools, how would the process unfold in a variety of settings? In particular, what parts of the design would stand out as particularly critical or important?

▓▓▓ *Process Is Content*

A number of years ago, Jonathon Gillette, SDP project manager for professional development, presented the elements of an SPMT to a group of educators. He was fairly new to the SDP, and it was his first time presenting the SPMT module with Comer in the room observing. He had prepared thoroughly and presented every element in detail: the number of people represented, the number of meetings, the types of agendas, and items usually discussed. At the end of the presentation, he asked Comer for feedback. Answering in his usual low-key manner, Comer replied, "You did a great job, Jack. (*Pause*). But you missed the whole point. In every interaction you are either building community or breaking community. The mechanisms, how you meet, are secondary."

In that one small statement, the entire presentation was reframed back to its center, its purpose: building community. The SDP mechanisms are not only a means to empowerment and sharing of power but also, essentially, a pathway toward community building. For the first time in school reform, the SDP process showed that it was important to focus on how reforms were accomplished. Not only did the means become as important as the ends; without proper attention to the means, one could never get to the ends. The guiding principles of collaboration, consensus, and no-fault—the process elements of the design—have helped to transform the way schools function. Over and over again, in countless reviews of schools that have successfully implemented the process, we have heard how central the process was to making changes. It allowed local expertise to emerge, it allowed local variations in implementation, and equally important, it imposed a discipline on the adults' interactions. That is, collaboration had to be modeled by everyone, no-fault had to be practiced when describing children and adults, and finally, there had to be enough agreement among all groups to reach consensus.

Although these guiding principles are process features, they are a central part of the content of the process. To alter one of them is to move in a substantially different direction. Take consensus, as an example. Consensus is more than a type of decision-making method. It is the means of transforming the way in which adults interact with one another. It requires strong listening skills; it requires adults to reach out beyond the opinions they already hold. It gives voice to the least powerful as well as to the most powerful. It provides a way for the inevitable subgroups in a school's community to connect with one another. It models that everyone is needed in order to make a real difference for students.

Replace this one feature with voting, and an entirely different dynamic emerges. People campaign rather than engage in dialogue. One group wins, while the other group loses. True believers create their opposites who have no stake in supporting the majority. Coalition building replaces community building. The genius of consensus is that it forces a transformation from fighting for one's subgroup (teachers, parents, or particular children) to being an advocate for the whole learning community.

Modeling the guiding principles in a school context that is often set in a larger context of fault finding, finger pointing, frustration, and failure is an enormous challenge. It requires a commitment to learning and enacting a set of interpersonal skills that are challenging to take on in the best of contexts. But not only can it happen, it has happened and continues to happen in schools that everyone has written off as hopeless. These schools have transformed themselves, and all have found the guiding principles to be their linchpin.

Organizational Structures Are a Critical Means of Sustaining Instructional Changes

One of the ongoing debates among reformers is the relative importance of changing or creating structures versus instructional interventions. One side points to the critical need to generate consent by pulling professionals into the decision-making process. The other side points to the volume of research that shows achievement gains deriving solely from direct interventions in classrooms.

To the SDP staff, this debate seems odd. Our experiences have shown us that both are critical, and our process has helped schools link the two in a wide range of ways. Some schools have spent a significant amount of time restructuring in order to gain sufficient consensus to move forward on instructional initiatives as a whole group. Some have used restructuring to organize what were already a host of ongoing instructional initiatives. Some have gone back and forth, first focusing on structure, then focusing on instruction. Some have used the structures to get a global picture of student strengths and needs.

In every case the structures were not the end but a means to working more effectively with students. In turn, instructional changes produced inevitable tensions that without facilitating structures would have gone underground until they had brewed into full-scale conflict. In one large high school, significant pedagogical changes had been introduced prior to the creation of an SPMT. By the end of the year, the teachers were at each other's throats. After implementing all nine elements of the SDP process, this school not only sustained its earlier changes, but leaped ahead with additional instructional shifts supported by the entire faculty. Recent improvements in achievement scores at the school underscore that success.

In another example, a fully implemented SDP elementary school chose to pursue a major constructivist initiative and hired a local consultant to provide the training. At the first training, the staff was immediately concerned that the methods offered did not fit with how they understood their children. They challenged the consultant to regard them as equal partners in creating a fit between the constructivist theory and the specific children at their school. Their unity and collaboration in creating a global picture of their students gave them not only the knowledge but also the confidence to issue such a challenge. As a result, they implemented a modified approach that enabled them to jump to third place citywide on higher-order thinking skills.

▰▰▰ *The Importance of a Developmental Foundation for Learning*

One key theory that Comer brought to bear in his process was the vital role of child development as a foundation for learning. Even in settings with superb curricula and teachers, instruction can flounder when teachers assume that their students have a developmental capacity that has yet to emerge. This is true of traditional instruction, and it is especially true of new, more experiential and cooperative learning techniques. Developmental strengths are vital to students' being able to work together, make judgments, and utilize their considerable natural curiosity in pursuit of increasingly complex questions.

A developmental approach stands in contrast to highly cognitive, highly controlled delivery systems—now increasingly seen dressed up by technology. For an individual teacher and for a school, taking development seriously is a major cultural transformation from an obsession with cognition to a commitment to overall human development. A developmental perspective moves one into the world of the child. It begins with the recognition that all children learn. John Holt pointed to this years ago when he described the enormously complex task of language acquisition that children acquire prior to school. But although children are engines of growth, the kinds of experiences they have are critically important, as some experiences enhance growth, while others undermine growth. Children are complex "wholes." They are not just a brain on a stick.

Depending on their life experiences, children come to school developed differently. Some come with great strengths; a focus of many researchers now is the resilience of urban children. Some come with significant developmental gaps: They have not had certain interactions with, conversations with, and guidance from adults. Some come with part of their development undermined by significantly traumatic experiences. For example, one kindergartener had learned to suppress all of his natural curiosity as a means of surviving his neighborhood. Since he was passive and extremely withdrawn, the teacher saw that her first task was to create different experiences for him so that he would simply dare to leave his seat.

Sometimes, just any developmental perspective helps. For example, in Maryland, a new performance-based assessment is becoming the basis of how the state rates individual schools. The tests are quite complex, involving cooperative learning groups that work together for a period of days and end with individuals writing up their results. In looking at the testing process, it is clear that the quality of interaction within the groups is critical. The state acknowledges this by requiring that students be randomly assigned. One of the testing grades is eighth grade. Developmentally, what do we know about eighth graders? We know they are the most peer-conscious, clique-forming of adolescents. Thus, they might find themselves working together with someone they don't know—or worse, someone they do know, and perhaps hate. Test scores have been low. Part of this is certainly the newness of the design and the fact that students do need to strengthen their writing. Therefore, many schools instituted activities targeted at strengthening this skill. Some others also chose to design a developmental intervention focused on students' being comfortable working with another student in their grade. Both modifications generate more effective learners.

The Importance of Child-Centered Planning

Planning has become a mantra for all school reform efforts. In the best circumstances, schools have been able to implement good organizational processes with ongoing cycles of assessment and review. From the SDP perspective, planning is vital, but planning must also reinforce a core idea that students are at the center of the process. Without clear guidelines, planning can become a vehicle for local adult agendas. Good planning must be "Comerized" and anchored to the specific students in that specific school. The SDP schools that have made significant achievement gains have child-centered planning processes.

In those successful schools the connections are made early on between structure and instruction. Most of them created curriculum subcommittees that immediately looked at ways of matching the student population to effective instructional choices. Some schools, as in Dallas, begin orientations of new SPMTs with a thorough examination of student strengths and needs. In essence, all are making the planning process a form of staff development in which the content is their students and the reward is deeper knowledge of how to make a difference for those children. Over and over again members of these schools have said that it was their deep engagement in the discernment process that made a difference. They chose the SDP approach because it did not prescribe the instructional or curricular answer, but generated a process to empower them to find their own answers for their own children.

▰▰▰ The Vital Importance of Ongoing Assessment, Monitoring, and Feedback

Many commentators on school change have pointed to the enormous challenge of changing schools on the fly—the equivalent of fixing a flat tire while driving a car. In addition, commentators have noted the messiness of change—its ability to overwhelm even the most skilled people. These descriptions match what we have experienced in the field. In many ways schools are overly busy worlds, and the sheer volume of efforts can soon remind one of the random, multicolored splatter of a Jackson Pollock painting. As supporters of change, we have steered schools over and over again back to the assessment and modification operation of the SDP process.

Assessment and modification, in SDP terms, is not just an annual review but a process of asking critical questions before, during, and at the end of every change process. Those questions include: What kind of changes are you looking for? How will you know if they have happened? How long will it take for them to emerge? What might be some early indicators? These questions are not only vital for good work—for the inevitable adjustments along the way—but also they are vital for sustaining the work. They alert those in the midst of change of the progress they have made. They anchor the school community to the larger picture even when the details are temporarily obscuring their vision. They allow an emphasis on the positive while people put themselves on the line to do even better. Although it is true that success breeds success, it is essential that what is being celebrated is truly a success.

▰▰▰ Relationships, Relationships, Relationships

Rebuilding the learning community is critical to the growth of its children, and relationships are at the core of that rebuilding. Reports from a number of schools mark the beginning of their transformations from the moment that relationships began to gel. Strong relationships are prerequisites of growth and learning, and the relationships between students and teachers must be supported by strong relationships among the adults. The world of the student is often radically different from the world of the teacher. Economic, ethnic, racial, and other differences are part of the fabric of every school in this country. It is crucial that the adults in each of those worlds make common cause and that children know of that shared mission. Too often parents and teachers end up pitted against one another, and like two quarreling parents, send double messages to their children.

Teacher-to-teacher and teacher-to-administrator relationships are also vital. The task of developing children is too difficult, too complex, to do alone. The larger school context—the building of experiences across grades—requires coordination and cooperation among all staff. Only with this kind of synergy can the impact be substantial enough to create the kinds of developmental outcomes children need to thrive in our current society.

The SDP emphasis on relationships is often mistaken for a "climate" program, or even a "feel-good" program. The goal is not just to feel good about one another. The point is that strong relationships are required for effective schooling. They are a means, not an end. And it goes beyond feeling good. Positive feelings are important—most schools have far too few positives as they often have to work in a context of constant criticism and blaming. But strong relationships carry negative and positive expressions. Sometimes the hard truths we hear from one another do the most to improve our work. Strong relationships take time, they take work, and they take energy. But they offer a means for more effective learning, which is a benefit to everyone.

Implementation

In the messy world of school change, how does the implementation of a comprehensive change process unfold? What are the most effective change strategies? How were our methods changed by our early experiences?

Preintervention or "Entry Planning" Is Key to Both Short- and Long-Term Success

Early in the life of the SDP, we entered districts in a variety of ways: as a result of court desegregation rulings, school-level interests, community interests, and at the invitation of superintendents. What we found in every one of these cases was that the preintervention period was brief, rushed, and uncoordinated across the various levels of a system.

For example, if we were invited in by a school, they would show eagerness for our program, they might get a letter of support from the superintendent, and we would be off to the races. Little time would be spent examining whether we were in fact the right choice for them. That was assumed. Further, little time would be spent generating a dialogue with the district central office. A simple blessing was sufficient.

We now know that not only is this short-sighted but also it fails to address issues of sustainability—issues that, if not addressed at the beginning, emerge only when funding ends or when a crisis emerges. Neither time brings the range of options available at the beginning of the process.

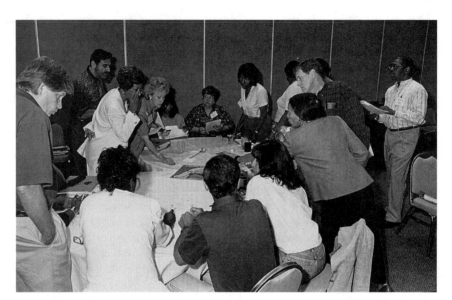

At the SDP Principals' Academy, adult learning teams, practicing and modeling consensus, collaboration, and no-fault are at the heart of the learning process. Photo by Laura Brooks.

Thus, we have begun to build for all our new schools and districts entry processes that help create a stronger context for immediate change and that lay the groundwork for long-term sustainability. Now, gaining entry means that both districts and schools will make specific commitments. But they are not a series of "hoops," each requiring compliance. Rather, a set of key questions triggers a structured dialogue among the district central office, the local school, and the national SDP office.

The entry of the Detroit schools into the SDP, overseen by Dr. Edward Joyner, was our most recent example of using a careful entry process to establish a positive climate for change *prior to actual intervention*. In this process, Detroit pulled together a high-level, mixed-stakeholder team that included the superintendent, key union leaders, key university partners, and a key foundation partner. Together, they examined the SDP process in detail through readings, through site visitations, and through SDP national orientation sessions. They asked questions about the fit of the process to their setting, where it lined up in other district plans, how it could be supported over a long time frame of up to 10 years, with both the inevitable superintendent and school board changes, and where the long-term resources would come from.

The entry process itself began to "Comerize" the group as they followed the guiding principles of consensus, collaboration, and no-fault. When they did decide to go ahead, all the stakeholders had had an opportunity to test their concerns, thus removing many of the immediate barriers to change. Finally, the entire group had a stake in the success of the program.

Although the entry process slows down the initial pace of change—the process takes up to a year—it more than makes up for that lost time in the overall alignment of a variety of stakeholders when the first school comes on board.

The Outside Change Agent Is Vital in Supporting Implementation

Again and again, reports from the field have pointed to the presence of a strong positive change agent outside the school as an important support for the changes inside the building. Principal leadership is still a key ingredient (it is described below), but the outside change agent is also a powerful factor. Principals themselves are often isolated and struggle to gain a perspective on how they are influencing their staff. An outside change agent can provide the feedback and coaching necessary for enacting new behaviors. In addition, the outside person can provide valuable process consultation to a team with well-established internal dynamics. Finally, groups in the middle of change often lose track of where they are and even lose track of the common vision under an avalanche of details. An outside person can offer important reminders and benchmarks of progress.

Linkage Between National Professional Development and Implementation

Early on, the SDP developed a national professional development program as a major part of the implementation of the process in schools. It began as a trainer of trainers model. In this design, we provided a national professional development curriculum for local change agents, who return to their districts and, in turn, train other local change agents. We had a lot of early success, especially when we broke the training up into two sessions, one in May and one in February. This allowed for implementation experiences between the first and second week of training.

Even with these early successes we began to see that three modifications were important for greater impact. First, the content of the SDP training had to be tightly tied to the work of implementation back in the districts. Thus, the more we were able to identify and define the tasks of early implementation (such as presenting the process to mixed stakeholders, establishing the three mechanisms, and beginning to make an impact on school culture), the more concentrated we could be in designing core lessons for each week of professional development. In essence, we were able to go deeper into fewer topics with greater carryover in the field.

Second, we knew that the structure of our professional development carried with it implicit messages about how our participants should do their professional development locally. If we used a traditional didactic approach, it was almost guaranteed that they would use the same approach with their local schools. We knew that such a traditional approach was not only *not* the most effective, but also it failed to convey messages about the importance of relationships and the importance of building on the expertise adults already had. Thus, we redesigned our professional development so that adult learning teams, practicing and modeling consensus, collaboration, and no-fault were at the heart of the learning process. Further, we were explicit in paying attention to affect—feelings—as well as intellect—thoughts. As a result, the professional development done locally has improved markedly.

Finally, we recognized that the single change agent faced enormous challenges back in the field. Now we invite a team of change agents that includes a lead district facilitator, the principals from the participating schools, and a key district central office ally. As a result, this team shares a common initial experience in learning, an experience that serves as both short- and long-term team building. When facilitators and principals begin on the same page, a great deal of tension and confusion is avoided.

The professional development model has in many ways now become a "coaching of coaches" model in that national staff members coach the acquisition and application of new knowledge rather than train others in what they should know. This shift carries the process back to the local site with the emphasis on relationships and local empowerment, which is much more consistent with the notions underlying the SDP.

Implementation Is Dissemination

One of the early challenges of any successful reform effort is spreading the word. When you feel that you have truly discovered ways of improving the opportunities for students, there is a tremendous urge to tell the world about it. Often, this approach fails to consider how others best learn about school reforms that work.

As a result, dissemination activities often take place in forums far away from the schools where the real action is happening. National conferences, districts' keynotes, policy forums, and national publications can get out the news that something good is happening. But, again and again, we hear that people only really learn what the process is all about when they visit our schools.

In hearing this feedback, we began to coin the phrase "implementation is dissemination." That is, people can best learn when they can experience a site that is involved in actual implementation. This framing has two significant implications. First, we as an organization have put most of our energies and focus into implementation rather than traditional dissemination activities. When faced with a conflict between writing, or working with a school, we have chosen the school. Of course, both are important, but we have a clear priority: If the schools fail to implement, then there is little to disseminate.

Second, we have organized demonstration schools, not exemplary schools for visitation. Most reformers want visitors to their exemplary schools, a title that often consciously and unconsciously makes difficult any discussion of the messier aspects of change. Demonstration schools, however, can be in different phases of change: early, middle, and mature. Even mature implementation schools may struggle with difficult aspects of change.

The key is to lift up the full complexity of change for others to see so that it is authentic and recognizable. It has been motivational for others to see someone else wrestling with similar problems and making some progress. It has led to deep conversations between teachers, parents, and administrators—conversations that often continue informally long after the site visits.

If the Principal Is the Key to Starting, the Collaborative Process Is the Key to Full Implementation and to Sustaining Change

A great deal of literature on school change has pointed to the critical role played by building-based leaders, especially the principal. The SDP experiences confirm those findings. Strong, effective leaders, especially those that model the guiding principles of consensus, collaboration, and no-fault, can speed implementation and generate tremendous transformational energy.

But another interesting lesson has also emerged. Effective SDP principals helped start the program, but it was their collaborative communities that carried forward faithful replication, even after the principal left. There are a number of effective, even exemplary principals, who are not in any way following the SDP process. These leaders are often charismatic and able to galvanize a community by the sheer force of their personality. They are able to restore hope, order, and achievement to even the lowest-performing schools. But their strengths as individuals are often what differentiates them from effective SDP principals. Even though many effective SDP principals are also charismatic, their focus is on developing leadership in *others*. In many ways, they are trying to make their leadership *less* important. They empower others and build community not around themselves but often through themselves.

Sustaining Change and Going to Scale

All successful reform programs, especially ones that have been around for a significant period of time, have eventually faced the difficult issue of sustaining changes. How do you sustain change over a number of years? How do you keep the energy alive after the initial excitement of success and make success a continued excitement while routine? How do you survive the inevitable changes in leadership both at the building and district level?

A second burden of success is the issue of replication and what is now called "going to scale." How do you provide adequate support for 100 schools when you have worked successfully in 10? How does that picture change when the number reaches 1,000?

▨ Concentrate Expansion Within a District

SDP initially accepted schools from anywhere and everywhere, which immediately created problems of logistics and ongoing support. We know that the key to real change is coaching, follow-up, and focus over the long haul. These are precisely the elements that are difficult to obtain, and when available, are quite expensive.

In addition, we began to understand more and more about the district office's influence, both short term and long term, on the change process in schools. With the SDP process, local ownership becomes strengthened as the community connects and begins to gain a deeper understanding of its particular students. In enacting the child-centered process, schools not only can, but want to, make instructional decisions for their buildings and spend their staff development resources accordingly. Such new operating processes inevitably conflict with standard district operating practices, such as staff development initiatives, general district instructional directions, and the kind and quality of data collected and fed back to schools.

Further, success in a district carries its own special burdens. Nothing upsets the status quo more than a low socioeconomic school succeeding. It challenges the assumption that the kids are the problem. There are jealousies and competitive forces that seek to undermine anyone who has truly pushed ahead. In addition, the kind of community empowerment achieved in some SDP schools creates political anxiety in the powers that be and has, at times, led to the dismantling of such schools.

Given these experiences, we became increasingly convinced that the districts needed parallel intervention. Interventions now needed to happen simultaneously on two levels—the schools *and* the districts—effectively doubling the intervention work load. Recognizing this fact, we began to target expansion within districts. That is, expansion was easier within a known district than it was if one had to learn all about a new district context. Thus, our school-to-district ratio became larger, and we concentrated on expanding within districts as well as in new districts that would enter the program prepared to work with a large number of local schools.

As noted above, with a new entry process and with teams coming to national training (teams that included a central district person), getting up to scale and sustainability were reframed in terms of organizing district standard operating procedures to support, rather than conflict with, local reform.

▨ Concentrate District Efforts Not Only on the Superintendent But Also on the "Middles"

Once we understood the importance of the district as the base for scale-up and sustainability, we also discovered the importance of those in the "middle." Part of this discovery comes as a result of the high turnover rates of most urban districts. Superintendents may start your program, but it is likely that none will last long enough to institutionalize it. But those in the middle—those in career central office positions—often have a long-term investment and a deep local knowledge as to how to effect as well as block change. This group has also been almost totally ignored in most reform efforts, and in some cases they have been actively avoided. As a result, the division between them and local reformers tends to increase diametrically: Local efforts move in one direction, while central office staff continue to exercise their responsibilities in another direction.

Superintendents often exacerbate this widening gulf as they see their role as one of blessing local initiative, rather than as leading central office staff in the changes needed to support local change. It is not surprising, then, to see one of two frequent scenarios: In one, a local building leader does not feel or act empowered by a superintendent's blessing because he or she knows it will directly conflict with another central office person—someone who will almost undoubtedly outlast the superintendent. In the other scenario, a building leader does move ahead and does engage that conflict, the mediation of which is often done in a "political," not a programmatic, context.

Our entry process now brings key central office staff into the reform process from the beginning as partners in designing long-term change. The burden of change is now spread to others outside the local context, and the child-centered agenda generated by effective local practice can begin to drive realignment of central office practice.

Systemic SDP

Many of our insights, including those concerning sustainability and going to scale, have brought us back to central office structures and processes. While we have worked to change schools one at a time and still feel this is essential, we have also learned, sometimes the hard way, that districts must engage in parallel reform. The onus of change must be shared, and the old structures must give way to ones that are in concert with new local processes.

Further, we have found that local barriers often create opportunities for building new central structures. The demands of good local change create the support demands that can shape a service-oriented central staff. That is, when there is effective implementation of the SDP, the same elements that can create conflict with central office staff create opportunities for systemic change. For example, consider the child-centered planning process. A key to that process is the collection of data about students, data on their cognitive development and on other areas as well. How will that be done? Who can design and implement it? How does that relate to other data demands in the system? These are all central office or systemic issues.

Another example is the Student and Staff Support Teams. The stripping of social services from most urban schools has forced deep reductions in personnel, who are often assigned to a number of buildings. Are they assigned to an SDP school only so that they learn new ways of operating? Are they reassigned each year or allowed to really understand the culture of each of their assignments? This again is a central office or systemic issue.

School principals from across the country and from abroad participate in the SDP Principals' Academy. Photo by Laura Brooks.

Increasingly, it has become clear that each of the systemic issues, if redesigned to support SDP implementation, in fact, supports any kind of effective local reform. All exemplary programs require aligned staff development, effective local planning, and collaborative practices. As districts themselves move toward more site-based management and local control, they need to find ways to become service deliverers. SDP school change can lead the way.

As a result, the national office of the SDP initiated its Systemic Initiative in 1994. This intervention targets both local schools and the central office as units of parallel change. In this initiative, we initially propose an additional, parallel process for the district central office staff. Adoption of the three guiding principles would directly affect the nature of interchange in a central office from one of fault finding to one of consensus, collaboration, and no-fault. Adaptation of integrative structures, such as the SPMT, to a central office context would establish a process of problem solving. It would bring any conflicts to the surface between building-based change efforts and central office staff, and would encourage the important participants to seek a solution, even when the solution would require some transfer of authority and accountability. It would also allow the creation of a vision of total improvement within an integrated district. The SDP would be both the foundation for this vision and the means by which a wide variety of initiatives can be integrated into the system.

Systemic SDP is a way to generate meaningful whole-district change. Essentially, it requires, at all levels of the system, the kind of major shift in adult behavior that will enhance significantly the intellectual and psychosocial development of our young people. Additionally, it demands a willingness to make any necessary changes in the structures and processes of school systems that will ensure that the well-being of students becomes the one nonnegotiable item in the school reform process.

Finally, it sets in motion, at the beginning, problem solving about both sustainability and going to scale. How will the initiative survive a change in superintendency? How will schools navigate changes in principals? How will the system retain a focus for years rather than months or weeks?

Our early experiences have been positive. Certainly we are aware that we have raised the complexity of early interventions. To some degree this has led to some slower beginnings. But we have found that central offices are themselves under enormous pressure to reinvent themselves. The systemic SDP process provides a means to making the central offices child-centered—they connect to local schools that are themselves becoming child-centered. In the end, a straight line runs from a child in a classroom to every administrator in the system. If the local reform breaks down, there is no connection for central office. If central reform fails, powerful but separated adult agendas will eventually undermine gains. Both local reform and central reform are essential. Both are possible.

▞▚▚▚ *Summary*

Changing schools and, in concert, school districts is an enormously challenging task. In many ways this task has been made more difficult over the last few years as budget cuts and social distress have mounted. The SDP has been in some of the most distressed schools in the country. At a recent Principals' Academy, we featured a panel of SDP principals from New Orleans, Oakland, Washington, D.C., Miami, San Diego, and New York City's District 13. Each had become principals in schools that were at the bottom of their districts. All had led remarkable transformations, and all had based their success on the SDP.

In listening to their stories, the themes that rang out echoed the original SDP design elements: relationships, process, community, assessment, and an unswerving focus on children. All found themselves making different instructional choices. All evolved in a variety of ways. But all could point to the SDP process as the heartbeat of their learning community.

Our challenge now is to have a panel of superintendents from each of our districts, districts that are themselves seen as distressed and intractable to positive change, and hear a similar set of stories about transformation. Such districts would each make different choices and evolve in different ways. But each would have the SDP process as its heartbeat and would have every school as a place where children gained the center stage.

Epilogue

Lessons Learned

JAMES P. COMER, EDWARD T. JOYNER,
AND NORRIS M. HAYNES

Before we end the story of the SDP for now, we would like to share with you that every member of the national office staff of the SDP, regardless of position or unit, contributed to this book. "Many voices telling one story" is the approach that guided us in writing this book. In collaborative work, team members bring with them to the project their own experiences, perspectives, preferred methods of working and expressing themselves, their often unspoken apprehensions and sense of the desired aims. Having lived in schools for 28 years, we know that a truly collaborative project culminates in a finer work than any one individual could have accomplished by himself or herself. We also know the moments of frustration, tension, and dismay when many "voices" gather together. We have learned that the way to overcome these moments is to consciously and deliberately keep the children in mind. By not allowing ourselves to diverge into our own concerns, we come to recognize that voices that at first seem to be talking about different subjects are in actuality in a mutual discourse about what is good for the children.

In this Epilogue, two very different voices are heard. One voice narrates the lessons learned in conducting research in schools. The other voice talks about lessons learned regarding school leaders and the qualities they bring to the task of making a difference in the lives of children. Both keep the children in mind, albeit in strikingly contrasting ways. Our experience in working collaboratively has shown us that a grander story is told when told by many together.

SDP national staff. Not pictured: Brian K. Perkins. (Photo by Laura Brooks.)

▰▰▰ *We Begin with Evaluation ...*

Our many years of documenting the process and outcomes of the SDP have provided us with important insights into critical issues related to the evaluation of educational change initiatives. The evaluation plan must take into account the unique circumstances in school districts and schools. Quantitative research and evaluation designs must always be accompanied by carefully structured ethnographic studies to derive the most valuable and richest information. Moreover, measuring program outcomes, such as improved student performance on standardized tests, is meaningless unless there is a commensurate assessment of the level and quality of program implementation. Our primary insight is that an evaluation is an intervention in itself. For example, to survey people's perceptions about parental involvement in schools broadcasts to them the message that we highly value parental involvement.

The natural contexts of school districts and schools are very different from the staid conditions of laboratories, where the scientist controls all of the inputs and is able to precisely measure the outcomes. In the evaluation of educational change initiatives, we are looking at people in their real-life settings. We have seen, in several instances, schools in which staff wanted to be part of the SDP process, but the schools were assigned to the control group! These staff members went ahead on their own to implement key elements of the process, which was good for the children, but it interfered with our research. This poses a dilemma for us and for the field of educational research. The scientific community values rigorously controlled experimental studies. To think that we can transpose exactly the same research and evaluation paradigms from laboratories to schools is a mistake for which the educational change movement could pay a high price in the form of the absence of rich, meaningful, and useful data.

External evaluators have intervened in schools in order to conduct research. External evaluators, with a few notable exceptions, often feel a sense of professional obligation and accountability to the scientific community to bring to the task an evaluation framework that is cast in the traditional laboratory mold. They often set out a research and evaluation plan that dictates to schools who should or should not implement an educational change program, when they should or should not implement, and even how they should and should not implement. Thus, the research itself becomes a major part of the intervention in an intrusive and disruptive way. This approach interferes with the organic, dynamic process of educational change. Our experience has been that findings resulting from this kind of external, decontextualized evaluation misrepresent the true impact of the program. Variations of implementation and the contextual factors may mediate program effects.

In their discussion of the quasi-experimental research design, Haynes and Bility (1994) note that it is characterized by the researcher asserting some measure of control over what may be controlled (such as *random selection* of students within a school), but accepting certain preconditions in the research situation (p. 16). For example, we are not able to *randomly assign* some children to private schools

Mrs. Kathleen Daly pictured with 1995 recipients of the Patrick Daly Award for Excellence in Educational Leadership. Pictured (from left): Herman D. Clark, Jr., Kathleen Daly, John F. Cooke, Princess D. Whitfield. Recipients not pictured: Alan L. Harris and Grace D. Nebb. (Photo by Laura Brooks.)

and other children to public schools. Our efforts have been carefully designed to combine appropriate quasi-experimental methodologies with qualitative ethnographies to give us contextualized rigor and robustness. We acquire comparative data within the natural contexts of the real world of schools.

⬛⬛⬛ *. . . We Continue with School Leaders*

When we think about the early days of the SDP in New Haven and reflect on the tremendous growth of the program, the premier lesson that we have learned from our 28 years of living in schools is that schools are able to be transformed, and, in turn, so are the life paths of the students. We have seen people modify the way they work and interact with each other for the children's sake. We have seen a school that was dubbed "Horrible Hine" turn into the "Thrill on the Hill" due to the efforts of the principal and the school community. The principal saturated her children with love. In her words, "You have to love them to get them to trust you, before you can teach them" (Whitfield, cited in Joyner, 1995).

Educators rarely see the ultimate outcomes of their efforts because development in children is incremental. Years later, as adults, people will speak of the teacher who opened their awareness to viable alternatives in their life decisions, but they rarely look up that teacher to say thank you. Joyner recalls that when he heard about Patrick Daly, a principal who was struck down when he left his school to search for a child who had run away, he thought about how people like Daly work their whole lives in schools and no one ever recognizes their achievements. As a first step to what we hope will become a wave in this country, the SDP petitioned Yale to sponsor an award with Yale's name on it to say thank you on behalf of the children to school people who provide children with safe passage through some very troubled times. Yale granted our petition because it has a soul and a special commitment to the community. This award, which we called the Patrick Daly award, has already been received by people plowing the ground in schools, and we will continue to say thank you to school people who are loving children, teaching them, anchoring their lives, and refusing to give up on them. We describe these educators as servant leaders.

We entered into the field of education to serve; to be servant leaders. We serve the needs of the entire school community. We have seen superintendents, principals, teachers, parents, and community members transforming the children in their schools and districts as a result of their actions. Islands of despair have been turned into places of hope because of the servant leaders in the schools.

The servant leader is visionary. This vision is grounded in our democratic principles. Now, of course, our democratic principles stem from our sense of ethics and our country's manifold religions. Ralph Tyler (1949) expressed this point when he noted that an educational philosophy in a democratic society emphasizes four democratic values:

Edward Joyner addresses principals from around the country and abroad at the SDP Principals' Academy. (Photo by Laura Brooks.)

(1) the recognition of the importance of every individual human being as a human being regardless of his race, national, social, or economic status; (2) opportunity for wide participation in all phases of activities in the social groups in the society; (3) encouragement of variability rather than demanding a single type of personality; (4) faith in intelligence as a method of dealing with important problems rather than depending upon the authority of an autocratic or aristocratic group. (p. 34)

We have a concept of the United States that says that what we should be trying to do is create a sense of oneness so that race, class, gender, and disability will not thwart children in their development. No child is expendable. To deny a child a good education is to affect that child's life chances. If the child's life chances are affected, then so, too, will be the child's opportunity to be happy and to contribute.

The servant leader is hopeful and faithful. We suffer in this country from a crisis of hope. We need to show people how to build things that will be sustained over time. The harvest is finished, the summer is over, but we are not finished, we are not safe. As servant leaders we must transmit a sense of hope to students, parents, and staff. We must be that vision. Servant leaders are always faithful, and faith is the sister of hope. It is the acceptance that something will happen, and, in our case as educators, that good and wonderful things will happen. Many in this country dwell on what they do not have. So every day the servant leader must infuse the ethos of the school with a dose of faith in the children. That faith broadcasts to them the conviction that they can accomplish by having faith in their abilities and their will to bring new things into existence. The servant leader needs to be faithful and hopeful because it is very difficult to function in many of the environments in which we work.

Servant leaders are honorable, persistent, and courageous. To be honorable means to be true to the principles of our profession. We see in schools men and women of honor who remain steadfast, immovable, and unshakable to their commitment to the highest ideals of education. Students have to be won over to the ideals of these educators. Servant leaders insist on quality in every aspect of the school. They are willing to leave the safety of the mainland to sail in shark-infested waters through stormy seas.

Servant leaders are thankful. We are thankful for the opportunity to be educational leaders, and we remember that from those to whom much is given, much is expected. We are thankful every day for the opportunity given to us to affect children's lives, to experience the beauty of looking into the eyes of children who are now heading in a positive direction, to hear their often unspoken words: "If it were not for you, I wouldn't be where I am now"; "Because of something you said, something you did, a time when you touched me, I can change and grow."

Servant leaders practice reflective thought. Educators must always study the results of their actions. By modeling the reflective process, we promote this quality among the staff, and, in turn, the students. We should seek knowledge, wisdom, a right spirit, and a clean heart as we reflect. Through reflection, we learn to be kind and just. The ancient sage, Simon the Just, used to say that one of the foundations of the world is the practice of loving kindness (*Sayings of the Fathers*, 1:2). We challenge educators and parents to consider what schools would be like if everybody accepted loving kindness as a principle and made it the foundation of every program and every decision made for children. To school people that talk about what the children cannot do or why they need to be punished, we say, show me the kindness. Where is the kindness in that decision? Where is the kindness in telling a child that he cannot achieve because he lives on the wrong street, or because he doesn't have a father in his house? We should insist that a respect for kindness and justice be reflected in all of our schools' activities. It is mandated; it is not negotiable. To this end, we must be action oriented. And as we act, we must act as servant leaders. To ask the best of children means that we always have to ask the best of ourselves.

References

Haynes, N. M., & Bility, K. (1994) Evaluating school development. *School Development Program Research Monograph*. New Haven, CT: Yale Child Study Center.

Joyner, E. (1995). Keynote address. SDP Principals' Academy.

Tyler, R. (1949). *Basic principles of curriculum and instruction*. Chicago: The University of Chicago Press.

About the Authors

███████ **Michael Ben-Avie, M.A., M. Phil.**

Michael Ben-Avie is a predoctoral research fellow with the Yale Child Study Center's School Development Program. He is currently a Ph.D. candidate and a staff member of the SDP's Research and Evaluation Unit.

███████ **James P. Comer, M.D.**

James P. Comer is the Maurice Falk Professor of Child Psychiatry at the Yale University Child Study Center, associate dean of the Yale University School of Medicine, and director of the School Development Program. His preventive psychiatry work in schools began in 1968. He has published more than ninety scientific articles, more than twenty chapters, and four books, the latest, *Maggie's American Dream: The Life and Times of a Black Family,* based on the life of his own family and his work in schools. He wrote a monthly article for *Parents* magazine between 1978 and 1993, and continues as a contributing editor. His pioneering work in school restructuring has been featured in numerous newspapers, magazines, and television reports.

Dr. Comer is a graduate of Indiana University, Howard University College of Medicine, University of Michigan School of Public Health, and was trained in psychiatry at the Yale School of Medicine.

He is a co-founder and past president of the Black Psychiatrists of America. He was a consultant to Children's Television Workshop *(Sesame Street)* and has served as a consultant, committee member, advisory board member, and trustee to numerous local and national organizations serving children. He has been the recipient of the John and Mary Markle Scholar in Academic Medicine Award, Rockefeller Public Service Award, Harold W. McGraw, Jr., Prize in Education, Charles A. Dana Award for Pioneering Achievement in Education, and many other awards and honors, including more than thirty honorary degrees.

Joanne Nancy Corbin, M.S.S.

Joanne Corbin is an assistant professor in social work at the Yale Child Study Center. She graduated from Wellesley College in 1982 with a B.A. in psychology. Ms. Corbin received a master's degree in social service from Bryn Mawr College in 1986.

Ms. Corbin is an implementation coordinator in the School Development Program and works with several school districts throughout the country including New Haven. She provides training on Mental Health Teams and child development. Within the School Development Program, Ms. Corbin coordinates the Consortium for Urban Education, a collaboration among Southern Connecticut State University, the New Haven Public Schools, and the Yale Child Study Center. The goal of the consortium is to prepare teachers for their work in urban environments. Ms. Corbin also addresses related areas within the School Development Program.

In addition, Ms. Corbin is a social worker in the outpatient department at the Yale Child Study Center. She works with children and families, and conducts seminars on family therapy and cross-cultural issues.

Ms. Corbin has worked extensively in the field of mental health since 1979, focusing on the psychosocial issues of children, adults, and families, with particular work in the area of mental retardation. She has also explored cross-cultural issues in mental health through her work at Mathari Hospital in Nairobi, Kenya.

Christine Emmons, Ph.D.

Christine Emmons was born in Grenada, a tiny Caribbean island. She received a teacher's certificate from the University of the West Indies in 1971, and a B.A. from the same university in 1979. Dr. Emmons received a master's in library science from the University of Western Ontario in 1984, and a Ph.D. in educational psychology from the University of Connecticut in 1992. Dr. Emmons was an elementary school teacher, and later librarian of the Education Resource Centers, in her native Grenada. She is currently an associate research scientist at the Yale Child Study Center and coordinator of research at the School Development Program.

Sara Gebreyesus, M.A.

Sara Gebreyesus, a research associate at the Yale Child Study Center, began working with the School Development Program in 1990. Ms. Gebreyesus graduated from Hunter College in New York City in 1987, with a B.A. in psychology and a minor in anthropology. Ms. Gebreyesus received paralegal training and a certificate at Baruch College in New York in 1987. She received her M.A. in psychology from Southern Connecticut State University in New Haven in 1992. She is currently working on her postgraduate work in educational psychology at the University of Connecticut in Storrs.

Ms. Gebreyesus has worked as a paralegal with public and private law agencies in New York. She has served as an interpreter for Tigrinya speakers in court and other nonprofit agencies. She has worked as a freelance legal and social document translator in Tigrinya language and has worked as an instructor in Tigrinya and Amharic in the African Languages Department at Yale University from 1992 to 1993.

Ms. Gebreyesus conducts case studies to document the SDP implementation process and evaluates the SDP training program in collaboration with the Research Team.

Jonathon H. Gillette, Ph.D.

Jonathon Gillette is senior implementation coordinator for the Comer Project for Change in Education. He is also project manager for the implementation of the first Comer/Zigler model school.

Dr. Gillette received his B.A. from Harvard University, an M.A.T. from Wesleyan, and a Ph.D. in administrative science from Yale University in 1985.

Dr. Gillette has taught at the high school and graduate school levels. He was a teacher at Hillhouse High School and directed Title VII and Title X federally funded programs. In addition, he directed the Hillhouse Freshman Program, which won a number of awards, including the State of Connecticut Humanities Council Awards for the Artist-in-Residence Program. He has taught group dynamics to graduate business students at Yale's School of Organization and Management.

Dr. Gillette has published a number of articles and is coeditor of *Groups in Context*. His special interests include organizational and group dynamics, school restructuring, job redesign, structural change in complex organizations, and race relations. He has worked as a consultant on a broad variety of issues, from site-based management in public schools to factory restructuring. He has also served as a consultant on race relations to a number of Fortune 100 companies.

Dr. Gillette is active in many community organizations. He is one of the founding partners of a recycling corporation dedicated to local economic development. He was recently named to the Board of the Housing Authority of the City of New Haven and has been active in the development of the citywide educational policy.

Norris M. Haynes, Ph.D.

Norris M. Haynes is associate professor of psychology, education, and child development at the Yale Child Study Center and research director of the School Development Program. He is also a member of the faculty in the Department of Psychology and the Yale Bush Center in Child Development and Social Policy. Dr. Haynes contributes significantly to the SDP's training and dissemination activities. He was responsible for designing the dissemination plan and for developing and preparing grant proposals in support of the SDP's national dissemination strategies. Dr. Haynes has served as the organizational liaison and is a member of the steering committee for the ATLAS Communities project.

Dr. Haynes earned a B.A. in psychology and a master's degree and advanced certificate in educational and counseling psychology from the State University of New York at Buffalo. He earned a Ph.D. in psychology and education from Howard University in 1978. He also holds a master's of business administration with a concentration in public health and health services administration.

Dr. Haynes has taught at the elementary and high school levels. He has been a professor at Howard University and adjunct professor at several other universities. He has worked as a senior psychologist and associate director of an educational and psychological research consulting firm in Washington, D.C. He has served as a consultant to many school districts, state departments of education, and colleges of education. He is a licensed clinical psychologist and has worked extensively with children and families.

Dr. Haynes is the recipient of many honors and awards including Outstanding Young Man of America; citation in several Who's Who publications; the Crispus Attucks Award for Educational Leadership; a Fulbright Scholarship; and the first Howard University Graduate School Distinguished Alumnus Award in 1994. He serves on a number of editorial boards for professional peer review journals and advisory boards for national psychological and educational research and intervention organizations and agencies.

Dr. Haynes is the author of many articles, book chapters, and a recent book, *Critical Issues in Educating African-American Children.* He is also the author of a book that is in press, *Promoting Motivation, Learning and Achievement Among Urban Middle and High School Students.* Dr. Haynes has also served as a guest editor for the recent special edition of *Educational Horizons,* an international journal on educational and psychological issues.

▨▨▨▨ J. Patrick Howley

Patrick Howley is presently project manager for implementation for the School Development Program. As project manager, he works with implementation coordinators and school district facilitators in planning and organizing implementation strategies for each of the school districts in the SDP network. As a member of the Professional Development Design Team, he develops and presents modules for the Leadership Development Programs and the Principals' Academy in the following areas: team building, clinical supervision, relationships, person-centered coaching, community building, and child development. In addition, he is a lead contact for the Principals' Academy held each summer at Yale. A major role of Patrick's work at SDP is helping to ensure that people develop and use effective human relationship skills.

Mr. Howley has had a long history working in schools. He has been an elementary school teacher, a junior high school counselor, a director of a high school gifted program, a coordinator for a federally funded project to develop teacher centers, and a human resource specialist for the University of

Connecticut. He has served on the faculty of numerous colleges and universities in Connecticut. He has taught courses at Sacred Heart University, and served on the faculty at Connecticut College supervising student teachers. At Southern Connecticut State University, he taught peer counseling, interpersonal group dynamics, and counseling procedures in the Counseling and School Psychology Department.

Before coming to the School Development Program, Patrick brought together his experiences as a classroom teacher, guidance counselor, a counselor in private practice, and his staff training and development work to consult independently with both schools and businesses in the areas of collaborative learning teams, coaching administrators, team building, community building, self-esteem, listening skills, and conflict resolution. He has served as a trainer for the State of Connecticut's Cooperating Teacher and Beginning Educator Support and Training (BEST) Programs. He also has been trained as an assessor in the assessment component of the BEST Program. In addition, he is a facilitator of problem solving for teams participating in Program Improvement Institutes in the Institute for Teaching and Learning of the Area Cooperative Educational Services.

Mr. Howley's main interest and training experiences have been focused on adult development. He has extensively studied the Enneagram, a development process. He has been trained in a process called focusing. He has been trained and certified to administer both the Myers-Briggs Type Indicator and the Heroic Myth Index, a model used for both personal and organizational development.

Edward T. Joyner, Ed.D.

Edward Joyner is the acting director of the School Development Program at the Yale Child Study Center. He received a B.A. in social science from Elizabeth City State University in North Carolina and an M.A.T. from Wesleyan University in 1973. He received an Ed.D. in educational administration from the University of Bridgeport in 1989.

Dr. Joyner has taught at both the high school and college levels. He was an assistant principal at Hillhouse High School and principal of Jackie Robinson Middle School in New Haven. He has published articles dealing with at-risk youth, and for local school districts has developed training manuals related to school change as a response to changing student and community needs.

Dr. Joyner has worked with Dr. James P. Comer to develop collaborative relationships between universities and public schools. Together they have also worked with the Carnegie Corporation to carry out interventions directed at improving middle schools. His special interests include school leadership, organizational behavior, and school–community collaborations. He has been an education consultant to local school districts, state departments of education, philanthropic foundations, universities and colleges, as well as the College Board and the Council of Chief State School Officers.

Louise P. S. Kaltenbaugh, Ph.D.

Louise S. Kaltenbaugh is assistant professor of education in the Department of Elementary and Secondary Education at Southern University at New Orleans. She is director of the Post-Baccalaureate Teacher Center for Urban Education and administrator of the SUNO/NOPS partnership. She teaches courses in reading and supervises first-year teacher interns. Her research and teaching interests are focused on the development of K–16 educational partnerships and the study of change through action research. She is both an assessor and a trainer for the Louisiana Teacher Assessment Program.

Dr. Kaltenbaugh received her M.A. degree from the University of New Orleans; an M.A.T. degree at Tulane University; and a Ph.D. degree in educational administration, higher education, from the University of New Orleans.

Robert D. Kranyik, Ph.D.

Robert D. Kranyik is the Charles A. Dana Professor Emeritus of Educational Management at the University of Bridgeport, College of Management. His specialties include management and leadership development, organizational development, and educational program design and management. His clients have included federal and state government agencies, corporations, trade associations, hospitals, universities, and school districts across the country. He is the author of more than fifty articles and several books. He has also written and edited autotutorial educational programs.

Dr. Kranyik received a B.S. in sociology and an M.A. in education from Fairfield University. He received a Ph.D. in educational administration from the University of Connecticut. He has also studied at New York University, the New School for Social Research, and Teachers College, Columbia University.

He provided leadership in the creation of the University of Bridgeport's doctoral program in educational management, a unique program that melds modern management concepts with interdisciplinary studies to produce leaders in education and training. His current professional interests include school site management, school leadership development, and the use of organizational development concepts in the improvement of education and training.

In 1974, Dr. Kranyik served as director of a competency-based teacher education program that received a Distinguished Achievement Award from the American Association of Colleges of Teacher Education. In the same year he was named an Outstanding Educator of America by Outstanding Educators of America, Washington, D.C. He is listed in *Who's Who in America, Who's Who in the East, Who's Who in American Education,* and the *Dictionary of International Biography.* He was a founder of Connecticut School Management Institute, which for 5 years provided professional renewal programs for school principals.

Edna N. Negron

Edna Negron is an implementation coordinator for the School Development Program. She was born in Ciales, Puerto Rico, and graduated from the University of Hartford with honors. She has spent her adult life in public education with an emphasis on the education of Hispanics. In 1985, she opened the Dr. Ramón Emeterio Betances Elementary School in Hartford, Connecticut, serving a student population of 600. Ninety-eight percent are minority students, of which 95% are below the poverty level.

While at Betances, Ms. Negron implemented the School Development Program and in 1994 received the SDP's prestigious Patrick Daly Award for Excellence in Educational Leadership. Ms. Negron participated in the development of state legislation for family resource centers and implemented the first urban family resource center in the country, which is modeled after Dr. Edward Zigler's "School of the 21st Century." With significant funding from the Travelers Companies Foundation, Ms. Negron developed a school-based clinic at Betances through a coalition of Hartford Hospital, the Travelers, Inc., and the Hartford Board of Education. In addition, while at Betances, she started "El Futuro en Nuestras Manos," a mentor program for fifth and sixth graders.

Prior to serving as the principal for Betances, Ms. Negron was the director of the Bilingual Education and Multicultural Department in the Hartford Public Schools. In that position she developed a bilingual education compliance plan for the U.S. Office of Civil Rights, which became a national model. She negotiated the *Ramos v. Gaines et al.* bilingual federal consent decree on behalf of the Hartford Public Schools and developed the existing board policy on bilingual/multicultural education.

Ms. Negron also developed and implemented a curriculum of equal benefits for LEP students K–12 that served 42 language groups. This included English as a Second Language, native language instruction, graduation requirements, identification, placement, and exit criteria. She developed New Arrival Centers designed for older LEP students.

From 1990 to 1993, she became the first Puerto Rican and Hispanic woman to be elected and to serve a complete term in the Connecticut State House of Representatives, representing the then sixth district. During her term she served as a member of the Education, Public Health, and Commerce and Exportation committees of the General Assembly and participated in Connecticut's current bilingual education legislation.

Deborah B. Smith, Ph.D.

Deborah B. Smith is Assistant Professor of Education in the Department of Elementary and Secondary Education at Southern University at New Orleans. She teaches courses in reading and supervises preservice teachers assigned to the schools involved in the Southern University at New Orleans, School Development Program, and New Orleans Public Schools Partnership. Her research and teaching interests are focused on curricular changes in K–16 educational settings based on action-research. She is an assessor for the Louisiana Teacher Assessment Program.

Dr. Smith received her M.Ed. degree from UNO and the Ph.D. degree in Curriculum and Instruction from Louisiana State University in Baton Rouge.

▓▓▓▓▓ David A. Squires, Ph.D.

David A. Squires is the program manager for curriculum, instruction, and assessment for the School Development Program. Dr. Squires earned a B.A. in English and an M.A. in education from Allegheny College. He taught English and creative writing at East Technical High School in Cleveland and Churchill Area High School outside Pittsburgh. After 7 years of teaching, he continued his education at the University of Pittsburgh, working at the Learning Research and Development Center for 3 years while completing a Ph.D. in curriculum and supervision with minors in reading/language arts and educational administration.

In 1979, Research for Better Schools, Inc., in Philadelphia hired Dr. Squires to develop research-based approaches to instructional improvement. He also worked with the Delaware State Department of Education to develop research-based standards for elementary and secondary schools. From this work, he published *Effective Schools and Classrooms: A Research-Based Perspective* through the Association for Supervision and Curriculum Development in 1983.

In 1981, Dr. Squires became the supervisor of curriculum and staff development for the Red Bank Public Schools, a pre-K through eighth-grade district in New Jersey, a position that also included districtwide responsibility for Chapter I, ESL, testing, affirmative action, school improvement, grants, and facilitation of the Comer School Development Program. Serving 70% minority students with 65% below the poverty level, Red Bank improved student achievement from below to above grade level over the next decade. Schools in the district received recognition for outstanding parent programs, demonstration grants for effective schools, and a national award for outstanding parent Chapter I programs in both reading and mathematics.

At the School Development Program, Dr. Squires is working on three projects: the curriculum alignment process in which schools examine their expectations, state and national standards, curriculum, texts, tests, and data gathering processes so that informed decisions are made about what to teach students; the "Developmental Pathways Study Process," a 2-year study that asks teachers, administrators, and parents to examine the life of a child for a year in order to know that child well; and strategic alliances with high-quality, research-proven instructional programs that promote children's development across the six developmental pathways.

Index